TRIAL ADVOCACY

IN A NUTSHELL

THIRD EDITION

By

PAUL BERGMAN

Professor of Law
University of California, Los Angeles

ST. PAUL, MINN.
WEST PUBLISHING CO.
1997

Nutshell Series, In a Nutshell, the Nutshell Logo and the WP symbol are registered trademarks of West Publishing Co. Registered in the U.S. Patent and Trademark Office.

COPYRIGHT © 1989 WEST PUBLISHING CO.
COPYRIGHT © 1997 By WEST GROUP
                    610 Opperman Drive
                    P.O. Box 64526
                    St. Paul, MN 55164–0526
                    1–800–328–9352

ISBN 0–314–21200–0

TEXT IS PRINTED ON 10% POST
CONSUMER RECYCLED PAPER

For Dad

*

III

PREFACE

This Third Edition of Trial Advocacy in a Nutshell explains and illustrates essential techniques for persuasively advancing a client's cause at trial. (No misleading book title here!) Like its predecessors, this edition eschews vague lawyer homilies in favor of specific questioning and argument techniques. At the same time, because no set of techniques is suited to every trial and every trial attorney's unique personal style, the book offers variations on those techniques and describes why and when they might be appropriate.

Unlike substantive rules, many principles of effective trial advocacy change little with time. For example, 18th century barristers undoubtedly cross examined witnesses based on the factors set forth in the Credibility Model (Page 25). (Admittedly, they would have been hard-pressed to describe the foundation for offering fax documents into evidence, Page 173!) So why the need for a Third Edition, other than to go where Professor Kenney Hegland has never gone before? The principal reason is my continuing experiences as a teacher of trial advocacy. I have increasingly come to appreciate that a persuasive case relies on more than effective oral courtroom skills. An advocate must also know how to develop convincing courtroom stories through the use of factual arguments supporting the stories' accuracy.

The Second Edition moved in the direction of describing the factual content of persuasive trial stories, and here I carry on this development by setting forth and explaining (in Chapters 2 through 5) four types of arguments that are likely to affect a judge's or juror's acceptance of a story in virtually every type of case. The four types of arguments consist of Credibility Arguments, Inferential Arguments, Normative Arguments and Silent Arguments. Organizing evidence according to these four argument types is essential to building persuasive trial stories.

Of course, developing persuasive arguments is of value only if those arguments influence an advocate's courtroom presentations. Thus, throughout the book I suggest methods by which advocates can incorporate factual arguments into what they say during opening statement and final summation, and the questions that they ask during jury voir dire, and direct and cross examination.

I have tried to improve upon the earlier editions in a number of other ways. For example:

* I devote a separate chapter to "Exhibits" (Chapter 8), and provide sample foundational showings for many common types of exhibits.

* I incorporate references to specific sections of the Federal Rules of Evidence into many of the illustrations and explanations.

* I follow up many of the transcript illustrations with detailed explanations, aided by numbering the questions and answers in these transcripts.

* I draw a number of illustrations from the criminal prosecutions of William Kennedy Smith, the Menendez Brothers and O. J. Simpson, which occupied so much of the media's and the public's attention during this decade.

* The text nowhere uses the term "deconstruction."

I am genuinely grateful for the numerous positive comments I have received over the years from the instructors, students and lawyers who have used earlier editions of the Trial Advocacy Nutshell. Like any other author of a successor edition, I hope that the improvements I have made do not mess up what readers have liked about the earlier editions. Therefore, let me assure old friends that I retain much of the substance and tone of the earlier editions. For example, the "Cross Examination Safety Model" (Page 187) remains at the heart of the cross examination chapter. Also, I continue to sprinkle nursery rhymes into the illustrations of many argument and questioning techniques. The nursery rhymes provide ready factual context, and add to the humor which many readers have told me they appreciate. Those readers who frown on mirth in lawbooks have the option of reading one of Kenney Hegland's books.

For those readers for whom this is important, I am pleased to report that none of the theories and illustrations used in the book were tested on animals. Also, no animals were harmed during the writing of the book, though two legal doctrines previously on the endangered species list did become extinct.

PAUL BERGMAN

Los Angeles, California
July, 1997

ACKNOWLEDGEMENTS

The people whose contributions are reflected throughout this book know who they are. However, that wasn't good enough for them. Thus, I first want to publicly acknowledge my UCLA colleagues, David Binder and Albert Moore. Together we wrote "Trial Advocacy—Inferences, Arguments and Techniques" (West Publishing Co. 1995), and the ideas that we jointly developed permeate this book. I am grateful to David and Al for years of friendship and counsel, and thankful that they are too busy playing golf to realize how much I've appropriated for this book.

I also want to thank Tal Grietzer, Michael Cobb and Professors Steve Derian, Susan Gillig, Christine Goodman and Al Moore for reading portions of the manuscript. Yes, you are entitled to your opinions. Catherine Halvorsen of the UCLA Law Library made up for my rudimentary computer data base searching skills and found the People vs. O. J. Simpson closing argument transcripts. Wendy Haro and Bunny Friedman remained cheerful despite my repetitive promises that each draft was the last. Thanks finally to my delightful daughter Hilary, who contributed in a way that I can no longer remember.

ACKNOWLEDGEMENTS

Now it's really too late for feedback from those to whom I sent drafts of Second Edition chapters. This still includes you, Avrom.

Finally, thank you to the UCLA School of Law for taking me out of the classroom so that I could write this book. At least I hope that was the reason.

OUTLINE

OUTLINE

OUTLINE

TRIAL ADVOCACY

IN A NUTSHELL

THIRD EDITION

*

CHAPTER 1

AN APPROACH TO LITIGATION

Trial advocacy may be the specialty that first drew you towards a career in law. Perhaps the most visible and enduring symbol of the American legal system, adversarial trials are also one of its most important. Trials activate the abstract rights devised by legislatures and courts, and the outcomes of trials often shape future social behavior.

Nevertheless, as a would-be trial advocate you may be intimidated by the imagery that often surrounds successful trial lawyers. Both the popular media and lawyers' own texts often portray courtroom advocacy as an art that you can succeed at only if it is your birthright to do so. Seemingly, successful litigators can master voluminous files, converse easily with experts of every stripe, hold juries spellbound by combining the story-construction skills of a Pulitzer Prize-winning writer with the performance skills of an Academy Award-winning performer, and have an unerring intuitive ability to ferret out mendacity. (You might recall famous barrister Sir Wilfred's "monocle test" in the classic courtroom film, "Witness for the Prosecution." By studying his client's reaction to the light reflected off his monocle, Sir Wilfred would determine the client's trustworthiness.) Together, this popular imagery might scare you into thinking that negotiating shopping center leases is not such an unsatisfactory legal career, after all.

Like all durable popular images, those concerning litigators contain germs of truth. Courtroom advocates do need to possess storytelling skills. And at times you may have to rely on your intuition when selecting jurors or cross examining witnesses. However, much of the "art" of trial advocacy consists of techniques that you can learn in the same way that you learned arithmetic and the Rule Against Perpetuities—well, arithmetic anyway. Those techniques are the subject of this Nutshell. In ensuing chapters you will learn how to develop comprehensible and persuasive trial stories, and how to present those stories effectively to judges and jurors.

A. AN ARGUMENT–CENTERED APPROACH TO TRIAL

This book focuses on techniques for preparing and presenting persuasive stories at trial. Discovery is complete, and you have some mass of information which is the basis of the evidence you will present at trial. Of course, a modern reality is that most cases settle before trial. Many litigators today resemble the admirals of Gilbert & Sullivan, who never went to sea. However, the techniques described in this book are important even in a climate of settlement. Only if you are comfortable trying a case can you be sure that a recommendation of settlement is based on a client's best interests, not your own discomfort with trial.

To try a case successfully, you'll need to combine the following skills:

- The "Basics:" Ability to apply evidentiary rules inside the courtroom.

- The "Sizzle:" Ability to use persuasive oral techniques, such as eliciting direct examinations in a way that emphasizes crucial testimony.

- The "Steak" ("Potatoes" for vegetarians): An ability to develop factual arguments (evidence marshalled pursuant to ultimate facts) supporting a story's accuracy and probative value.

This book explains and illustrates each of these skills. It begins, however, with the last: argument preparation. Most trials call upon a factfinder (judge or jurors) to resolve competing versions of history. A prosecutor offers evidence that a defendant committed a crime; the defendant offers an alibi. A plaintiff contends that a doctor botched an operation; the doctor claims to have properly performed the surgery. Your primary advocacy job in such cases is to persuade a factfinder of the accuracy of your client's historical story, and to demonstrate how that story proves (or from the defense perspective disproves) controlling legal elements such as "lack of due care," "identity" or "intent."

To help you carry out these tasks, this book presents methods for developing arguments drawn from a story's factual content. An argument is a bundle consisting of one or more items of evidence linked to a discrete ultimate fact. Depending on a cases's complexity, you may develop as few as one or two, or many, arguments. Arguments help you organize a mass of evidence into manageable and persuasive chunks, and are the primary tool for convincing a factfinder that your client's story is accurate and legally compelling.

B. THE RATIONALITY OF EVERYDAY EXPERIENCE

Searching for explanations of trial outcomes, some commentators take refuge in polemics—e.g., "if you're rich, you win." Others take refuge in pedantry, proposing that jurors be made aware of complex mathematical fact-finding models based on statistics and probabilities. Tending to occupy a middle ground, lawyers take refuge in traditional intuitions—e.g., "develop a theme;" "keep the jury's attention on the witness during direct." Despite the multitude of such intuitions, litigators often qualify them with the proviso, "Trial is always something of a crapshoot."

This book examines persuasion from a fourth perspective, which regards fact-finding as rooted in the rationality of everyday experiences. Judges and jurors draw inferences (arrive at conclusions) based on generalizations drawn from everyday experience. For example, when a factfinder infers from evidence that "Sara was late for a meeting" that "Sara was speeding," the factfinder implicitly relies on a generalization that "People who are late for meetings are likely to speed." That generalization is based on the factfinder's experiences with how people in our culture commonly behave when they are late for meetings.

Thus, the book's answer to the polemicist is that, in most cases at least, a trier attempts to develop a story about what really happened, as opposed to applying cultural or ethnic stereotypes. Its response to the pedant is that until such time as precise inferential calculations are available, a litigator's task is to persuade using the tools of everyday reasoning. And its reply to an intuitive approach is that intuition informed by factual analysis is the basis of professional skill.

C. PERSONAL CHARACTERISTICS OF EFFECTIVE LITIGATORS

Many law students and recent graduates wonder whether they are personally suited to life inside courtrooms. Fortunately, effective courtroom advocacy is not the exclusive domain of any one type of personality or background. Here are some of the most important traits which effective litigators are likely to have in common.

1. Self–Confidence

Self-confidence is an important characteristic, whether you want to be a successful seller of shoes or of historical events. Studies tend to suggest that lawyers who speak confidently and assertively carry greater sway with jurors than do passive-sounding lawyers. However, perhaps only a faulty zipper can undermine self-confidence as quickly as courtroom procedures. You approach a court clerk to file a motion, only to be told with a withering look that, "You file those *after* calendar call." Or, a judge uses some shorthand jargon with which you are unfamiliar: "Do you want this set down for a 352 motion?" Your discomfiture is made even worse by your sense that everybody else in the courtroom knows exactly the correct procedures.

The answer to maintaining self-confidence in the face of such adversity is surprisingly simple. You need only say, "I don't know." The earth will not cease to spin. Too many advocates who have only recently acquired the hallowed title of "attorney" feel like they are expected to know everything, and that any admission of ignorance is a badge of incompetence. In fact, courtroom procedures vary so much that you will constantly meet unfamiliar ones. Ask the clerk how and when to file your papers, and tell the judge that you're uncertain of what a 352 motion is. Amazingly, you will not be thought incompetent—you will learn something!

2. Willingness to Learn About Diverse Subjects

Many attorneys specialize in narrow subject matter areas such as real estate financing, corporate buy-outs, and motion picture contracts. As a litigator, you are more likely to "specialize" in whatever is the subject matter of your current cases. You may try a case on behalf of a buyer seeking rescission of a land sale contract one month, and on behalf of an employee allegedly fired as a result of age discrimination the next. Even if you specialize in personal injury matters, your practice is likely to be diverse. You may have one case in which the issue is whether an accident is the cause of your client's tinnitus, and another in which the issue is whether kidney failure resulted from surgical malpractice.

To be a successful trial advocate, you must be willing to learn about whatever "industry" is involved in a case. If the alleged victim of age discrimination worked in an automobile assembly plant, you will have to learn about the plant's operations. To represent your tinnitus victim, you may need to learn almost as much about tinnitus as a doctor. Thus, you will come into contact with diverse kinds of people engaged in diverse activities. If you can look forward to constantly learning about new areas of life, you are well on your way to success in trial advocacy.

3. Common Sense

If you are like most people, you probably think you have common sense, which you might think of in this context as enabling you to "think not like a lawyer." However, law school can interfere with your ability to use common sense. Law school often creates complexity where none is apparent on the surface. For example, you may think a torts opinion relatively straightforward, only to find out in class that the author of the opinion muddled legal doctrine and masked a political value choice in case precedents. Examining law in law school is much like looking at a drop of water under a microscope. What looks on the surface to be a static mass is teeming with movement and change.

To be successful at trial, you generally must move in the other direction, from complexity to simplicity. For instance, you may need to convince a factfinder that what seems to be a unique and complex series of events is consistent with their everyday experiences and conforms to a few directly applicable legal principles. Using common sense can help you develop arguments that respond to the way that a lay juror is likely to think about a case. An intricate argument about a series of psychological ailments that have allegedly rendered a person hopelessly allergic to dogs may be met by the response, "Then why was he holding a leash?" Simple explanations grounded in everyday experiences are most likely to persuade a judge or juror.

4. Integrity

While integrity is an essential characteristic for all attorneys, courtroom advocates are perhaps faced with more temptations to stray than others. Your ethical responsibility to represent clients "zealously" in an adversarial system may tempt you to sacrifice long-term integrity to accomplish short-term goals. For example, a client may suggest that you tell him how to testify. Or, you may be tempted to make a spurious evidentiary argument to which you know your inexperienced adversary will be unable to respond adequately.

Resist such temptations. Even in large urban areas, the percentage of attorneys who try cases is small, and reputations spread quickly. You have ethical obligations to the court, to your adversary, and to future clients, and you should not compromise your personal standards for any client.

D. TRUTH AND THE ADVERSARY SYSTEM

The social legitimacy of trials depends on the popular notion that they represent a "search for truth." In our rationalistic system of justice, factfinders are supposed to base their verdicts on "what really happened." Yet lawyers must acknowledge deep public skepticism about trials and lawyers. Many people see lawyers as willing to subvert truth in order to win, and verdicts simply as reflections of factfinder biases.

Unfortunately, lawyers must also acknowledge that for a variety of reasons the adversary system cannot in most cases claim to produce objective reality. For example:

• Substantive and evidentiary rules themselves distort reality by shaping the stories that lawyers can tell. For example, substantive rules focus on discrete moments of time (e.g., when a robbery may have been committed or a libelous statement made) and thereby circumscribe the scope of reality that a factfinder hears. Similarly, evidence rules which forbid or admit character evidence according to the situation affect the scope of reality.

- Witnesses filter events through fallible powers of observation and memory, and often through personal biases.

- Even our language distorts reality, because words have a limited power to convey real events. For example, a witness who was on the wrong end of a gun will probably be unable to communicate fully the emotions and feelings aroused by the experience.

Against this background, you must frankly acknowledge the legitimacy of adversarial techniques. For example, you have an obligation to a client to try to select a sympathetic factfinder, to help witnesses shape testimony in pretrial conferences, and question friendly witnesses in a way that avoids mention of damaging evidence. With objective reality unprovable, you must rely on such techniques to persuade a factfinder of the accuracy of your arguments.

CHAPTER 2

CONSTRUCTING ARGUMENTS

Trying a case resembles painting a house. For either to be done competently, the main activity (painting, eliciting evidence) is likely to be dwarfed by the preparation (sanding, discovery). This and the next three chapters of the book explain how to prepare for trial by constructing arguments. (You're on your own when it comes to painting.) You've gathered evidence and investigated the adversary's case. It's now time to organize that evidence into arguments that you hope will persuade a factfinder (judge or jury) to rule in your client's favor.

You'll learn how to construct (and respond to) four types of arguments: Credibility Arguments, Inferential Arguments, Normative Arguments and Silent Arguments. These arguments are the tools by which you can convince a factfinder that your client's story (version of events) is more believable than an adversary's, and that your desired legal consequences follow from those events. Together, the four types of arguments:

- link stories' concrete happenings ("the defendant bought rat poison a week before the victim's death") to abstract legal elements ("the defendant intended to kill the victim").

11

- identify the evidence you'll offer and emphasize during direct and cross examination and the contentions you'll make during opening statement and final summation.

- respond to the kinds of factual determinations that factfinders have to make in nearly every case (i.e., evaluating the credibility and probative worth of evidence).

- help you communicate the evidence and contentions that you think are most likely to appeal to a particular factfinder.

Arguments do not dictate a fixed content of trial presentation. Rather, they enable you to organize and communicate your case in a way that maximizes its persuasiveness, no matter what evidence you consider most important and whether it be "rational" or "emotive." Two attorneys preparing the same case for the same party might reasonably develop different arguments because of disparate views about what will have the greatest appeal to a particular factfinder.

This chapter explains the foundational steps of argument preparation. You'll follow these steps no matter which type of argument you want to prepare, because they are necessary to link the abstract language of legal rules with concrete stories. The following three chapters describe how to tailor arguments according to the type of factual assertion that you want a factfinder to accept (or from a defense perspective, refuse to accept).

A. STEP 1: FORMULATE STORIES

The first step in argument construction is to formulate the stories that you will elicit at trial. This is standard trial preparation. Prior to trial, examine such sources as witness statements, depositions and documents. Then with an eye to evidence rules, determine what information you will elicit from individual witnesses and meld all of it into a client's overall story. If you represent a plaintiff, the overall story will have to consist of sufficient information to carry the burden of proving each disputed legal element. If you represent a defendant, the overall story will revolve around the specific elements you intend to contest at trial.

For example, a plaintiff's story in a civil negligence action may have to include facts sufficient to prove "duty," "breach of duty," "cause in fact," "proximate cause" and "damages." A defendant's story, by contrast, may pertain only to "duty" or "damages."

The story concept is not unique to trial. Stories are simply interconnected events arranged chronologically. While they typically emerge piecemeal from different witnesses and in question-answer rather than narrative form, trial stories are much like those you learned as a youngster, such as "Goldilocks" and "Dante's Inferno." You may develop arguments both for witnesses' individual stories and a client's overall story.

The storytelling mode is hardly surprising. Stories are the basic coin of informational exchange in our society. Whether you are telling a friend what happened when you dined in a fancy restaurant, or a factfinder what events constitute a robbery or a breach of contract, you almost always tell a story.

Everyday experience and social science research confirm that factfinders also tend to rely on stories when making decisions. Factfinders sometimes select between parties' competing stories. Other times they assemble the parties' competing stories into their own composite versions of "what really happened." But whichever path a factfinder follows, the factfinder is likely to understand what happened in the past in story terms, and to evaluate legal principles in terms of that understanding. The factfinder's story may not represent "objective truth," but with objective truth unattainable the legal system is content for cases to be decided according to probabilities.

Outlines: Prepare chronological outlines for each witness' story and a client's overall story, and keep them in a trial notebook or folder. It's easy to get caught up in evidentiary technicalities and procedural wrangles, and these outlines will help in the courtroom when you question witnesses or deliver arguments.

Defendants As Storytellers. Defendants as well as plaintiffs typically put forth and try to establish the accuracy and probative worth of stories. (A common exception to this practice is criminal defendants who instead of offering an affirmative story try to poke holes in the prosecution's case and "rest on the prosecution's burden of proof.")

Example: A plaintiff sues a former employer for wrongful discharge, claiming that the employer wrongfully terminated the employee for being absent from work to serve on a jury. In addition to denying the plaintiff's claim, the employer is likely to offer its own version of "what really happened" (e.g., "the plaintiff quit;" "the plaintiff was fired for reasons having nothing to do with jury service").

Example: In the widely-publicized "Menendez" trials of the 1990's, two brothers were charged with planning to and intentionally killing their parents. The brothers not only denied the prosecution's claim, but also offered evidence of "partial self-defense," claiming that they reasonably though erroneously feared that their parents were going to kill them.

Because defendants typically offer stories of their own, argument preparation typically is as important for defense as for plaintiffs' lawyers.

B. STEP 2: IDENTIFY CRUCIAL FACTUAL PROPOSITIONS

The next step in argument preparation is to link stories to discrete legal elements by identifying factual propositions (sometimes called "ultimate facts" or "material facts"). Then determine the factual propositions whose accuracy is crucial to a case's outcome.

1. Factual Propositions Defined

Factual propositions bridge the gap between stories and legal rules. Stories describe concrete happenings, and are largely devoid of legal concepts. Legal rules and their constituent elements are abstractions, devoid of concrete factual content. This is hardly surprising. Elements have to be stated in broad abstract terms if laws are to cover a wide variety of possible conduct. But as a result of this reality, a factfinder has to see the connection between concrete stories and abstract rules. Factual propositions establish the connection by restating abstract legal elements in case-specific factual terms. In chart form, the factfinder's task looks like this:

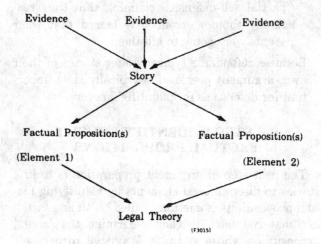

This diagram (based on an off-tackle play developed by the 1938 Chicago Bears) emphasizes that a factfinder constructs a story based on the evidence that the factfinder sees and hears. A factfinder then has to make a mental connection between a story and legal rules.

Consider these examples of factual propositions:

- In a breach of contract action, a factual proposition satisfying the element "not of merchantable quality" would be, "The bicycles had square wheels."

- In a tort action, a factual proposition satisfying the legal element "breach of care" would be, "The contractor used roof supports made out of balsa wood."

- In a murder prosecution, a factual proposition satisfying the legal element of "identity" would be, "Johnson fired the gun."

Since defendants often proffer evidence to support defense versions of events, defense attorneys too formulate factual propositions. Defense counterparts to the above propositions would be:

* "The bicycles had round wheels" or "The bicycles met all contract specifications."

* "The roof supports were made of solid oak."

* "Johnson was asleep at home at the time of the murder."

2. Need for Factual Propositions

Factual propositions are an important intermediate step between stories and legal elements. By identifying factual propositions:

- Representing a plaintiff, you make sure that a story has at least one material fact for each required element.

- Representing a defendant, you target the element or elements you hope to disprove. (Defendants relying on affirmative defenses also make sure that a story has at least one material fact for each element of the affirmative defense.)

- You identify the actual testimony whose accuracy you will try to establish. Generally, witnesses cannot testify using the abstract language of elements. For example, a witness cannot testify that, "The collision was the proximate cause of my hearing loss," or that "Eric committed waste all over the premises." However, witnesses often can testify to material facts: "Sanna backed out of her driveway at a speed of 85 m.p.h." (This would be a material fact for "breach of duty" in a negligence action.)

- You create a map of the evidence you will emphasize and the inferences you will try to communicate to a factfinder throughout trial, including opening statement, direct and cross examination and final summation.

3. Identifying Factual Propositions: An Illustration

The following simple example demonstrates the process of linking stories to abstract elements by identifying factual propositions. Assume that you represent plaintiff Ron Knaplund in a fraud action, and that your overall story is as follows:

Ron wanted to buy a collection of baseball cards as a graduation present for his daughter Kris. On August 26, Ron attended the annual Mammoth Baseball Card and Chili Cookoff Show at the downtown Sheraday Hilton Hotel. One of the merchants at the show was Lefty O'Righty, a retired baseball player. Ron told Lefty that he wanted a valuable set of cards to give as a graduation present to his daughter, a lifelong baseball fan. Lefty told Ron that he had unusual collections of first edition baseball cards, including sets of "Left–Handed All–Star Shortstops" and "Catchers Who Became Nuclear Physicists." Lefty assured Ron that all cards were original and authentic, and Ron paid $7,000.00 for all 3 sets. Ron later took the sets to be appraised, and learned that the cards were all reproductions, worth at most a few hundred dollars. Ron seeks compensatory and punitive damages, as well as damages for emotional distress.

O'Righty's version of events is quite different, and the dispute will have to be resolved through trial.

To identify factual propositions, first list the elements of a fraud action. Those elements typically consist of: (1) making of a representation; (2) falsity of the representation; (3) scienter; (4) reasonable reliance; and (5) damages. As usual, the elements are abstractions, not tied at all to Ron's unique factual story. Then, based on Ron's story, convert each element to a factual proposition.

Here are some of the factual propositions you might formulate based on Ron's story:

Element 1: Making of a Representation. *Factual Proposition:* On August 26, Lefty O'Righty told Ron that all of the baseball cards that Lefty was selling were original and authentic.

Element 2: Falsity of Representation. *Factual Proposition:* The baseball cards that Lefty sold Ron were reproductions.

Element 3: Scienter. *Factual Proposition:* Lefty knew when he told Ron that all of his cards were original and authentic that they were reproductions.

Stories can produce multiple factual propositions for a single element. For example, if Lefty made more than one misstatement to Ron, you might identify multiple factual propositions for element 1.

4. Identify Crucial Factual Propositions

In theory, you might develop arguments to support all of the factual propositions you hope to prove at trial. Certainly, a plaintiff (or a defendant seeking to establish an affirmative defense) needs to offer sufficient evidence to sustain the burden of proving each factual proposition. However, in many cases you needn't develop arguments for all factual propositions.

a.   Representing a Defendant

Representing a defendant, you develop arguments only for the factual propositions you intend to dispute. For example:

- You represent a criminal defendant in a robbery case, and will put forward an alibi defense at trial.

- You represent a defendant in a civil fraud action, and will contest only the reasonableness of the plaintiff's reliance.

In each of these situations, you might limit argument preparation to factual propositions for the single element you intend to contest.

b.   Representing a Plaintiff

Representing a plaintiff, you too can limit argument preparation to contested propositions-if you are confident of which propositions a defendant will contest. Often you will have a basis for making this judgment. For example, a pretrial conference order may define the scope of proof. The thrust of a civil defendant's pretrial discovery or a criminal defendant's preliminary hearing cross examination may be a harbinger of trial arguments. Depending on your relationship with defense counsel, you may even choose to rely on personal conversations. Of course, in case of doubt, you'll have to develop arguments for all factual propositions you'll pursue at trial.

C.   STEP 3: IDENTIFY IMPORTANT EVIDENCE

Once you've identified a case's important factual propositions, you're ready to build the arguments through which you'll try to convince a factfinder of their accuracy. The starting point for each type of argument is an item of important evidence. Just as the longest journey begins with a single step, an argument typically begins with the strongest item of evidence you can identify for the accuracy of a factual proposition. Focus on a specific factual proposition-not on a substantive rule of law and not even on a constituent abstract element. Ask yourself: "Based on depositions, witness statements, etc., what's the strongest item of evidence I can offer that this proposition is accurate?" That's the evidence upon which you'll develop an argument. When you have a number of strong evidentiary items linking to the same factual proposition, you may develop arguments based on each. However, too many separate arguments may tax the patience and attention-span of a factfinder.

Professional judgment is your best guide to strong evidence. Looking to such factors as every-day experience, local community norms and sentiments and an adversary's specific contentions, determine what you consider to be the strongest evidence that tends to prove a factual proposition. Though fixed guides to "strongest evidence" do not exist, keep in mind the following guidelines:

- Don't be a prisoner of your own experiences and values. What counts is what a likely factfinder will view as strong evidence.

- Consider both the rational and the emotional impact of evidence when determining strength.

- Direct evidence usually constitutes strong evidence, for direct evidence accepted as accurate by a factfinder conclusively proves a factual proposition.

- Don't base an argument on evidence of doubtful admissibility.

- Your initial selection needn't be determinative. Unlike the builders of the Leaning Tower of Pisa, prior to trial you can scrap an argument tilting the wrong way and start over with a different evidentiary item.

With this foundational approach in mind, turn now to the process of constructing actual arguments.

CHAPTER 3

CREDIBILITY ARGUMENTS

This chapter describes how to construct arguments persuading a factfinder to accept your client's version of disputed evidence. Adversaries commonly offer disputed versions of important evidence. For example:

- In a criminal case, a prosecution eyewitness identifies the defendant as the robber. The defense offers evidence that the eyewitness is mistaken and puts forth an alibi.

- In a civil personal injury case, the plaintiff claims that the defendant was late for a meeting and was therefore speeding. The defendant denies being late for a meeting.

Credibility arguments grow out of evidence bolstering your version of disputed evidence and attacking your adversary's version.

A. CREDIBILITY MODEL

The factors in the Credibility Model set forth below identify the types of evidence upon which you'll typically base credibility arguments. As the famed evidence scholar Wigmore long ago pointed out, these factors potentially apply to every case, no matter what its substantive background or factual context.

Credibility Model

Credibility of Testimony

   Consistency with Common Experience

   Internal Consistency

   Consistency with Established Facts

Credibility of Witnesses ("Source Credibility")

   Expertise

   Motive or Bias

   Reason to Recall

   Demeanor

Three caveats in connection with the model. First, the model works both ways. The same factors are the bases of arguments that your witnesses are credible and that your adversary's witnesses are not. For example, you might support your witness' credibility with an argument that the witness is neutral, and attack an adverse witness' credibility with an argument that the witness has given inconsistent accounts of events.

Second, each credibility factor potentially operates independently of the others. Thus, you can strengthen a credibility argument by combining two or more factors into a single argument. For example, you might argue that your version of a dispute is accurate because your witness was neutral (had no bias or motive) and testified in a direct and forthright manner.

Third, I thought of recommending the mnemonic "CICEMRD" to help you remember the credibility factors, but decided not to after spraining my tongue in three places trying to pronounce it.

B. CREDIBILITY OF TESTIMONY

1. Consistency With Everyday Experience

Rich testifies that he knows his best friend by his initials only; he does not know what the initials stand for. Jenni testifies that while stopped at an intersection waiting for the light to change, she noticed and can recall the license plate number of a car that made a left turn and proceeded through the intersection without incident. Eileen testifies to what took place during an important meeting, but cannot remember where or when the meeting took place.

Without knowing anything about these three people, or the story contexts to which these pieces of information pertain, you are likely to conclude that all three lack credibility. Based on everyday social experience, you expect people to know what their best friends' initials stand for and where important meetings take place, and that they do not pay rapt attention to every car that passes their line of sight. Factfinders bring such experiences into courtrooms, and use them to evaluate testimony. Thus, you can bolster your version of disputed evidence with an argument that your version is consistent with everyday experience, and attack the adversary's version by arguing that it is inconsistent with everyday experience.

"Objection," you might say. "Often, neither I nor a factfinder will have experienced a witness' precise situation. Therefore, we can't evaluate testimony according to our own experiences."

"Objection overruled!" Analogy is as powerful a reasoning tool in fact-finding as it is in traditional appellate case analysis. Perhaps a factfinder has never known a best friend by initials only. But in all likelihood, the factfinder has known people by nicknames, and in the case of best friends has known what the nicknames stand for. The factfinder is likely to use the experience in the analogous setting to evaluate the witness' testimony.

Factfinders even commonly evaluate expert testimony in the light of their own experiences. For example, an expert may testify that a physically abused child's failure to complain or run away was an example of "Child Abuse Accommodation Syndrome." However, when evaluating the evidence, a factfinder may reason, "That doesn't make sense. I've known of a couple of children who were overly disciplined, and they sure let others know about it right away." Or, a factfinder may disbelieve the expert because of the expert's poor demeanor while testifying. In either case, the factfinder evaluates the expert testimony using everyday reasoning.

The factors in the Credibility Model primarily constitute familiar applications of everyday experience reasoning. For example:

- When you ask a factfinder to distrust testimony from a biased witness, you call on the factfinder's personal experiences with the effect of motive on people's honesty and perceptual ability.

- When you argue that an adverse witness' story has changed from one telling to the next and is therefore not believable, you call on a factfinder's personal experiences with the effect of alterations in stories on their accuracy.

When developing credibility arguments, be careful not to become a prisoner of your own experiences. Experiences are not uniform, certainly across subcultures and even within a single subculture. Therefore, a factfinder's reaction to important evidence will not necessarily comport with yours. One way to overcome "experience blinders" is to test a friend's or a colleague's reaction to a credibility argument before trial. You should also try to learn something about a factfinder's relevant experiences, and to the extent possible select a factfinder whose experiences are compatible with your arguments.

For all of its ubiquitousness, everyday experience reasoning can lead to injustice. Though a factfinder may have an accurate sense of how things *usually* happen, in any specific situation the uncommon may be true. Car alarms occasionally function properly; you may every so often stand in the supermarket line that moves the fastest. The factfinder whose everyday experience leads to disbelief of the uncommon may arrive at a verdict that fails to reflect what actually happened.

However, just because you are the proponent of evidence that conflicts in some respects with a factfinder's experience does not mean that you are helpless. Credibility arguments rest on generalized beliefs, and generalizations are by definition subject to exceptions. Thus, you may counter an adversary's "inconsistency with experience" argument with evidence that constitutes an exception to a generalization.

For example, return to the "initials only" situation. Assume that your alibi witness knows your client, supposedly the witness' best friend, by the witness' initials only. You realize that the adversary is likely to attack the witness' credibility with an argument that "People generally know the full names of their best friends." If the witness can explain why that generalization does not apply in this instance, you may counter the credibility argument by preparing an argument based on the "exception evidence." The testimony on which your argument would be based would look something like this:

Q: Do you know Mr. Cooper by any name other than "J.B.?"

A: No.

Q: Did you ever ask him what "J.B." stands for?

A: No, I never have.

Q: Among your friends and neighbors, is it unusual for people to be referred to by their initials only?

A: No, lots of people only use initials. It's a kind of a tradition in my ethnic group to use initials. I've got maybe 5 or 6 friends that I know only by their initials.

Based on such testimony, you would prepare an argument that, "People generally know the full names of their best friends-except when people in their ethnic group commonly use initials only."

2. Internal Consistency

When we determine credibility according to everyday experience, we evaluate evidence based on beliefs about the functioning of the "outside world." Another common way to evaluate the credibility of evidence is from "within." Most people accept a generalization that credible stories "hang together"—they are internally consistent and remain constant from one telling to the next. We are likely to view witnesses who speak with a forked tongue to be either mistaken, a liar, or a reptile. Thus, you can bolster your version of disputed evidence with an argument that it is consistent with other parts of a story and has not varied, and attack an adversary's version by arguing that it is internally inconsistent.

An internal inconsistency may first appear at trial when an adverse witness' testimony is materially different from a prior statement. In such situations, you obviously cannot prepare an internal inconsistency argument prior to trial. However, you can prepare such an argument when you notice an inconsistency in a witness' pretrial story. For example, assume that you are a defense counsel in a criminal case, and that the police report contains the following information:

"Witness Ramirez was in the store at the time of the robbery. Ramirez initially stated that he did not see the robbery take place. However, the day following the robbery Ramirez identified the defendant as the robber during a photo identification."

In this situation, you might prepare an argument that Ramirez's in-court and photo identifications are unreliable because they are inconsistent with Ramirez's earlier statement that he didn't see the robbery.

Statements need not be directly contradictory to serve as the basis of an internal inconsistency argument. If the only way you are willing to attack testimony, "The light was red," is with "The light was green," you will make internal inconsistency arguments about as often as a New York cabbie drives five blocks without honking. Statements may detract from credibility even if they are only somewhat contradictory. For example, assume that an adverse witness has asserted, "The first bowl of porridge was too hot." You might base an inconsistency argument on either of these statements:

* "There was one bowl of porridge on the table."

* "I was so busy I didn't have time to eat."

If you recognize an internal inconsistency in your witness' story, prepare to counter an adversary's argument by seeking out a possible explanation from your witness. For example, as the prosecutor in the robbery case above, you might ask Ramirez why he initially told the police that he didn't see the robbery. Ramirez might reply, "Because I was scared of getting involved." You might offer the explanation at trial to undercut the adversary's argument.

3. Consistency With Established Facts

Most people find it easier to choose a restaurant if they first decide what kind of food they want to eat or what neighborhood they want to visit. Similarly, resolving factual disputes is easier for a factfinder who can compare disputed evidence to "established facts." You can argue that your version of disputed evidence is credible because it is consistent with established facts, and attack an adversary's version by arguing that it conflicts with such facts.

Factfinders may regard facts as established for a variety of reasons. Parties themselves may establish facts as true by stipulation, or a judge may establish facts as true by taking judicial notice. More often, a factfinder simply regards information as established because of the source from which it comes—a document or a neutral, straightforward witness.

For example, assume that you are the prosecutor in a rape trial. A woman will testify to a violent act of rape; the defendant will claim that they engaged in consensual intercourse. An emergency room physician will testify for the prosecution to certain injuries the doctor observed on the woman about 30 minutes after the alleged rape. The factfinder in this situation is likely to regard the injuries as an established fact. You may therefore bolster the woman's version of events by arguing that it is consistent with the doctor's testimony, and attack the defendant's version by arguing that it conflicts with the testimony.

C. CREDIBILITY OF WITNESSES ("SOURCE CREDIBILITY")

1. In General

Everyday experience teaches that our belief in information is in part influenced by what we know about its source. For example, your belief in the accuracy of statistics may be influenced by whether the speaker is a politician or a statistician. Social science research generally validates the effect of a speaker's personal attributes on the credibility of messages. In one well-known experiment, groups of listeners heard a speech on issues of the day. Some groups were told that the speaker was affiliated with unpopular groups like the American Nazi Party. Other groups were told that the speaker was from a mainstream, popular group such as the League of Women Voters. Though all groups heard the same message, people's beliefs in its accuracy varied dramatically depending on the speaker's identity.

In trial, your ability to control your witnesses is limited. Of Eleanor Roosevelt, Albert Einstein and Jimmy the Weasel, you know the one who is likely to be a percipient witness on your client's behalf. Also, evidence rules constrain your offering significant evidence of a client's or witness' good character. Perhaps only as part of selecting an expert witness can you consciously pick and choose based on personal background factors. Thus, you will often need to develop credibility arguments based on the factors set forth below.

2. Specific vs. General Credibility Evidence

A "source" credibility argument may pertain to a witness' entire testimony. For example, you may argue that a witness' bias undermines the believability of the witness' entire story. Or, a source credibility argument may concern only specific evidence. For instance, apart from a witness' overall credibility, you may argue that the witness' driving an open convertible enabled the witness to hear what was said after an auto accident.

Classifying credibility arguments as either specific or general, while loads of fun in its own right, often affects examination strategy. A typical questioning goal is to elicit evidence in such a way that the factfinder realizes its probative value. Thus, you'll often want to elicit specific credibility evidence along with the event to which the credibility evidence pertains. For example, you'd elicit evidence that a witness was driving an open convertible when you elicit evidence about what the witness heard following an auto accident.

Linking evidence to credibility arguments can even affect the admissibility of evidence. For example, assume that you'd like a factfinder to be aware that a witness to an auto accident has lived in the same house for 20 years. Unless you demonstrate how the evidence relates to credibility, a judge may regard it as improper character evidence. However, the evidence may be admissible if you argue that the information is relevant to the perceptual ability of the witness when it comes to describing an accident that occurred in front of the witness' house.

3. Lying or Mistaken?

Whenever you attack an adversary's story with a credibility argument you have to decide whether your "bottom line" will be that the adversary's witness was lying or mistaken. In general, factfinders are more responsive to the latter than the former. (Of course, exceptions exist. In 1995's famous murder trial of O.J. Simpson, for example, jurors who heard testimony that police officer Mark Fuhrman lied about having used the word "nigger" undoubtedly agreed with the defense argument that Fuhrman had lied about events at the murder scene.)

4. Expertise

Factfinders are likely to believe testimony from witnesses with perceived expertise. For some readers, mention of "expertise" connotes the image of people wearing white jackets with stethoscopes in their pockets. Other readers may think of doctors. However, a more accurate scope of expertise is conveyed by Will Rogers' quote, "All of us are dumb, except in different areas." This credibility factor does not just apply to those witnesses who qualify as experts under Federal Rule of Evidence 702. You can base an "expertise" argument on any information from which a factfinder might infer that a witness' knowledge adds to the probative value of testimony.

Here are examples of testimony on which you might base non-expert expertise arguments:

- A bartender's opinion that a patron was or was not under the influence of alcohol.

- A rutabaga farmer's testimony about the appearance of a rutabaga crop just before it was harvested.

- An eyewitness who had the closest and least-obstructed view of an event.

5. Motive or Bias

The motivations which are the common sources of credibility arguments are familiar to anyone conversant with Aristotle, Shakespeare, or TV soap operas. We all recognize that a witness' testimony may be colored by such considerations as money, love, friendship, money, jealousy, hatred, and money. Perhaps on rare occasions you have even detected your own inclination (always unexercised, of course), to fudge a bit in your own self-interest. On the other hand, you may cherish a "neutral" witness with the same rapture with which a botanist cherishes a prize rose.

Though attorneys routinely base credibility arguments on evidence of motive or neutrality, recognize that almost every witness is potentially open to a charge of bias. For example:

- Many witnesses are open to the charge of having a personal or professional interest in a case's outcome, since most of us spend the bulk of our time with people with whom we have a personal or employment relationship.

- Experts are open to bias charges because they are paid for their time, and future employment may hinge on an expert's willingness to give a favorable opinion.

- Even when employees must seek compensation for work-related injuries through a state's workers' compensation fund, employers are open to bias charges because future insurance premiums may rise if an employee is successful.

- Witnesses with no prior connection to a party may be open to a charge that they are psychologically committed to an initial telling of events, and will obstinately stick to that version even when confronted by contradictory information.

With most witnesses potentially open to charges of bias, you will often have little difficulty developing bias credibility arguments. Of course, the same thing will be true for your adversary. Thus, you should regularly dust your own witnesses' stories for bias problems and be prepared to address them. With a garden-variety bias charge that would apply equally to all similarly-situated witnesses, you can often reply to an attack with a few dismissive words during final summation: "Of course my client's main witnesses were his mother and father. In whose company would you expect a two year old to be?"

Another common tactic is to confront a bias attack head-on during direct examination of your own witness. Attorneys commonly refer to this tactic as "taking the sting out of cross examination." You defuse the adversary's likely attack by referring to it first and in a way that downplays its significance. For example, here you take the sting out of an expected bias attack based on your witness' financial stake in a case's outcome:

Q: Turning your attention to the meeting at which Julie, the general partner, disclosed the liens on the Orange property, please describe what happened.

A: Well, she began by distributing an analysis prepared by her attorney. She said the limited partners would have to come up with another $200,000 if they wanted to hold onto the property. She said she was fully extended, and had no obligation to contribute further financial resources.

Q: Were you a limited partner in the Orange property deal?

A: No.

Q: How did you happen to be at that meeting?

A: Well, I was in a related limited partnership, the Lemon property. Julie was also the general on that one, and I knew that whatever happened with the Orange partnership would affect me.

Q: Are you presently in litigation with Julie on the Lemon property?

A: Yes.

Q: Is your testimony at all affected by the fact that what happens to Julie in this case may affect the outcome of the Lemon property litigation?

A: No. Of course I don't want to lose my money, but I realized going in that the investment was pretty speculative, so I didn't really invest that much. Also, this is a business dispute, and Julie and I are still friends.

Q: O.K. Let's return for a moment to that meeting. After Julie distributed her attorney's analysis....

Bringing out the potential financial motive yourself suggests that the evidence is of little probative value. Moveover, on direct unlike on cross, the witness can explain the situation in response to open questions. Eliciting information about the meeting before going into the potential bias may also be helpful. Social science research suggests that the effect of motive is diminished when a listener hears information before learning of the motivation.

6. Reason to Observe or Recall

Most people in our culture believe in cause-and-effect; things happen for a reason. For example, the nightly stock market report is hardly complete without an explanation: "The industrial index went up 30 points today on news that inflation is low in cholesterol." Applying this attitude to witness testimony, belief about the accuracy of testimony is often affected by a witness' having a reason to observe or recall an event. You can bolster credibility with an argument that a witness has a particular reason to observe or recall a past event, and attack credibility by arguing that no such reason exists. For example:

- In a breach of contract action, you offer evidence from a waiter that during a May 1 lunch meeting, the waiter heard Binder agree to sell golf equipment to Moore. The waiter offers a reason for recalling the conversation: "They were giving me golf tips all through lunch so I was around their table during most of the lunch hour." You might argue based on this explanation that the waiter had a reason to hear the conversation and that the waiter's version of events is therefore credible.

- In a medical malpractice action, your adversary offers evidence from Andrea that when she was in a hospital emergency room waiting for an MRI, Andrea overheard another patient tell the admitting nurse that "It's been longer than an hour since I had dinner." You might prepare an argument attacking the credibility of Andrea's story on the ground that Andrea has no reason to recall or recollect what an unrelated patient told the nurse.

7. Demeanor

Demeanor is the collection of physical traits and idiosyncracies that factfinders often regard as adding to or subtracting from credibility. For example, you may argue that a factfinder should distrust the testimony of a witness who hesitates repeatedly or looks to opposing counsel before answering, and trust the testimony of a witness who is forthright during both direct and cross examination. You can prepare demeanor credibility arguments (preliminarily, at least) when, as is often the case, you've had a chance to interview or depose a witness before trial.

Attorneys often try to improve their own witnesses' demeanor. For example, you may try to incorporate a tangible exhibit into a direct examination. Many people take on added confidence and are more comfortable when they can hold and refer to exhibits. Or, you may issue a flurry of pretrial instructions such as to how to dress (professionally), how to respond to questions (succinctly, without volunteering information) and where to look (occasionally directly at judge and jurors).

Such tactics sometimes backfire. Demeanor is the sum total of a person's traits and appearance.

Change a single element, and you may detract from credibility. The instruction to use eye contact can backfire if a witness stares at the judge continuously while testifying. The witness whose manner of dress is rumply and whose language tends to be salty may lose credibility when constrained by "suitable" attire and the rules of grammar. Witnesses are often nervous enough trying to remember their testimony; your instructions may only add another level of complexity.

Nevertheless, you can take a variety of steps to help witnesses project as credible a demeanor as possible:

- Take witnesses on field trips. You can bolster witnesses' confidence in their memories by accompanying them to the scenes of important events, and help relax them by taking them to the courtroom where a trial will take place. In the latter situation, avoid asking questions that reveal your own lack of experience: "Say, witness, why is that person behind the high desk wearing a black robe?"

- Rehearse testimony, both your direct and an adversary's anticipated cross. Ask questions the same way in your office that you will in court. When attorneys complain after trial that "the witness' bad demeanor really took me by surprise," the reason is often that the attorneys first surprised the witness. For example, don't ask narrow, specific questions during rehearsal and then expect witnesses to elaborate in response to open questions at trial. You're the professional. Adapt to your witnesses, don't make them adapt to you.

● Give in-court reminders when necessary. For example, when a witness is so nervous that the witness is having difficulty telling an intelligible story, many judges would allow you to say something like, "Many people are a bit nervous when they testify. Please just relax, listen to what you're asked, and answer as best you can." Or you may tell a witness whose gaze has been transfixed on you, "Now, please look directly at the jurors and tell them whether you ever ..." Or in a desperate situation, "Please retake the oath, this time without keeping your fingers crossed."

If despite such techniques your witness' demeanor remains a potential issue, you can address it during final summation. In particular, you might suggest to a factfinder that it's unfair and irrational to evaluate a witness according to demeanor. Consider this argument:

"Opposing counsel will probably argue that Kevin is not credible, because he was nervous and had trouble answering some questions. Does that strike you as a fair way to decide my client's future? Someone who's not a professional witness, who has never testified at a trial before, who answers a subpoena, is understandably nervous and opposing counsel wants you to disregard everything he says? Wouldn't you expect a person in Kevin's position to be a bit nervous? Let's not get sidetracked, let's look at what Kevin had to say ..."

Here, you not only ask the factfinder to reject what you characterize as an unfair argument, but also you cast the nasty adversary as the proponent of the unfair argument.

This chapter has described the kinds of evidence you can look to when developing arguments supporting the accuracy of your client's version of important disputed evidence. The next chapter describes arguments supporting your desired legal conclusions.

CHAPTER 4

INFERENTIAL ARGUMENTS

This chapter describes a process for developing inferential arguments. An adversary can accept your version of important evidence yet contest its inferential significance. For instance, your adversary in a personal injury case may concede that a driver was late for a meeting, but contend that being late did not cause the driver to drive carelessly. An inferential argument seeks to persuade a factfinder to infer the conclusion "drove carelessly" from the evidence "late for a meeting."

Making Both Credibility and Inferential Arguments. When an adversary disputes an item of important evidence, you may have to develop two arguments: a Credibility Argument to convince a factfinder to accept your client's version of the dispute, and an Inferential Argument convincing a factfinder to draw your desired inference. For example, your personal injury case adversary may deny that the driver was late for a meeting. If so, you may need to develop a credibility argument that the driver was late, and an inferential argument linking that evidence to your desired inference, "drove carelessly."

A. INFERENCES DEFINED

An inference is simply a mental link between information and a conclusion (factual proposition). All of us draw inferences every day and have done so since early childhood. For instance, perhaps you winced as a child when your parents told you that "company is coming for dinner." If so, it's because you inferred from that information that you would have to eat late, sit quietly at the table, go without TV, etc. And if you're happy to receive a message to return an opposing counsel's phone call, perhaps it's because you infer that your settlement offer has been accepted.

While inference-drawing is a familiar activity, few us think about the process by which we draw inferences. Understanding that process will enable you to develop inferential arguments supporting your desired inferences and undermining those of your adversaries.

B. INFERENCES AND CIRCUMSTANTIAL EVIDENCE

Inferential arguments come into play when you build an argument around an important item of circumstantial evidence. Inferential arguments are not necessary for direct evidence, which if accepted as accurate by a factfinder establishes a factual proposition without the need of an inference.

Example: A witness testifies in a murder case that "The defendant is the person who pulled the trigger." If believed by the factfinder, this testimony establishes the element of "identity" without the need for an inference. (Readers inclined towards cynicism might protest that since a factfinder must infer that direct evidence is accurate for a factual proposition to be proved, the concept of direct evidence is a myth. But why let cynics spoil a good dichotomy?)

By contrast, circumstantial evidence proves a factual proposition only via one or more inferences. For example, evidence that Hansel and Gretel had a violent quarrel tends to prove that Gretel killed Hansel the next day only if the factfinder infers that the quarrel motivated Gretel to kill Hansel. Thus, if you're prosecuting Gretel for murder you may want to develop an inferential argument linking the evidence ("violent quarrel") to your desired conclusion ("murder").

Inferential arguments would be unnecessary if circumstantial evidence always gave rise to a single and obvious inference. Alas, items of circumstantial evidence typically give rise to numerous and even conflicting inferences. Thus, you cannot assume that factfinders who believe that your evidence is accurate will draw your desired inferences. For example, a factfinder who accepts evidence that Hansel and Gretel had a violent quarrel the day before Hansel's death may have a "so what" reaction, simply failing to see any connection between a violent quarrel and murder. A factfinder may even draw an opposite inference favorable to the defense, reasoning that the violent quarrel so frightened

Gretel that she stayed as far away from Hansel as possible. Inferential arguments, then, are often necessary if you are to convince a factfinder to draw your desired inference. As luck would have it, the process of developing such arguments begins with the next section.

C. IDENTIFY AN EMBRYONIC ARGUMENT

Inferential arguments, like credibility arguments, begin with what you consider to be an important item of evidence. To begin developing an inferential argument, simply link the important evidence to a desired factual proposition. You thereby create an "embryonic argument," which you will try to carry to full term with additional evidence.

Example 1

Important evidence: Julian was 20 minutes late for a meeting.

Factual proposition: Julian was speeding.

Embryonic argument: Julian was 20 minutes late for a meeting; therefore he was speeding.

Example 2

Important evidence: The bloody glove found at a murder scene does not fit the defendant's hand.

Factual proposition: The defendant is not the person who committed the murder.

Embryonic argument: Evidence that the bloody glove did not fit the defendant's hand shows that the defendant did not commit the murder.

If you think that an embryonic argument is so strong that any factfinder is certain to accept it, you may move on to arguments for other factual propositions. However, left to their own devices and often at the behest of opposing counsel, factfinders often draw inferences that you do not anticipate. Most of the time, therefore, you need to identify additional evidence that strengthens an embryonic argument.

D. IDENTIFY A GENERALIZATION UNDERLYING YOUR DESIRED INFERENCE

Identifying the generalization underlying the link between an item of evidence and a factual proposition can help you to strengthen an embryonic argument. All inferences are based on generalizations. Whenever you or a factfinder draw an inference, you implicitly adopt a generalization about the behavior of people and things. For example, when you infer that a driver who was late to a meeting was driving carelessly, you implicitly rely on a generalization such as, "People who are late to a meeting sometimes (or often) drive too fast." Similarly, when you link a glove's lack of fit to a defendant's innocence, you implicitly rely on a generalization such as, "People whose hand does not fit a bloody glove found at a murder scene have not committed the murder."

Referring to generalizations during trial. Explicitly identifying generalizations is primarily a tool for strengthening embryonic arguments. You need not always refer to generalizations when arguing to a factfinder at trial. For example, during final summation you may argue that "The fact that the driver was late for a meeting strongly supports our contention that the driver was speeding," without mentioning the underlying generalization. See Chapter 10, "Closing Argument."

Multiple generalizations. Sometimes you can further strengthen an embryonic argument by recognizing that two (or sometimes more) generalizations connect an item of evidence to a factual proposition. For example, assume that you have identified the following embryonic argument: "Because Carol's children were roughhousing in the back seat of her car, Carol was driving carelessly." Underlying this argument might be two generalizations: (1) "People who drive while their children are roughhousing in the back seat of their cars are sometimes angry;" and (2) "People who drive while they are angry sometimes drive too fast." By more precisely identifying the mental path a factfinder should follow, multiple generalizations can sometimes help you produce a stronger argument.

E.   STRENGTHEN AN EMBRYONIC ARGUMENT WITH "ESPECIALLY WHENS"

Having identified an underlying generalization or two, you strengthen an embryonic argument by marshaling additional evidence suggesting that the generalization is especially likely to be accurate in your particular case. To identify additional evidence, add "especially when" to a generalization and examine a case file for information supporting its accuracy. The result is a full-term inferential argument that converts a statement about what is generally true into an assertion about what is true in a particular case.

Example

Embryonic argument: Julian was 20 minutes late for a meeting; therefore he was speeding.

Generalization and especially whens: People who are late to a meeting often drive too fast, especially when ...

- the meeting is an important one.
- they have no way to inform the other attendees that they are late.
- they are to lead the meeting.

Assume that you can offer evidence of each of these "especially whens." Your resulting inferential argument is that "Julian was 20 minutes late for an important meeting that he was to lead. He had no way of informing the other attendees that he was going to be late. You should conclude from this evidence that Julian was speeding."

Identifying "especially whens" is closely analogous to identifying important evidence. Relying on professional judgment and looking to factors like everyday experience and local community norms, you determine what evidence a factfinder is likely to find pertinent and persuasive. Also keep in mind the following:

- You can often include evidence of doubtful admissibility when developing an inferential argument. If an "especially when" is not admitted into evidence, the argument proceeds without it.

- An "especially when" sometimes will strike you as stronger evidence for a factual proposition than the evidence with which you began an embryonic argument. If so, reconstruct the argument putting the former "especially when" at its center. (The former "strong" item will probably become an "especially when" in the new argument. Well, fame is always fleeting.)

For instance, assume that an "especially when" in your argument about the driver who was late for a meeting is, "the meeting concerned the driver's child's failure to comply with conditions of probation imposed after the child was convicted of a crime." You believe that an argument centering on the subject matter of the meeting will be more persuasive than the one based on the driver's being late for the meeting. If so, simply reconstruct the argument to emphasize the former "especially when." The new argument would go something like this: "People who are on the way to a meeting with a probation officer concerning their child's failure to comply with the conditions of probation often drive too fast, especially when they are late for the meeting and have no way to inform the probation officer that they will be late." (If you were a "perfect thinker," you might have based an argument on the "probation officer" evidence in the first place. However, few of us are perfect thinkers. Your views about what evidence is most important often fluctuate, even during trial when you gauge a factfinder's reaction to evidence.)

F. ATTACK AN ADVERSARY'S ARGUMENT WITH "EXCEPT WHENS"

Just as you often attack the credibility of an adversary's important evidence, you typically also seek to undermine its probative value. To do so, identify an adversary's likely embryonic arguments and add "except when" to the generalizations underlying those arguments. The evidence you identify tends to detract from a generalization's usual accuracy, and thereby undermines the adversary's argument. (While you should think through an adversary's case thoroughly enough to identify the adversary's likely embryonic arguments and underlying generalizations, you needn't go so far as to identify an adversary's "especially whens." Normally, you can undermine an adversary's inferential arguments by looking for "except whens" to generalizations underlying embryonic arguments.)

For example, assume that you're prosecuting the defendant in a murder case. You're confident that the defense will base an argument on circumstantial evidence that a bloody glove found at the murder scene did not fit the defendant's hand when the defendant tried it on at trial. The generalization underlying this argument is, "People whose hand does not fit a bloody glove found at a murder scene have not committed the murder." To counter the argument, add "except when" to the generalization and examine the file for evidence suggesting that what might be generally true is not true in this particular case. "Except whens" that you might identify include:

- "Except when a year has elapsed between the date of the murder and the date the defendant tried on the glove, and the glove shows signs of shrinkage."

- "Except when blood from the defendant and the victim is on the glove."

- "Except when a search of the defendant's residence turned up numerous gloves of varying sizes."

Assuming that you offer such evidence at trial, you would have the basis for an argument such as:

"The fact that the glove didn't appear to exactly fit the defendant's hand in no way disproves that the defendant committed the murder. A year has elapsed since the date of the murder, and you heard evidence that the glove clearly shows signs of shrinkage. Furthermore, recall that a search of the defendant's residence turned up numerous gloves of varying sizes, showing that the defendant would wear gloves even if they didn't fit perfectly. Finally, blood from both the defendant and the victim is on the glove. Thus, you should ignore the supposed lack of fit between the glove and the defendant's hand."

G. RESPOND TO AN ADVERSARY'S LIKELY "EXCEPT WHENS"

Just as you can, an adversary is likely to put forward "except whens" to attack your arguments. If you can anticipate an adversary's likely attacks in advance, you have a chance to offer evidence responding to them during trial.

For example, assume that you represent the defendant in the "late for a meeting" negligence case. You plan to argue that the factfinder should infer that the defendant was driving carefully, based in part on evidence that the defendant was driving with an expensive glass vase in the car. Thinking about how the plaintiff is likely to reply to this argument, you think it likely that the plaintiff will cite the defendant's being late for a meeting. That is, the plaintiff will argue that "People who have expensive glass vases in their car sometimes drive carefully, except when they are late for a meeting." To respond to this argument, try to generate evidence explaining away the impact of the "except when." One way to generate such evidence is to confront a client or witness with the adversary's argument and ask for a response. Here, for example, you might ask the defendant, "The plaintiff will probably argue that it didn't matter that you had the vase in the car, what really affected your driving was that you were late for a meeting. How can we answer that?" (or, "Is there anything in particular that led you to drive at a safe speed even though you were late for the meeting?") You can respond to the adversary's argument by including the evidence you uncover in the defendant's direct or redirect examination:

Q: You've told us that when you started out, you were late for the meeting with Samantha. Why didn't this affect how you drove?

A: I had told Samantha's secretary a few days earlier that I might be late, so I wasn't that concerned. Also, a meeting I had scheduled for later that day had fallen through, so I had no time pressure to finish the meeting by a certain time.

CHAPTER 5

NORMATIVE AND SILENT ARGUMENTS

This chapter describes how to prepare the final two kinds of arguments which you can use to try to influence factfinders at trial.

A. NORMATIVE ARGUMENTS

Many factual propositions make assertions about past events. Consider these examples of "historical" factual propositions:

- In a tort action, for the legal element breach of care, "The contractor used roof supports made out of balsa wood."

- In a murder prosecution, for the legal element of identity, "Johnson fired the gun."

- In a murder prosecution, the defense version of the legal element of identity, "The defendant was at home at the time of the murder."

The factfinder can accept or reject each of these factual propositions strictly according to its view of history: does each proposition accurately assert what happened in the past?

Some legal elements, however, require factfinders to make normative as well as historical judgments.

That is, some elements call on factfinders to evaluate the propriety of past events in the light of community norms. Consider these examples:

- A prosecutor in a police battery case may have to prove that a police officer used "excessive force" when making an arrest.

- A plaintiff in a breach of contract action may have to prove that the defendant's breach was "material."

- A plaintiff in a negligence action may have to prove that the defendant acted "unreasonably."

- An employee in a wrongful termination case may have to prove that the employer lacked "just cause" to sack the employee.

In each of these cases, a factfinder would have to do more than decide what happened in the past. In addition, a factfinder would have to evaluate the legal propriety of what happened according to its view of community values and standards. "Normative arguments" assert your positions on the normative aspects of legal elements.

For example, assume that a factfinder concludes in a wrongful termination case that an employer sacked an employee for reporting drunk to work on two occasions in a three week time span and for misplacing a purchase order. That determination doesn't end the factfinder's task. The factfinder still has to decide whether those delinquencies constitute "just cause" for termination. In making this normative determination, a factfinder acts as the "conscience of the community." The "just cause" determination reflects a value judgment about appropriate behavior by employers and employees.

A normative argument consists of the reasons that a normative standard has or has not been satisfied. Typically, normative arguments demonstrate why a party's conduct was fair and reasonable (or unfair and unreasonable). As with credibility and inferential arguments, such arguments rest on what you think a factfinder will see as important evidence supporting the accuracy of your normative claims. Evidence bearing on the fairness and reasonableness of a party's conduct tends to satisfy one of the following factors:

- The evidence identifies positive or negative consequences (or potential consequences) flowing from a party's conduct; or

- The evidence shows that less restrictive alternatives were (or were not) available to a party; or

- The evidence demonstrates that a party's conduct did (or did not) conform to the customs and practices of a particular trade, industry or profession.

The evidence that you identify pursuant to any one of these factors become the bases of arguments in support of your normative position.

For example, assume that you represent a plaintiff who has sued a police officer for using excessive force in making an arrest. Your "historical" factual proposition is that the officer struck your client with a baton at least five times after the defendant was immobilized on the ground. Your normative arguments that the force was "excessive" might be as follows:

- Consequences: the plaintiff suffered multiple skull fractures as a result of the baton blows. (The *potential* for multiple skull fractures would also support a consequentialist argument, albeit a somewhat weaker one.)

- Alternatives: A backup officer who could have helped immobilize the plaintiff without the need to resort to head blows was on the scene.

- Industry practice: Local police department practice is to immediately handcuff an immobilized suspect.

Developing such arguments in advance of trial enables you to make sure that you have evidence proving (or disproving) the normative aspects of factual propositions. Along with the other arguments, you also contribute to the outline of your most important evidence.

Like the factors in the Credibility Model, the factors you can use to influence a factfinder's normative judgment also cut both ways. For example, the defense attorney in the "excessive police force" prosecution might argue that the officer's actions did not have negative consequences. That is, the defense might argue that the force was not excessive because the baton blows did not (and did not have the potential to) result in skull fractures. Rather, the fractures occurred when the arrestee's head struck the ground, and might have occurred even in the absence of baton blows.

B. SILENT ARGUMENTS

Factfinders are sometimes influenced by arguments that legal rules do not allow to be made explicitly. For example, a factfinder may believe a witness in part because the factfinder and witness are members of the same ethnic group, or disbelieve a witness who talks with a non-U.S. accent. The arguments which promote these conclusions are silent. Because no rational connection links ethnicity or accent to trustworthiness, neither party can put forth such arguments at trial. However, they are a reality of trial. In our polyglot society, all people have the peace of mind of knowing that they belong to groups which are distrusted by members of other groups.

To Kill a Mockingbird. To Kill a Mockingbird (1962) is perhaps the best film ever made about the effect of racial prejudice on the outcome of a trial. The film, set in the early 1930's, depicts the rape conviction of an innocent African–American man by an all-white Southern jury. Atticus Finch, the defendant's lawyer, is a heroic figure. However, Atticus is unable to dislodge the jurors' silent arguments linking credibility to racial identity.

So inherent are silent arguments in the trial process that you may seek to capitalize on them without realizing that you are doing so. You make silent arguments when you decide what to wear to court, when you advise a client of how to dress for trial and when you confer respectfully with a client within a factfinder's view. Sometimes silent arguments are more obvious, as when a prosecutor's office assigns a trial deputy who is of the same ethnicity as a defendant. Implicit in the trial deputy's participation is the argument, "I wouldn't be prosecuting this case if the defendant weren't really guilty."

The following considerations may help you to counter silent arguments that may be directed against a client you represent:

- Take time before trial to think about whether your client is likely to be the victim of a silent argument. Silent arguments potentially arise in every case, not just in emotionally-charged ones. Whether a client (or a witness) is a landlord, a tenant, a debt collector, a youth, or anything else, prejudice is always a risk of trial.

- In a jury trial, consider addressing silent arguments during jury voir dire. For example, you might ask, "Will each of you promise not to give less than full weight to Ms. Beilen's testimony simply because her accent might make her a little difficult to understand?" Few jurors would refuse to give such a promise. By making the promise explicit, however, you make it less likely that jurors will subconsciously be influenced by the witness' accent.

- Make a motion in limine (pretrial motion) to exclude evidence which might give rise to a silent argument. Obviously, you can't exclude evidence of a witness' accent or a party's ethnicity. But assume that a witness was a member some years earlier of an unpopular social group. If membership in the group has only a scant connection to the case, consider making a motion seeking to exclude the evidence. Under a rule such as Federal Rule of Evidence 403, you'd ask the judge to exclude the evidence of group membership because the danger of unfair prejudice outweighs its probative value.

- Offer "individualizing evidence." Often, silent arguments grow out of stereotypes concerning the perceived attributes of social groups. If you can show that a member of a burdened group does not share the perceived attribute, you may overcome a silent argument.

Example: Your client is a low-income tenant. You fear that the factfinder thinks low income tenants irresponsible, and is therefore inclined to disbelieve your client's story. You may overcome this argument by looking for opportunities to offer evidence of the tenant's responsible behavior. The factfinder can keep its general prejudice, and you gain by showing that your client is an exception to the general stereotype. (Your personal preference might be to attack the stereotype head-on by arguing that any general hostility by the factfinder to tenants is unfair. However, your primary duty is to an individual client. The head-on approach didn't work for Atticus Finch, and it probably won't work for you either.)

- Address the silent argument explicitly during final summation. Most people consider themselves fair and unbiased; it's always the other slobs who cause the problems. Thus, when you raise the possibility that a silent argument might influence a factfinder, and argue the unfairness and irrationality of such an argument, a factfinder may consciously reject it. Though conscious intent may not forever eliminate subconscious prejudice, it may for a brief moment counteract it.

CHAPTER 6

OPENING STATEMENT

Together, opening statement and final summation bookend your presentation of evidence. Each gives you a chance to address a factfinder directly. As opening statement precedes evidence, it formally functions as a roadmap or outline that helps a factfinder follow your overall story and the legal significance of your evidence. In the words of nearly every judge who's ever donned a robe, opening statement is not the time to argue the merits of your case. However, opening statement needn't be a bland recital of evidence to come. If you don't describe your case during opening in a way that makes a factfinder want to rule in your client's favor, your chance of ultimate success is slim.

A. PUT FORTH A THEME

A theme is a succinct assertion that captures the fairness and justice of a legal claim. A theme conveys the message that beneath all the testimonial complexity is a simple truth that merits a favorable verdict. Stories typically emerge piecemeal through different witnesses, and evidence rules normally prevent witnesses from giving opinions about the significance of evidence. Thus, a theme is generally your only opportunity before final summation to convey the justness of your case in a sentence or two.

To develop a theme, try to reduce a client's over-all story to a key sentence or two and provide a reason for events happening in the way you claim they did. Examine these possible themes:

- A prosecutor in a criminal case: "In an effort to scare a family of bears into thinking that their house was haunted and selling it cheap, the defendant broke into the house, destroyed furniture, ate food and rumpled beds."

- A defendant in a criminal case: "This is a case in which coercive police tactics have caused two highly suggestible witnesses to misidentify a completely innocent person." (Note that this theme does not depend on the defense offering its own version of events. Even a defense attorney who intends to rely entirely on poking holes in the prosecution's evidence could articulate this theme.)

- A plaintiff in a civil wrongful discharge case: "This is a case in which Susan Davis, a five year employee of the bank who consistently received outstanding performance evaluations, was fired by a supervisor who was trying to shift blame for a bad loan to her."

- The defendant in the same civil wrongful discharge case: "In this case my client, the Conglomerate Bank, protected its depositors and employees by discharging an employee who decided to finalize a big loan to get herself promoted to branch manager. Her false reports led the bank to make a loan it would never have made otherwise, causing the bank to lose nearly half a million dollars."

Each theme briefly describes what happened, and suggests why events took place as you claim. Each thus provides the factfinder with a succinct way of thinking about a case from your client's perspective. Of course, you need to echo a theme throughout a case. For example, it does little good to say during opening statement that a loan supervisor fired an employee in an effort to shift blame for a bad loan, and then introduce evidence showing that the supervisor's true motivation was a romance gone sour.

B. SET FORTH YOUR STRONGEST ARGUMENTS

At the conclusions of trials, factfinders have to link factual stories to abstract legal elements. Since arguments marshal evidence according to factual propositions, you can help the factfinder make this link during opening statement by identifying at the beginning of an opening statement the crucial arguments on which you will ultimately rely.

For example, assume that you represent the defendant in the misidentification criminal case. Your strongest argument is based on evidence that before a showup, the witnesses were told that "your information really helped to nail the right guy." You've constructed the following argument:

"People who have been told before viewing a suspect that their information has really helped to nail the right guy often misidentify the suspect as the culprit, especially when ...

• the statement is made by a police officer;

• the suspect is the only person the witnesses are asked to identify;

• the suspect and the witnesses are of different racial groups;

• the crime was committed at night and the witnesses were 50 feet away;

• the witnesses observed the culprit for at most a moment or two.

After setting out your theme, you might refer to this argument during opening statement as follows:

"You'll hear critical evidence that before viewing the defendant, the witnesses were told that their information really helped to nail the right guy. This led them to misidentify the defendant as the culprit, especially when you also consider that the statement was made by a police officer, the suspect was the only person the witnesses were asked to identify, the suspect and the witnesses are of different racial groups, the crime was committed at night and the witnesses were 50 feet away and the witnesses observed the culprit for at most a moment or two."

Observe that the above example does not refer to the generalization underlying the argument ("People who have been told before viewing a suspect that their information has really helped to nail the right guy often misidentify the suspect as the culprit.") However, you may often choose to do so.

C. SUMMARIZE YOUR STORY

The main portion of an opening statement typically consists of an overview of the evidence you will present at trial. One overview option is to proceed "witness-by-witness," summarizing the testimony each witness will give. A major down side is that a witness-by-witness overview tends to be boring; even writing the sentence wasn't much of a thrill. Moreover, a witness-by-witness overview fails to provide a factfinder with an overall chronology of events, and obscures the relationship between evidence and crucial arguments.

A second overview option is to set forth evidence according to arguments. This option allows you to emphasize the most important evidence, but at a cost of obscuring an overall story. For example, look back at the sample argument at the end of Section "B" above. That argument does not provide a story about what happened.

A third overview option is to provide a chronology of important events, melding the testimony from all witnesses into a single overall story. A "story" overview responds to the way in which judges and jurors commonly approach decision-making, which is to organize testimony into a story reflecting their beliefs about what really happened. A story overview also helps factfinders understand and recognize the importance of testimony as it emerges during a trial. The following suggestions may help you to provide an effective overview:

- Generally, relate events in the order of their occurrence. Whether you are describing a movie's plot, trying to remember where you left a set of car keys or trying to explain to a factfinder the events culminating in litigation, chronology is usually the clearest method of communication. You may have to vary from this method in complex cases. For example, if numerous events relating to different aspects of a case are happening during the same time span, consider providing a separate chronology for each aspect.

- Use concrete, everyday language that engages a listener's interest. For example, compare the potential civil plaintiff's overviews below. The case involves a bicycle rider who was injured when the quick-release mechanism on the front wheel of the bike allegedly malfunctioned and caused the bike to collapse.

Excerpt A: "Though I remind you that what I say is not evidence, I expect the evidence will show that my client rode his bike at a normal speed and in a normal manner across railroad tracks. The evidence will further show that the uneven surface resulted in the bicycle's bumping up and down as it crossed the tracks, loosening the quick-release mechanism on the front wheel, so that the bike gave way under my client and he my client fell to the ground."

Excerpt B: "Joy was out for a bike ride on a typical late summer day. School was approaching, but she and her two friends had a few more days to relax and enjoy summer vacation. They decided to see a movie matinee, and headed down Bolas St. towards Beloit Ave. They were pedaling at a normal rate of speed, as they had plenty of time to get to the movie. Michael rode across the tracks, and then MaryAnn. Of course they bumped up and down a bit, but they had no problem at all. Then Joy pedaled across. Suddenly her bicycle began to shake and bounce. Just as Joy got across the tracks, the quick-release mechanism on the front tire came loose and the front wheel collapsed. Joy was thrown to the ground."

Excerpt A does little to create empathy or drama. The injured rider is abstractly referred to as a "client;" phrases such as "what I say is not evidence" and "the evidence will show" distance the factfinder from the incident; and the language is flat and legalistic. Excerpt B, by contrast, refers to "Joy" by name, helping the factfinder see her as a person, not a legal abstraction. The language is conversational and vivid, and the story unfolds much as it might outside of court. Without breaking any rules, or playing on false sympathy, Excerpt B is more likely to make the factfinder want to rule in Joy's favor.

- Incorporate arguments into an overview. Assuming that you've already mentioned your most crucial arguments at the outset of an opening statement, you may refer to others at the point in a chronology where you mention the evidence on which the argument is based. For example, in the bicycle case, assume that you have developed an argument based on the design of the quick-release mechanism, which includes a couple of "especially whens." You might set forth the argument at the point in the story when you mention the mechanism:

"Just as Joy got across the tracks, the quick-release mechanism on the front tire came loose and the front wheel collapsed. Quick-release mechanisms are prone to collapse when made from recycled soda cans, especially when ..."

D. OPENING STATEMENT PITFALL: ARGUMENT

Remember that argumentativeness is a principle opening statement no-no. You're not supposed to analyze credibility or explain the inferences or conclusions that you want a factfinder to draw from testimony. A good rule of thumb is, "If a witness will not testify to it, you probably cannot refer to it during opening statement." Compare these examples:

a. "Little Jimmy was standing but ten feet away from where the collision occurred, and had an unobstructed view of what happened."

b. "Little Jimmy, standing but ten feet away from where the collision occurred, had the best opportunity of all the witnesses to observe what happened, and therefore his testimony is particularly credible."

Example "a" refers to factual testimony that a witness will give, and thus is proper in opening statement. However, example "b" is improperly argumentative. No witness will testify that Jimmy had "the best opportunity ... to observe," or that he is especially credible. The assertions refer to inferences that the factfinder is to draw.

However, many judges permit seemingly forbidden argument during opening statement. In part, the reason is that attorneys often fail to recognize and object to improper argument (or won't object to yours so that you won't object to theirs). In addition, judges have wide discretion when it comes to ruling on the propriety of opening statement, and one judge's proper factual assertion is another's improper argument. By analogy, consider the philosophy of the great Rodin, who said that to sculpt an elephant one had only to start with a large block of marble and chip away whatever was not an elephant. Final summation is like Rodin's block of marble, and judges vary greatly when it comes to ruling on how much argument you have to chip away.

Because you can never be certain of what a judge will consider to be improper argument, the best tactic is to err on the side of argumentativeness. If an adversary objects, and if the judge sustains the objection, you can apply the chisel to the remainder of an opening statement. In the meantime, look for chances to identify your desired inferences and conclusions during opening statement. For example, you'll probably be allowed to tell a factfinder that your two witnesses are "neutral and unbiased," and assert that an adversary driver "was not paying enough attention to the road."

Definitional niceties aside, be aware that proper opening statement is sometimes in the ear as well as the eye of the beholder. Using an argumentative tone of voice increases the likelihood that a judge will sustain an "improper opening statement" objection.

E. OPENING STATEMENT PITFALL: EXCESSIVE DETAIL

Excessive detail is an enemy of a persuasive opening statement. You need to include enough details to make a story comprehensible and appealing. Yet excessive details obscure important evidence and are tedious. Moreover, just as an overly detailed movie preview can destroy any interest you might have in seeing a film, so may excessive details in opening statement cause factfinder inattentiveness to your witnesses. A factfinder may think, "Why should I bother paying attention to the witness? The attorney already covered this stuff." Too, if witnesses simply repeat what you've already said during opening, the witnesses may appear to be following a well-rehearsed script.

In the abstract, rules separating "good" details from "excessive" details are nonexistent. The arguments you've developed before trial are generally your best guides. Include the details that support important arguments, otherwise try to limit yourself to summary descriptions of past events.

F.   OPENING STATEMENT PITFALL: PROMISES YOU CAN'T KEEP

What you say during opening statement is not evidence. Therefore, you should not refer to information that you may not be able to offer into evidence in an effort to make a persuasive opening splash. The consequences for violating this principle include:

- If the information is very prejudicial, the judge may grant an adversary's request for a mistrial and impose sanctions on you and your client.

- An adversary can undermine your arguments during final summation by pointing out your failure to deliver on promises you made during opening statement.

The following considerations will help you to avoid such negative consequences:

- Be alert to "waffling." If a friendly witness is reluctant to provide information, or includes information in a story on some occasions but not others, do not refer to the information during opening statement. Witnesses who waffle in the comfort of your office may turn to batter when placed under oath and leave you with egg on your face.

- Don't refer to information that will come from potentially unavailable witnesses. For example, don't refer to information that you hope to elicit from a six year old child who was exposed to measles on 14 different occasions in the weeks prior to trial and who has a sore throat and a high fever the day before trial. Otherwise, your adversary may be able to argue as follows:

"Ms. Cardozo promised in her opening statement to prove that my client, Mr. Palsgraf, drove through a red light. She promised to produce a neutral witness, someone who had no relationship whatsoever with her client, who would say that. Well, you've heard her evidence, all of it. Where was this witness she promised you? All we saw was a little kid whose face was so swollen that the kid could not say a word. Do not be misled by the story you were promised by Ms. Cardozo during her opening statement. Examine the evidence, and you will find a very different story."

- Be hesitant to refer to information you expect to elicit from an adversary's witnesses. If the adversary fails to call a witness, you may have to choose between two unappetizing alternatives: having to call an adverse witness yourself, or failing to keep a promise you made during opening statement.

- Do not refer to evidence of doubtful admissibility. For example, a prosecutor should not to refer to a defendant's prior misconduct (perhaps as evidence of motive) if there's a good possibility that the judge will exclude the prior misconduct as improper character evidence. As an alternative to omitting mention of doubtful evidence, you may make a motion in limine seeking a pretrial ruling that evidence is admissible.

G. SHOULD YOU VOLUNTEER WEAKNESSES?

An issue that often arises during opening statement is whether to refer to weaknesses in your arguments that are certain to arise at trial. It sometimes makes sense to "take the sting out" of an adversary's claims by first airing them yourself and showing that "we have nothing to hide." And ignoring known weaknesses makes you susceptible to an adversary's final charge that your opening statement was misleading. However, trotting out a number of potential weaknesses may prevent you from making a persuasive opening statement. The decision will have to rest on your best professional judgment.

For example, assume that you are the prosecutor in the popular comedy courtroom film, "My Cousin Vinny." Three prosecution eyewitnesses will testify that they saw the defendants going into and leaving a convenience store right around the time that the store clerk was shot and killed. However, none of the eyewitnesses actually saw the shooting. Should you tell the jury that you have no eyewitnesses to the actual shooting? If one of the eyewitnesses was a bit groggy from just having awoken, should you mention that to the jury?

In this situation it seems sensible to mention the lack of eyewitnesses to the shooting. Jurors might naturally expect such testimony, and you'd want them to understand at the outset that you have a strong case without it. On the other hand, to mention the grogginess seems unnecessary. Most witnesses are subject to potential credibility attacks, and to refer to them during opening statement may plant doubts in a factfinder's mind that are hard to overcome.

H.　"THE EVIDENCE WILL SHOW …"

"The evidence will show" is an opening statement-deadening mantra that attorneys sometimes chant repeatedly in an effort to avoid a charge of "arguing during opening statement." In reality, the phrase accomplishes little. The assertion, "All the adversary's witnesses are lying fools" is no less argumentative if preceded by, "The evidence will show." You don't need the phrase to tell a non-argumentative story:

"Ladies and Gentlemen, this lawsuit grows out of events that took place in September, three years ago. In that month, Consolidated Integrated Associated Amalgamated, a mom-and-pop manufacturer of aluminum extrusions, realized that it did not have enough scrap metal on hand . . ."

If you really must, remind a factfinder once at the outset that you will be talking about what the evidence will show, and then consign the phrase to the scrap heap.

I. VISUAL AIDS

Trials are a heavily oral medium, yet most people are visual learners. (Studies indicate vision accounts for about 85% of learning.) Therefore, visual aids tend to add persuasive impact to arguments. During opening statements, visual aids that you can use include:

- Tangible objects (murder weapons, photos, documents) that you intend to offer into evidence during trial. (Remember, don't display items of doubtful admissibility.)

- Charts setting forth expected testimony. The chart is not itself evidence, but simply an illustrative adjunct to an opening statement. Pulling out the same chart during closing argument is an effective way to demonstrate that you've lived up to your evidentiary promises.

J. OPENING STATEMENTS BY DEFENSE COUNSEL

Defense attorneys typically can elect to immediately follow plaintiffs' opening statements with their own, or to wait until just prior to the defense case-in-chief. Delaying a defense opening statement has some advantages. By waiting, you may keep plaintiffs in the dark as to the evidence you will offer and the arguments you will advance. Moreover, delay gives you a chance to fine tune a statement to reflect the evidence that actually emerged during a plaintiff's case-in-chief. And, to the extent that opening statement provides an overview of your case, the picture may become muddied by lapse of time and plaintiffs' stories.

Nevertheless, as a defense attorney you should almost always elect to make an opening statement before the plaintiff presents evidence. In civil and increasingly in criminal cases, pretrial discovery and negotiations usually eliminate the "surprise" element of delay. Also, an immediate opening statement helps a factfinder realize the significance of testimony you elicit during cross examination of plaintiff's witnesses. Finally, going first gives plaintiffs a built-in advantage in the battle for factfinders' minds. An immediate defense opening can reduce this advantage by preventing a factfinder from getting locked in to the plaintiff's version of events.

One possible option is a "mock opening statement," with which you emphasize the importance of the factfinder keeping an open mind without revealing evidence or arguments. Consider this example:

"I will make my remarks very brief, you'll hear the evidence later. As you listen to the plaintiff's witnesses, remember that when we get a chance to offer evidence you will hear a very different version of events. The rules allow plaintiffs to present evidence first. Listen to that evidence carefully, but keep an open mind so that you can listen to our evidence just as carefully. I am confident that when you weigh all the evidence you will conclude that the plaintiff has not met the burden of proof and render a judgment for the defendant."

Though largely conclusory and lacking reference to any actual testimony, the statement's brevity may cause a judge to allow it. However, if you are allowed to conduct voir dire questioning, you can cover much of the same ground at that time. In general, opening statement is too important a persuasive opportunity to waste with a mock opening.

K. IDENTIFYING THE "BOTTOM LINE"

The conclusion of an opening statement is an opportunity to tell a factfinder of your desired result. An explicit bottom line provides closure to a story and helps a factfinder understand the significance of testimony. For example, jurors in a criminal case may have one attitude towards your evidence if they think that you will ask for a not guilty verdict, and quite another if they know that your goal is a lesser-included offense. As a plaintiff in a civil case, you can identify a bottom line even if you choose not to specify the exact damages that you seek: "At the conclusion of the case, we'll ask you to award damages in the amount you think fair to compensate Ms. Miller for her medical expenses, lost wages and pain and suffering."

L. EYE CONTACT

No matter how impressive an opening statement looks on paper, it loses much of its impact if you read it to a factfinder. Your own lecture hall experience tells you that you're likely to pay more attention and be an "active listener" when a speaker talks directly to you instead of burying a head in paper. Write out an opening statement if you must, but when in the courtroom bring only an outline or refresher notes with you.

M. OPENING STATEMENTS IN JUDGE–TRIED CASES

The extent to which the techniques in this chapter apply to bench trials depends in part on whether an "all-purpose judge" hears a case. A judge assigned to preside over a judge trial on the day of trial is often as factually in the dark as jurors would be, and you might present much the same opening that you would to jurors. All-purpose judges generally handle cases from initial filing onward, and thus are likely to be familiar with the relevant factual issues. All-purpose judges may even urge you and an adversary to forgo opening statements altogether. However, you should be reluctant to waive opening altogether. A modified argument limited to your crucial arguments is a good fall-back position.

CHAPTER 7

DIRECT EXAMINATION

Success at trial typically depends on credible direct examinations. This pronouncement may seem heretical if your trial images come from movies and TV, where cross examinations are routinely a show's emotional high point. Even the biographies of legendary lawyers tend to emphasize their mastery of cross examination. In most cases, however, direct examination is your best opportunity to convince a factfinder that your arguments are accurate.

A. GENERAL PRINCIPLES

Effective direct examinations generally adhere to the general principles set forth below.

1. Testimony Is in Story Form

An effective direct examination elicits evidence in story form. Stories generally describe events in chronological order, provide a descriptive background for those events, and explain why the events took place. Stories are effective on direct examination for several reasons. They are a familiar form of communication, they provide clarity and give meaning and credibility to isolated events, and they stimulate witness recall. As a result, stories tend to

84

convey the important impression that a witness is describing events that actually took place.

In outline form, direct examination stories often look like this:

Event #1: Earliest Event in Story

    Details of Event #1; Reasons for Its Occurrence

Event #2

    Details of Event #2; Reasons for Its Occurrence

Event #3 (etc.)

Of course, this outline is an oversimplification. For example, you needn't offer explanations for the occurrence of every event, nor elicit details of unimportant events. The distinction between "events" and "details," moreover, is often a matter of personal taste. Think of Goldilocks, who enters the bears' home and sits on three chairs. You might regard "sitting on the too hard chair" as a separate event, or as a detail of a larger event, "sitting on chairs." However, definitional purity is unimportant. The underlying technique is to move stories forward in time by focusing on what you regard as important events, and to elicit details and explanations pursuant to your arguments (General Principle No. 2, below).

The following simple illustration demonstrates the story form of direct testimony. Assume that you are the prosecutor in a murder case, and call Marcus Nieman to testify to events preceding the killing. After brief background questioning, the testimony proceeds as follows:

1. Q: Mr. Nieman, calling your attention to the date of March 12 of last year, at around 6:00 P.M., where were you at that time?

2. A: I was taking the dog for the evening constitutional, and I was on the block next to where I live.

3. Q: Do you recall the name of the street?

4. A: Yes, Nutmeg Street.

5. Q: Can you please briefly describe that part of Nutmeg Street?

6. A: OK. It's all residential, mostly older apartment buildings two or three stories high.

7. Q: Did anything unusual happen during your walk that evening?

8. A: I'll say. I saw that lady over there (pointing to the defendant) run out of a car and into one of the apartment buildings.

9. Q: How far from the defendant were you when you saw her run out of the car?

10. A: No more than 15 feet, I'd say. About the same distance as from me to you.

11. Q: What was the lighting like?

12. A: It was twilight, not yet dark. I had no trouble seeing her.

13. Q: Please describe exactly what you saw.

14. A: OK. She pulled up to the curb really quickly, that's why I noticed her at first. She ran out of the driver's side of the car and I saw a gun

in her left hand. I was pretty scared, so I ducked behind a tree. I peeked out and saw her go into the building.

15. Q: Can you tell us which building she ran into?

16. A: At the time I just noticed that it was a three story brick building. I went back later to check the address, it's 11358 Nutmeg.

17. Q: Can you tell us anything more about the gun?

18. A: I don't know much about guns, just that it was a pistol, not a rifle or anything like that.

19. Q: What happened after the woman ran into the building?

20. A: I ran back to my place to call the police. The dog wasn't too happy about finishing the walk early. By the time I went back a couple of hours later, the police were there and the building had been sealed off.

Nieman's testimony provides the essential elements of a story. You might pick out three events, which emerge chronologically: walking the dog (No. 2); seeing the defendant run from a car to a building (Nos. 8–18); and heroically running home (No. 20). Some details tend to add context and reality to the story (No. 6), but most support your arguments (e.g. No. 12 supports Nieman's credibility.). Finally, credible stories often describe why events took place, so Nieman also explains why he happened to notice the defendant in the first place (No. 14).

Chronology does not require witnesses to remember the order of events with mathematical precision. A witness may be uncertain about a story's beginning:

"I'm not certain when we first contacted Fledgling to talk about the paint contract, but it was sometime in the early summer."

Chronology is even possible if a witness cannot recall approximate dates, but can recall when events occurred with respect to each other:

"I'm not sure when it happened, but I am certain that the chicken came before the egg." or "I'm certain that the roof leaked before the first snow that year."

2. Testimony Illustrates Arguments

When telling stories to social friends, you undoubtedly emphasize some portions of those stories more than other portions. Social settings give you the freedom to emphasize (or ignore) whatever you like. Inside a courtroom, adversaries offer competing stories. Thus, at trial you should emphasize the evidence supporting your arguments. Your goal is to "illustrate" arguments for a factfinder, which means helping a factfinder see the linkage between an item of evidence and an argument during direct examination.

Emphasizing evidence supporting arguments during direct examination is necessary because of the

need to focus a factfinder on the accuracy of your
arguments throughout a trial. Judges routinely admonish jurors not to form opinions until a case is
finally submitted to them. Illustrating arguments
during direct examination would be less necessary if
jurors were able to obey this directive. However,
judges might just as well admonish jurors not to
think about pink elephants. Research indicates that
judges and jurors (like the rest of us) evaluate
information continuously as they take it in. Moreover, psychologists talk of "mind sets," which once
formed are difficult to alter. For example, if it
would take "X" amount of data to convince a completely neutral factfinder, it might take "X + 3" to
convince one who has formed an unfavorable mind
set. Test this yourself by comparing the impressions
you get of two people from the following pair of
adjectives:

a. Generous, trustworthy, humorless, self-centered, obnoxious.

b. Obnoxious, self-centered, humorless, trustworthy, generous.

Though the words are identical, their differing
arrangement may have led you to form a more
favorable impression of person "a." And that favorable impression might well translate into a mind set
favorable to "a" that "b" would find difficult to
overcome.

The "continuous evaluation" and "mind set"
phenomena combine to make it important that you
illustrate arguments during direct examination. If a

factfinder fails to see the linkage between evidence and your arguments until final summation, your persuasive efforts may be too late. The following techniques can help you to illustrate arguments during direct examination:

- Emphasize events important to your arguments by eliciting more details about those events than about unimportant events. Give cursory treatment to or even skip over unimportant events. (Despite the wording of the oath, witnesses never tell the "whole truth." You have to be selective, so be selective in a way that emphasizes your arguments. The resulting story is no less truthful. By way of analogy, consider two maps of the United States, one showing the states according to their geographical borders and the other according to their populations. Both maps may be accurate, yet look very different because they were drawn with different purposes in mind.)

- Juxtapose evidentiary items pertaining to the same argument-even if you have to abandon chronology to do so. For example, assume that the fact that a witness was driving a convertible with the top down enhanced a witness' ability to overhear an important remark. To illustrate the connection between the "top down" evidence and your argument on behalf of the witness' credibility, juxtapose the "top down" evidence with testimony about the important remark. The direct might go as follows:

Q: And what was it you heard?

A: I heard Jones say, "...."

Q: How were you able to hear what Jones said?

A: I drive a convertible, and the top was down.

Had you elicited evidence chronologically, you probably would have elicited the "top down" testimony well before the testimony as to what Jones said. This would make it harder for the factfinder to see the connection between the testimony and the argument. (Your ability to juxtapose items of evidence for a single argument is of course diminished when those items are scattered through the testimony of two or more witnesses. Unfortunately, evidence rules allow only one witness to testify at a time!)

3. Testimony Emerges in Response to Open and Closed Questions

An effective direct examination is both witness-centered and attorney-centered. You are witness-centered when your questions invite witnesses to relate events in their own words to impress on factfinders that your witnesses are credible and knowledgeable. You are attorney-centered when your questions focus witnesses on evidence supporting your arguments. This section explains questioning methods to achieve these dual goals.

a. Open Questions

Open questions are witness-centered. They call witnesses' attention to topics and invite witnesses to discuss those topics in their own words. Examples of open questions include:

- "Please describe what happened after Mr. Dumpty reached the top of the wall."

- "Please tell us what was said in that conversation."

- "Describe the appearance of the left palm two months after the surgery."

- "After you fell down and saw the steamroller, what happened next?"

The answers to such questions tend to enhance witnesses' credibility. Rather than appearing to give memorized, programmed responses, witnesses choose their own words. Open questions focus the factfinder's attention on the witness rather than on you (unless you inadvertently ask questions while wearing a bright red rubber nose.) Moreover, open questions conform to the most familiar form of social dialogue. On social occasions, we usually ask questions like, "What happened?" We don't say, "I want to find out what happened, but don't tell me. Let me ask a lot of questions." Thus, open questions typically form the backbone of effective direct examinations.

Nevertheless, open questions are subject to two major limitations. First, despite your best pretrial preparation efforts, some witnesses will not answer open questions credibly. Their answers may obscure your arguments (by omitting important information, for example) and draw objections (by referring to improper or extraneous information). In such situations, you may have to largely abandon open questions and conduct more of an attorney-centered direct examination. Consider these examples:

- *The Detailer*. Some witnesses provide so many details in response to open questions that the responses sound canned and memorized. Consider this example:

  Q: What happened after you arrived at the wall?

  A: This odd-shaped person was sitting on top of the wall. The wall was at least 15 feet high. How long he had been sitting there, I couldn't say. He looked odd to me because his body was oval-shaped, and he was very pale. But he looked like a good egg. He kept yelling, "I'm going to jump" in a very high-pitched voice. He must have said this at least 10 times in the minute that I watched before he jumped ...

Such an answer is unlikely to be credible. The witness provides so many details that the answer sounds artificial and rehearsed.

- *The Partisan*. Some witnesses use the freedom that open questions provide to vilify an adversary or unleash social commentary. Again, credibility suffers:

  Q: What happened after you got to the wall?

  A: Well, that wall has been a deathtrap for years. Dumpty is the fifth person I can remember who has gotten stuck on it in the last year.

Will the king ever do anything except send his men out on horses each time a tragedy occurs? Anyway, there he was ...

This witness' partisanship suggests that the witness is more likely to fit events into the witness' preconceived ideas than to describe accurately what actually happened.

- *The Digresser.* Some witnesses lack the law's sense of logical relevance, and get side-tracked:

Q: OK, you're at the wall. Then what happened?

A: Getting to the wall wasn't easy, I'll tell you. There were horses everywhere; all the king's horses must have been out on the streets. When I saw Mr. Dumpty up there, I got really frightened. It reminded me of the time my brother ...

Such answers quickly exhaust a factfinder's patience.

A second limitation of open questions is at the same time one of their benefits: they elicit less-than-comprehensive answers. The answers to open questions typically allow you to probe for the omitted details, thereby emphasizing your arguments. The typical probing mechanism is closed questions.

b. Closed Questions

Closed questions seek to elicit specific items of evidence. While closed questions do not suggest a desired answer, neither do they invite witnesses to describe events in their own words. Examples of closed questions include:

- "What color was the car?"
- "How long did this conversation last?"
- "What reason did the chicken give for crossing the road?"
- "You mentioned the word yute. What's a yute?"
- "When the tree fell, did you hear a noise?"

Closed questions are attorney-centered. With closed questions you can focus witnesses on specific portions of events, and elicit evidence supporting your arguments. Closed questions are important direct examination tools because witnesses do not ordinarily supply all your desired information in response to open questions (nor would you want them to!). Closed questions allow you to probe for additional details, most often those details supporting your arguments.

For example, consider this open question and response:

Q: After you arrived at the wall, what happened?

A: Well, this odd-shaped person kept saying things like, "I'm going to jump. I'm going to jump." After a few minutes he pitched forward and fell all the way to the ground. By that time the king's men had arrived on their king's horses, but it was too late.

As is typical, the response to the open question is conclusory enough to allow you to pursue additional details with closed questions. For example, assuming the details were important to your arguments, you might ask questions such as:

Q: You say the person was odd-shaped. What was his shape?

Q: What was his tone of voice when he yelled, "I'm going to jump?"

Q: Can you estimate how many king's horses were there?

Closed questions are also an effective way of directing a witness around events you want to omit from a story. For example, assume that a witness' "complete" story would consist of conversations that took place on the 1st, the 10th and the 20th of a month. The conversation of the 10th is unimportant to your arguments, so you'd like to move the testimony directly from the conversation of the 1st to that of the 20th. An open question might be ineffective. If you ask, "What happened next?" after concluding testimony about the conversation of the 1st, you're likely to hear about the conversation on the 10th. A closed question is probably a better choice: "Do you recall another conversation that took place on the 20th?"

c. Analysis of Sample Direct Examination

The following example demonstrates how you can combine open and closed questions into an effective direct examination. Assume that you are prosecuting a shoplifter for stealing items from a supermarket. Your witness is Marla Engel, the market's security guard. The defendant denies the theft, and claims to have entered the store with the items which the guard says were stolen. Thus, the key evidence is disputed, and you've used the Credibility Model (Chapter 3) to develop an argument supporting the accuracy of Engel's story. Pursuant to this argument, you want to emphasize Engel's physical ability to observe the theft and Engel's reasons for observing the defendant's movements. A portion of the direct may proceed as follows:

1. Q: Where was the defendant when you first observed her?

2. A: She was in the frozen food aisle.

3. Q: Did anything in particular call your attention to the defendant?

4. A: Yes.

5. Q: And what was that?

6. A: She was carrying a large satchel-type purse. She had placed it on the child's seat of a shopping cart, and I noticed that the top of the purse was open. The type of purse she was carrying and the fact that it was open caused me to watch her movements.

7. Q: Can you please explain why this caused you to watch the defendant's movements?

8. A: Well, in my experience people who are planning to take merchandise without paying for

it often hide the merchandise in large purses or bags.

9.   Q: What material was the purse made of?

10.   A: It was a multicolored soft cloth of some kind.

11.   Q: And what were its dimensions?

12.   A: At least 18 inches from top to bottom and about that long at the handle. The bag was much wider on the bottom that at the top.

13.   Q: Where were you at the time you saw the defendant?

14.   A: I Was in an observation room with a one way mirror.

15.   Q: Please describe this observation room.

16.   A: Sure. The room I was in is above the dairy case. The one way mirror part is about 10 feet long and six feet high. It has a desk with four television monitors connected to hidden cameras.

17.   Q: How far from the defendant were you when you saw her?

18.   A: I'd say 10 to 12 feet.

19.   Q: And were you watching her on one of the monitors or through the one way mirror?

20.   A: Through the mirror.

21.   Q: Ms. Engel, please describe what happened after you first noticed the defendant ...

This direct examination excerpt combines open and closed questions to allow a witness to tell a story in her own words while illustrating the prosecution's arguments. The story is chronological, starting with the point at which Engel first observed the defendant (No. 2). In response to open questions (Nos. 5 and 7), Engel describes the purse and explains why its appearance was suspicious (Nos. 6 and 8). Because the appearance of the purse supports a credibility argument, you ask closed questions to elicit additional details (Nos. 9 and 11). You also use closed questions to direct Engel to a new topic, her own location (No. 13). You allow the witness to describe this room in her own words (No. 16), elicit additional details with closed questions (Nos. 17 and 19) and then move to a new portion of the story with an open question (No. 21).

No less than closed questions, open questions can also be an effective way of emphasizing the portions of stories that promote your arguments. For example, assume that the type of purse that the defendant was carrying is important to an inferential argument that the defendant entered the market intending to steal merchandise. In the example above, you elicited a description of the purse with two closed questions (Nos. 9 and 11). In the alternative, you might have used open questions:

Q: Please describe this purse in more detail.

A: It was large and bulky, filling up over half the area of the child seat portion of the shopping cart. It was made of soft cloth and it was open at the top.

Q: When you say it was open at the top, what do you mean?

B. DEVIATING FROM CHRONOLOGY

As you saw in Section A above, it often makes sense to deviate from chronology to illustrate arguments by juxtaposing items of evidence pertaining to the same argument. This section examines other common situations in which you might deviate from strict chronology.

1. Front Load Important Events

The "primacy" principle suggests that a factfinder's attention to a witness' testimony is often at its height at the beginning of a direct examination. Thus, a useful technique is to "front load" an event that occurs late in a witness' chronology and which is of particular importance to your arguments. "Front loading" important events tends to maximize a factfinder's attention to and retention of your version of important events.

For example, assume that you represent Derian, a defendant charged with murder. Derian contends that a gun went off accidentally while Derian and the alleged victim were playing a game. On direct examination, you want Derian to describe his relationship with the alleged victim, as the relationship helps to explain how and why the accident happened. However, your most important argument grows out of Derian's version of the accident itself. If you elicit events chronologically, the factfinder will not hear about the accident until after Derian describes the relationship. In this situation, you may choose to front load the accident. Begin Derian's direct examination with an account of the accident. Note that you can modify the chronology without abandoning it altogether. After eliciting Derian's version of the shooting, you can go back to trace the relationship chronologically. In outline form, Derian's story might look like this:

Event #1 (The accident-last in time)

    Details of Event #1; Reasons for Occurrence

Event #2 (Earliest event in story)

    Details of Event #2: Reasons for Occurrence-if important

Event #3 (next event in story)

    Details of Event #3; Reasons for Occurrence-if important

Etc.

A variation of the front loading technique is to begin a direct with a summary reference to the evidence supporting your principle argument, and then proceed chronologically. The factfinder gets a "preview" of your version of a key event, which may heighten the factfinder's attention when you later cover the event in detail.

For example, assume that you represent the defendant in a libel action. The libel consisted of a tabloid article harming a celebrity's career by allegedly falsely stating that the celebrity (who became famous for reasons no one can recall) had a normal upbringing and had always been a faithful spouse and parent. The defendant admits authoring the article, but claims that the allegedly libelous language was not in it when the article was submitted to the publisher for the final time. To emphasize the defendant's factual position with only a minor deviation from chronology, you might begin the defendant's direct as follows:

(Preliminaries have concluded)

Q: Let me begin by handing you Plaintiff's Exhibit #1, the article. Do you recognize it?

A: Yes, this appears to be the article in its published form.

Q: Do you see the underlined language, "Skylen had a normal upbringing, and has always been a faithful spouse and parent."

A: I do.

Q: Did you write those words?

A: I did not.

Q: Were they in the article as you finally submitted it to your publisher?

A: They were not.

Q: Let's go back to the beginning, and hear how you came to write the article. First ...

This sequence of testimony elevates the author's denial to the beginning of direct, but saves the detailed testimony about the author's version of the article for its proper chronological place.

2. Elicit Multiple Chronologies

Stories often consist of separate strands of events occurring over roughly the same time period. When a single witness will testify to events from different story strands, you can use "mini-chronologies" to facilitate factfinder comprehension. That is, elicit each strand of events as a separate chronology.

For example, assume that a manufacturer's offering of a new product for sale is preceded by economic feasibility studies, design and manufacture of prototypes, consumer surveys, and patent applications. These pre-sale activities probably occurred simultaneously, not sequentially. A single chronology of the pre-sale events would intermingle all events, perhaps preventing a factfinder from understanding what actually took place. "Mini-chronologies," separate stories for each pre-sale activity, are a good way to facilitate factfinder understanding. In outline form, the direct would look like this:

Story No. 1 (Economic Feasibility Studies)

Event #1

Details of Event #1; Reasons for Occurrence-if important

Event #2

Details of Event #2; Reasons for Occurrence-if important

Etc.

Story #2 (Prototypes)

Event #1

Details of Event #1; Reasons for Occurrence-if important

Event #2 (etc.)

3. Avoid Artificial Chronologies

Sometimes, trying to establish an order of events will do more to undermine a factfinder's comprehension than to facilitate it. When numerous events take place in a short span of time, you risk the wrath of the judge and the credibility of the witness by trying to set out a chronology that defies belief:

"Now, you've been describing the clash between the Ostrogoths and the Visigoths. When the archer you've referred to as Leon exited his horse, was that before or after the 23rd cannon from the right was fired?"

In such situations, you are often better off treating an activity as a single event, and eliciting details of that event without regard to chronology.

For example, assume that you want a witness to testify to a number of topics that were discussed in a single conversation. Instead of trying to proceed chronologically through the conversation, you might go topic-by-topic without regard to chronology. Instead of posing time-ordered questions (e.g., "What did you next discuss?"), ask topical questions (e.g., "What else did you talk about during this conversation?")

At other times, the exact order of events may be unimportant. For example, assume a will contest case in which the issue is whether a testator disinherited a child because of an insane delusion, or based on a reasonable belief. The executor, seeking to uphold the will, offers evidence that the testator disinherited a son because the son was addicted to gambling, was an unfaithful spouse, took drugs, and liked to eat coconut. The issue is the testator's awareness of the son's alleged behavior. Here, the chronological relationship among the alleged behaviors is irrelevant so long as it all antedated the making of the will. In such a situation, you would again proceed topically, eliciting evidence about the testator's knowledge without trying to establish a time sequence.

C. STARTING DIRECT EXAMINATIONS

1. Personal Background Questions

Customarily, you begin direct examinations by eliciting personal background information about a witness. This portion of the examination is usually quite short, at least when the background has no direct bearing on the subjects to which a witness will testify. Background questioning can become more extensive if the information is relevant to a witness' credibility, or if you are trying to qualify a witness as an expert.

Personal background questions tend to put a witness at ease, allow a trier of fact a few moments to become familiar with a witness before hearing what she has to say, and add to a witness' credibility. Typical subjects of background inquiry include a witness' place of residence and employment, and general job duties. Whether you are allowed to elicit more by way of background (e.g., a witness' marital and parenthood status, or how long the witness has lived at the same address) usually depends on time considerations, each judge's philosophy about the importance of personal background questioning, and whether the information has any bearing on issues in dispute. However, background concerning a witness' charitable good works is almost certainly improper character evidence.

For example, examine this potential bit of background questioning:

Q: Ms. Gillig, how are you employed?

A: I work in the local British consulate offices.

Q: What are your general duties there?

A: I arrange visas, coordinate official visits, and do some public speaking.

Q: Where do you reside?

A: On Eastbourne, in the Larchmont section of the city.

Q: And how long have you resided there?

Opp: Objection. Irrelevant.

Judge: Counsel, any response to the objection?

Q: Yes, Your Honor. This matter involves an incident that occurred in Ms. Gillig's neighborhood. The length of time she has lived in the neighborhood bears directly on her familiarity

A: I did.

Q: What were you doing when you first saw him?

Perhaps event and identity are both in dispute. But if the fact that the witness was at a certain location is not in dispute, you may begin on that point:

Q: Ms. Franklin, I know this constant starting over is hard on you, but it's not easy being an example in a book. Do you recall being on the corner of the intersection of Beach and Desert Avenues in early March of this year?

A: I do.

Q: Which corner were you on?

Finally, you might call a witness' attention to the date of an occurrence:

Q: Ms. Franklin, do you recall the date of March 12?

A: I do. At least, I did when you called me up here.

Q: Where were you on that date, around 3:00 P.M?

A: I was at the corner . . .

Be warned, however, that despite thorough preparation, witnesses tend to forget dates when they take the stand. "The 12th? Is that my aunt's birthday?" Try to set scenes without relying on a date, if at all possible.

with the spot where the incident took place, and thus adds credibility to her testimony.

Judge: I'll allow it, but do move on.

Q: Ms. Gillig, do you remember the question?

A: Yes, I've lived there . . .

In the absence of a relationship between the objected-to question and an issue in dispute, the objection may well have been sustained.

When, as in the example above, evidence that you might think of as "personal background" is relevant to a disputed issue, you can add to its probative value by eliciting it along with the testimony to which it relates. In the example above, for instance, you might have delayed asking Gillig how long she has lived in the neighborhood until you elicited testimony about the incident.

Finally, note that the background questions above are largely closed. Usually, you do not want witnesses launching into extended accounts of their lives. However, when qualifying experts you are more likely to employ open questions. Questions such as, "Please describe your experience in the field of animal psychology" allow experts to do exactly what they are paid to do—impress factfinders with their expertise.

2. Scene–Setting Questions

Having concluded personal background testimony, you can begin to elicit a witness' story. However, according to an ancient authority, "All beginnings are hard," and direct examination sometimes is no exception. Consider this possible opening foray:

Q: Now, Ms. Franklin, tell us what if anything unusual happened on the afternoon of March 12.

Opp: Objection. Vague.

Judge: Sustained.

Q: Ms. Franklin, did you see the defendant commit a robbery on the afternoon of March 12?

Opp: Objection, leading.

Judge: Sustained.

At this point, you may feel like opening your briefcase and putting away your papers as you contemplate a less public venue for making a fool of yourself. To avoid such pitfalls, follow personal background questioning with scene-setting questions.

Scene-setting questions begin a story on an undisputed contextual aspect of an event. Because the undisputed context is "preliminary matter," you can ask a leading question. A question or two about the context sets the scene, and direct is underway. You may set a scene by calling a witness' attention to:

• the first event in the witness' story;

• a person who participated in that event;

• the date of that event; or

• the location of that event.

At least one of these contextual features is bound not to be in dispute, and therefore acceptable as "preliminary." For example, return to the testimony of Ms. Franklin above. Assume that the defense is mistaken identity. You may set the scene for Franklin's testimony by calling her attention to the event itself:

Q: Ms. Franklin, I want to call your attention to a robbery that you observed. Do you recall it?

A: I sure do.

Q: What first called your attention . . .

With little ado, you are launched into the story. However, if the witness has been a lightning rod for robberies, the "event" question may have to be more specific:

Q: Ms. Franklin, I want to call your attention to a robbery you witnessed in which the victim was dressed as the Easter Bunny. Do you recall it?

Next, assume that the defendant admits to having been at the scene of the robbery, but denies having participated in it. There being no issue of identity, you might set the scene using that contextual evidence:

Q: Ms. Franklin, I want to call your attention to the defendant, seated over here. Do you see him?

A: I do.

Q: Did you see him on the afternoon of March 12?

If all are preliminary, you may combine a number of contextual details into one question:

Q: Ms. Franklin, I want to call your attention to a robbery that took place on the afternoon of March 12 on the corner of Beach and Desert. Do you recall that incident?

Once a scene is set, one way to continue is with "scene-change" questions, which simply ask witnesses in what way a scene you have set out has changed. Because the witness, not you, describes the change, you avoid any issue of "leading." For example, assume that the scene you have set is one in which a witness is walking down a country lane. You may proceed as follows:

Q: Mr. Wolfe, did you continue walking down the lane?

A: No, I did not.

Q: Why not?

A: I noticed a little clearing and straw lying all over the ground. Going closer, I noticed a flute in the middle of the straw, and some hairs that looked like chin whiskers.

Q: What did you do then?

A: . . .

If none of these scene-setting techniques works, you may continue putting your books and papers into your briefcase.

Set scenes continuously. The scene-setting technique is one you can use throughout a direct examination, whenever a witness' testimony moves to a new event. The technique can help factfinders follow a story, and may even pull them into a story as they visualize events as a witness describes them.

D. LEADING QUESTIONS

1. Drawbacks

After "mommy" and "daddy," "Objection, leading" is typically the third phrase uttered by toddlers who eventually go to law school. Thus, you undoubtedly know that leading questions suggest a questioner's desired answers, and that they are generally improper during direct (and redirect) examination. Their vice is that they allow an attorney to testify through the mouth of a friendly witness.

Leading questions often are simply assertions with a phrase tacked on at the beginning or the end to convert them into questions. Examples of leading questions are:

- "The car was red, right?"
- "Isn't it true that you never saw the document?"
- "A tree falling in a deserted forest still makes a sound, doesn't it?"

However, questions need not be so obviously leading to qualify as improper during direct examination. If a question incorporates disputed evidence, a judge may regard it as leading even though on its surface it is not. For example, assume in a negligence case that an important dispute centers on the color of the light when a blue car entered the intersection. You ask a witness:

"Was the light red when the blue car entered the intersection?"

On the surface, the question is not leading; it does not direct the witness to answer "yes" or "no." However, a judge would likely regard it as leading. The light's color is a central dispute in the case, and the witness and not the attorney should refer to it. The proper question would be, "What color was the light when the blue car entered the intersection?"

Perhaps more than their impropriety, the biggest danger of leading questions is that they tend to detract from a witness' credibility. Consider this brief example:

Q: Mr. Wall, you live on Walnut St. in Walla Walla?

A: Yes.

Q: You were in the U–Serve U–Pay gas station on the afternoon of May 4?

A: Yes.

Q: A robbery took place at that time and place?

A: Yes.

Q: You were standing near the cashier when someone rushed in with a gun and demanded all the money in the register?

A: Yes, that's right.

Q: Did the person then take the money and run?

A: Yes.

Q: And the person you saw robbing the gas station the person is seated over there? (pointing to defendant)

A: Yes.

Evidence rules to the side, this examination offers the factfinder no basis for believing the witness. The examination creates the impression that any utterance by the witness longer than one word might destroy the questioner's case. Imagine, for example, the stirring closing argument the prosecutor might make based on the testimony above:

"You remember the testimony of the eyewitness, Mr. Wall. He testified without hesitation, and I quote, 'Yes.'"

From this perspective, the "worst" direct may not be one filled with leading questions that repeatedly draw objections, but rather one filled with leading questions that do not.

2. Advantages

Given that the legal system has developed exceptions to many of the Ten Commandments, the existence of exceptions to the "no leading questions on direct" rule should not surprise you. Leading questions are both legally proper (see Federal Rule of Evidence 611) and effective advocacy in a variety of direct examination circumstances. One common circumstance arises when witnesses have "infirmities" that make it difficult for them to testify in their own words. (See Federal Rule of Evidence 611 (c)). For example, young children may be too frightened by the courtroom atmosphere to choose their own words, and witnesses who are elderly or ill may not have the strength or attention span to do so. A judge will normally permit you to lead when it is evident that responding to leading questions is the only efficient or possible way for a witness to testify.

Judges typically also allow you to use leading questions when you elicit "preliminary matter." Thus, you can effectively use leading questions to set scenes before focusing on stories' important details. For example, you can use leading questions when eliciting routine personal background information:

Q: Mr. Attila, you are a barbarian?

A: Yes.

Q: And you've been a barbarian for eight years?

A: That's right. Well, nine if you count my senior sacking and pillaging internship.

Subsidiary aspects of events are often non-controverted, and therefore qualify as preliminary matter. For example, a dispute may involve what was said during at a certain meeting. However, the parties may agree that the meeting took place and the general purpose for the meeting. If so, you may focus the factfinder quickly on your version of the dispute by setting the scene quickly with leading questions:

Q: You attended a meeting on the 26th of August, correct?

Q: Menkel and Meadow also were at that meeting?

Q: The purpose of the meeting was to discuss the buyout proposal?

Q: Now, please tell us what took place ...

In a number of circumstances, you may also use leading questions to repeat testimony that a witness has already given. For example, perhaps argument over an objection consumed time, and both witness and factfinder will appreciate a reminder as to where they are in the story:

Q: Sorry, Ms. Resnik. I realize that, sitting there for the last three weeks, you've become something of an expert on the business records hearsay exception. Before the interruption, you had just told us that you designed the firm's accounts receivable computer program, correct?

A: Ah yes, I remember it well.

Q: And that you prepared the manual which is Defendant's Exhibit B?

A: Yes, that's right.

Q: And you trained Mr. Houston as to how to use the program?

A: Yes.

Q: All right. Now let me ask you . . .

Similarly, judges will often allow you to repeat a witness' most crucial testimony with a leading question or two at the conclusion of direct:

Q: To conclude, Mr. Tobias, you inspected the condensers immediately upon their arrival in the plant?

A: Yes.

Q: And you found none that were defective?

A: Correct.

Q: I have nothing further at this time.

Finally, you may use leading questions when a witness is unable to recall evidence. Forgetfulness is not uncommon. Many a litigator can tell of the person whose clear memory during pretrial preparation went to pieces on the witness stand. When your questioning indicates that a witness has general recollection of an event but is unable to recall some details, judges have discretion under Federal Rule of Evidence 611 to permit leading questions. For example, assume that a witness has begun to describe the events leading up to an auto accident, and you expect the witness to testify that the driver of the blue car was talking on a cellular phone. You silently curse your fate as the witness has an unexpected failure of recollection, but use a leading question to get the information you are after:

Q: What else did you notice about the blue car?

A: I think that's about it, I'm not sure.

Q: I apologize if my question wasn't clear. I'm asking you about the driver of the blue car, and want you to tell us what else you noticed about the driver.

A: Nothing that I can think of now.

Q: Well, did you see an object in the driver's hand?

A: I just don't remember.

Q: Could the driver have been talking on a cellular phone?

A: Yes, that's right, the driver was talking on a cellular phone. Sorry, I just drew a blank for a second there.

In this example, you don't jump to the leading question at the first indication of forgetfulness. Instead, you approach cautiously, like a cat circling an unknown object. Ordinarily, a subtle clue is enough to jog most witnesses' memories. When necessary, however, you can resort to a leading question.

E. NARRATIVE QUESTIONS

1. Broadening the Scope of Witnesses' Answers

Narrative questions (or more precisely, "questions that call for a narrative response") are the broadest form of open questions. Judges tend to regard questions as narrative when they ask witnesses to describe a series of events that unfolded over time. Consider these examples:

- "Please describe the events culminating in the contract."

- "Tell us everything you can remember about the robbery."

- "How did the final design of the spacecraft come about?"

The value of such questions is that they maximize witnesses' opportunity to tell stories in their own words. However, because narrative questions allow such a wide scope of response, judges often sustain objections to them. Beyond the basic fear of listening to lengthy answers from people who have not attended law school, judges also protect counsel's right to know what information is sought, in case all or part of the information is objectionable. On the other hand, evidence rules favor witness-centered direct examinations, with witnesses describing events in their own words. No fixed line separates open from narrative questions, and Federal Rule of Evidence 611 gives judges much discretion when ruling on "calls for a narrative" objections.

Judges are most likely to allow narrative responses by "professional" witnesses-forensic experts, police officers and the like. Judges tend to trust such witnesses to answer succinctly and in accord with evidence rules. If you want to ask narrative questions of an ordinary lay witness, a judge might grant you similar latitude if you first show that the witness is similarly precise. Consider this example:

Q: Now, Ms. Ihori, where were you at about 6 P.M. on the afternoon of June 1?

A: I had just arrived at the Star and Garters Tavern, and was getting ready to work the evening shift.

Q: Please tell us what happened.

Opp: Objection, the question calls for a narrative response.

Judge: Sustained.

Q: Were there any customers in the tavern when you arrived?

A: Two or three, as I recall. It was pretty quiet.

Q: Did you notice Ms. Ray, the lady seated over there?

A: As I recall, she entered the tavern shortly after I arrived.

Q: Did you see where she went after she entered the tavern?

A: She sat down in a booth near the jukebox.

Q: Did you approach her?

A: Yes, I went over to get her order.

Q: And then what happened?

Opp: Objection, question calls for a narrative response.

Judge: I'll allow it.

A: One of the customers . . .

The second "what happened" question is no less narrative than the first. But perhaps because the witness has demonstrated in response to narrow questions that she can be trusted to answer succinctly, the judge allows the critical information to emerge through a narrative response.

Also, many judges permit "pseudo-narratives." Pseudo-narratives also ask witnesses to describe events in their own words, but contain limiting features. Consider these questions:

- "Did anything *unusual* happen?"
- "What *next* occurred?"
- "*Then* what happened?"

The italicized words impose subtle limits. The first limits a witness to whatever was "unusual." (Of course, the question may puzzle the convenience store clerk who is testifying in the 57th robbery in which the clerk has been victimized.) The others suggest a temporal limit: the witness is not supposed to relate an entire series of events. The subtle limits that pseudo-narratives impose provide a useful way to elicit testimony in a witness' own words while avoiding objections (or at least avoiding sustained objections).

2. Objecting to an Adversary's Narrative Questions

From a defensive standpoint, it's often in your interest to prevent narrative responses by an adversary's witnesses. You may be unable to object to improper evidence before the jury hears it, and a witness' narrative ability may add to the witness' credibility. Thus, when an adversary asks a very broad question, you can object: "Objection, Your Honor. The question calls for a narrative response." (The Federal Rules of Evidence basis for this objection is again Rule 611, which gives a judge broad control over the method of interrogation.)

Some witnesses are prone to giving narrative responses regardless of the form of a question. For example, a witness asked to estimate the speed of a car may break into an answer rivaling in length Hamlet's soliloquy. You have the right to interrupt an answer and object that "The witness is narrating," or that, "There is no question pending." For the sake of the court reporter, try not to talk at the same time as the witness. Stop the witness' answer before stating your objection. A good technique is to stand, then say "excuse me" and perhaps hold up your hand.

F. ADDITIONAL EMPHASIS TECHNIQUES

This chapter has already described a number of emphasis techniques, including front loading important events (see Page 100) and eliciting the details of important events with a combination of open and closed questions (see Page 96). This section sets forth additional emphasis techniques.

1. "No, No, No"

One way to add impact to a story about what did happen is to ask a series of closed questions about what did not happen. For example, assume that you represent a patient who claims that a doctor negligently prescribed the wrong medication. The doctor has testified to discussing the side effect of "dry mouth" with the patient; the patient claims that this conversation never took place. "No, no" questions can point up the conflict, as in this direct of the patient:

Q: Did you talk to the doctor on Feb. 3?

A: No.

Q: Did the doctor talk to you on Feb. 3?

A: No.

Q: Did anyone in the doctor's office talk to you on Feb. 3?

A: No.

Q: Was dry mouth ever mentioned to you as a potential side effect of the drug?

A: No.

Like a symphony that presents the same tune in slightly different forms, this series of questions elicits the same information from different perspectives. It thus allows you to emphasize evidence without running afoul of the "asked and answered" objection.

2. Points of Reference

To use the "point of reference" technique, incorporate evidence from a previous answer into a subsequent question. The repetition provides emphasis and allows you to clarify stories. However, use the technique only occasionally. You don't want to give a factfinder the sense that you're unfairly gilding the lily, or raise an objection that "counsel is testifying."

For example, consider this direct examination excerpt:

Q: What happened next?

A: The other guy ran behind a truck. He reappeared a few moments later with brass knuckles on his right hand.

Q: After he reappeared with the brass knuckles, what happened?

Here, you incorporate the witness' "brass knuckles" testimony into your next question. The point of reference allows you to repeat the testimony, and to clarify the chronology.

In the example above, you used a point of reference to move the story ahead to "what happened next." You may use the same technique to elicit further description of already-given testimony. For example:

Q: What happened next?

A: The other guy ran behind a truck. He reappeared a few moments later with brass knuckles on his right hand.

Q: You say that he reappeared with brass knuckles. Can you describe these brass knuckles?

The point of reference technique is especially useful when witnesses give ambiguous testimony. For example, a witness describes the converging paths of six cars into an intersection, and states, "The car was going 35 m.p.h." Or, describing a dispute between two women, a witness testifies, "She called her a no-good endomorph." The testimony leaves a factfinder unable to understand to which car or person each witness is referring. Point of reference questions can clear up the ambiguity:

- Q: You testified that a car was travelling at a speed of 35 m.p.h. To which car were you referring?

- Q: Which woman called the other a no-good endomorph?

You may also use a point of reference to keep chronology clear when a witness omits mention of an event:

Q: What happened then?

A: The wolf huffed and puffed and blew down the house of straw.

Q: Then what happened?

Q: The wolf began to huff and puff at a house made of bricks.

Q: After the wolf blew down the house made of straw, but before the wolf began huffing and puffing at the brick house, did anything else happen?

Finally, a point of reference is also a method of pointing up conflicts between your version of events and an adversary's:

Q: If Mr. Shakespeare testified earlier that the soup contained eye of newt and toe of frog, wool of bat and tongue of dog, would you agree with him?

A: No, definitely not. The actual contents were ...

Note that you refer to Shakespeare's testimony in the form of a question. Compare this interrogatory:

Q: Mr. Shakespeare testified earlier that the soup contained eye of newt and toe of frog, wool of bat and tongue of dog. Do you agree with him?

Many judges would regard your assertion as to Shakespeare's testimony as improper. You would be testifying, not posing questions.

3. Provide Examples of Conduct or Conditions Over Time

Witnesses frequently testify to conditions or behavior that spanned lengthy periods of time. For example:

- In a personal injury case, a plaintiff may testify that "my back hurt for at least six months."

- In a will contest case based on a testator's incompetence, a friend may testify that "the deceased regularly forgot things during the last two years of his life."

- In a landlord-tenant breach of warranty of habitability case, a tenant may testify that "the roof leaked whenever it rained."

Such conclusory assertions tend to have little impact, and they prevent factfinders from building concrete stories about "what really happened." On the other hand, a witness cannot describe each and every event giving rise to the conclusion. An effective compromise is to emphasize important events by eliciting testimony about specific examples upon which conclusions are based. For example, after the friend in the will contest case testifies that the testator was always forgetting things, you might ask questions such as:

- *If you want to proceed chronologically through a few examples:*

  "Do you recall the first time that you noticed the testator's forgetfulness?"

  "Was there a later time that you noticed the testator's forgetfulness?"

- *If you want to elicit a few examples without regard to chronology:*

  "Do you recall a specific example of the testator's forgetfulness?"

  "Can you recall another example of the testator's forgetfulness?"

  "Can you tell us about any other times that the testator was forgetful?"

A few specific examples emphasize the underlying events that form the basis for a conclusion without taxing a factfinder's credulity or attention span.

G. WITNESS ORDER

When you conduct direct examination of two or more witnesses, the small size of witness boxes demands that only one testify at a time. Hence, you must decide in what order they will testify.

Almost always, order of witnesses is purely a tactical decision; few rules mandate a particular order. One ordering possibility is suggested by the familiar principles of primacy and recency. These principles suggest that we remember best what we see or hear first and last. (So much for submerging discussion of these principles in the middle of the book!) The application of these principles to trials is by no means clear, because the experiments from which they were derived tend to consist of people staring at rows of letter combinations, and then trying to recall as many combinations as possible. To the extent that the results of such experiments apply in trial settings, you might think of beginning and ending with your "strongest" witnesses. Witnesses whose testimony is less significant, or whose manner of testifying is less than stellar, might be grouped in between.

You may choose among a variety of factors when deciding which witness is "strongest." Ideally, both your first and last witnesses will be the founders and heads of charitable and religious organizations, and will have available videotaped recordings of the opposing party declaring, "It was all my fault, and they should get at least 10 times what they've asked for." Unfortunately, stories tend to be either unassailable on cross but of secondary significance, or impeachable on several grounds but of vital legal significance. Which of these common types of stories is "stronger" is a matter for your judgment.

You may also measure strength according to the tone you are attempting to set for your overall story. For example, if the primary appeal of a case is to a factfinder's emotions, a strong witness might be one who will describe events that create feelings of empathy for your client. If the primary appeal is rational or scientific, your strongest witness might be an expert. In a civil case, your strongest witness might be the adverse party, examined as a "hostile witness." See Federal Rule of Evidence 611(c). On the other hand, a witness who was a losing contestant on "Wheel of Fortune" would probably never be considered a strong witness.

A strong witness may also be one who can provide a chronological overview of important events. Just as during Opening Statement, a chronology can help a factfinder understand the relationship of individual items of evidence to your arguments. For example, assume a civil suit for damages growing out of a typical urban traffic nightmare which resulted in cars littering the road for hundreds of feet. Representing the plaintiff, you've developed an argument based on Arlene's testimony that shortly before the accident the defendant said, "I've got to hurry, I'm late for the meeting." Arlene's credibility is unassailable, but her story is limited to the statement. A second witness, Jeff, was a passenger in the plaintiff's car. Jeff can describe the accident from beginning to end. However, the defendant can attack Jeff's credibility based on Jeff's friendship with Arlene and the fact that Jeff had drunk a couple of beers shortly before the accident. Who is the "stronger" and therefore lead witness, Arlene or Jeff? Perhaps the latter, because he can provide an overall chronology of events.

At the "recency" end of a case-in-chief, you may prefer to call a client as your last witness. Judges often exclude witnesses from the courtroom until after their testimony. Excluded witnesses cannot listen to the testimony of other witnesses. Parties, however, cannot be excluded. A client who testifies last, therefore, has the benefit of hearing the direct and cross of all the other witnesses before testifying.

Unfortunately, the order of witnesses is not always within your control. Situations such as these are common:

- The medical expert who was to be your first witness has to perform emergency surgery and is unavailable until the second day of trial. Judges often refuse to grant continuances for such reasons, insisting that you have backup witnesses available. A judge's need to keep up with a calendar is likely to outweigh your desire to fashion the order of witnesses.

- The testimony of Janet, a witness you want to call first, may rely on an exhibit whose foundation can only be laid by Ron. You might have to call Ron before Janet. However, consider these options:

• Ask the judge to permit Janet to testify concerning the exhibit, on the condition that if the proper foundation is not subsequently laid, Janet's testimony will be stricken.

• Ask opposing counsel to stipulate to the exhibit's admissibility.

• If neither of these options is available, call Ron first for the limited purpose of laying a foundation for the exhibit. Ask the judge for permission to delay the remainder of Ron's testimony until later in your case-in-chief. Opposing counsel may object under Federal Rule of Evidence 403 that calling and recalling witnesses will produce undue delay, but the judge has discretion under Rule 611 to grant the request.

H. SHOULD YOU ELICIT HARMFUL EVIDENCE?

Litigators are frequently advised to "take the sting out of cross examination" by eliciting harmful evidence during direct examination. Doing so implies that "we have nothing to fear from the harmful evidence." Moreover, when you elicit harmful evidence on direct you can provide a witness an immediate chance to offer an explanation that reduces its impact. By contrast, when harmful evidence comes out on cross, the explanation may not come out until redirect examination. That may be too late for you to rehabilitate a witness.

For example, assume that a witness will testify, "The light was green." However, during an earlier speech before the Conference of Priests, Ministers and Rabbis (all of whom are available to testify for your adversary), the witness said, "The light was red." Why allow your gleeful opponent to attack the witness with the inconsistency on cross? Better to bring it out openly during direct, when perhaps you can elicit an immediate explanation:

"The reason I made the statement at the conference was to make the point that you can tell a lie without being struck down by lightning. Hey- what was that flash?"

Nevertheless, routinely eliciting harmful evidence during direct examination is a mistake. First, you may elicit harmful evidence of which your adversary has no knowledge. Just as some people are so personally conscious of a physical blemish that they wrongly assume that everyone else is as well, so may you pessimistically credit an adversary with knowledge of harmful evidence.

Second, even an adversary who is aware of harmful evidence may not elicit it during cross examination, for fear that the witness will have an explanation that eliminates a seeming inconsistency.

Third, passing over harmful evidence gives a witness a chance to produce a favorable "mind set" in a factfinder. As discussed earlier in the chapter, once you create a favorable mind set, that mind set may remain despite the introduction of the harmful evidence during cross examination. However, if you routinely elicit harmful evidence during direct, you may prevent a factfinder from developing a favorable mind set in the first place.

I. CONCLUDING DIRECT EXAMINATIONS

The concluding portion of a direct examination offers you another chance to emphasize evidence supporting your arguments. To do so, ask a witness to repeat an item or two of evidence. Repetition does risk an "asked and answered" objection. However, judges have discretion to permit repetition, and often allow it if you are brief. Your questions should "signal" that you are winding up:

Q: Just a couple of more questions, Ms. Woods. Again, how many weeks of work did you miss?

A: Sixteen.

Q: And what was your family's income during those sixteen weeks?

A: Nothing.

Q: No further questions at this time.

When you promise a "couple of questions," be sure to abide by the promise!

J. CUMULATIVE WITNESSES

Cumulative witnesses become an issue when more than one person is available to tell essentially the same story. For example, cumulative witnesses may be spouses or business partners who participated nearly equally in the transactions resulting in a lawsuit. Or, cumulative witnesses may be those who attended a raucous political demonstration and can testify that a client did not throw rocks at the police. In such situations, you have to decide whether to call cumulative witnesses. (You may have an ethical obligation to consult with a client before making this decision. See Standard 4–5.2 (b), ABA Standards for Criminal Justice). Either way, risks exist. If you call cumulative witnesses:

- A factfinder may infer that calling Witnesses #2 and 3 indicates your lack of confidence in Witness #1.

- Using "a chain is only as strong as its weakest link" reasoning, a factfinder may tar one witness with the poor credibility of a cumulative witness.

- Just as a word that you repeat over and over begins to lose meaning, so may evidence that is repeated lose meaning, or at least emotional impact.

On the other hand, if you do not call cumulative witnesses:

- A factfinder may infer that the testimony of other witnesses you might have called would have been harmful. (A commonly-given jury instruction advises jurors of the permissibility of such an inference.)

• You may create a rift in an attorney-client relationship, if a client does not accept your explanation for deciding that the client or a witness is cumulative.

When faced with an unappetizing choice of calling or not calling cumulative witnesses, consider the following compromise approaches:

• Call cumulative witnesses, but elicit a complete story from only one or two and ask others to repeat only key evidence.

• Call only one or two witnesses, and ask opposing counsel to stipulate to the testimony of the others. The stipulation would be in this form: "If they were called and sworn as witnesses, A, B and C would testify as follows: ... "This form of stipulation permits opposing counsel to stipulate to testimony, without in any way conceding the accuracy or the credibility of the stipulated testimony.

K. ADDRESSING SILENT ARGUMENTS

As you know from Chapter 5, silent arguments are preconceptions and stereotypes that are likely to influence a factfinder even though they are not a subject of explicit argument. If you think it likely that your client or witness will be victimized by a silent argument, direct examination gives you an opportunity to address it. You'll need to identify the source of the preconception or stereotype, and think about whether you can offer testimony to counter it.

For instance, assume that your client is a debt collector. You think it possible that the factfinder will distrust the client because of a preconception that debt collectors use devious collection practices to extract more than they deserve. While you may not eliminate the factfinder's bias, consider including in your direct examination evidence that might suspend the bias in your client's case. For example, examine this bit of testimony:

Q: What happened next?

A: I sent the debtor a letter explaining that our only remaining option was to attach the bank account.

Q: Why did you send this letter?

A: My business practice is to advise consumers of the steps I can take in an effort to work out a payment schedule whenever possible.

Such testimony may incline a factfinder to view your client as an exception to the general rule, and to evaluate the evidence fairly without regard to the silent argument.

Evidence rules may not always allow you to address silent arguments during direct examination. Or, as where you think a factfinder may be biased against a witness with a heavy accent, you may be unable to think of evidence that counters the preconception. Surfacing the issue and asking clients

and colleagues for ideas will maximize your chance
of countering silent arguments.

L. ADDRESSING NORMATIVE ARGUMENTS

As you also know from Chapter 5, normative
arguments are based on evidence demonstrating
that a community standard (such as "reasonableness") has (or has not) been satisfied. Assuming
that you have developed normative arguments prior
to trial, you will typically offer evidence to support
them during direct examination.

For example, assume that your client is an employer who has been sued for wrongful discharge for
sacking an employee who reported drunk to work
on two occasions in three weeks and during that
time misplaced a purchase order. The employee may
concede that these events took place but make a
normative argument that they do not constitute
reasonable or sufficient grounds for discharge. During the employer's direct examination, you'll want
to offer evidence supporting your normative arguments as to why the conduct justified discharge. For
example, normative arguments are often based on
evidence of "positive or negative consequences flowing from conduct." Thus, you may ask the employer
such questions as:

- "What was the effect in the workplace of the
  employee's coming to work drunk?"
- "What happened as a result of the employee
  misplacing the purchase order?"

A second typical basis of normative arguments consists of evidence about the availability of alternative responses to conduct. To develop such arguments here, you might ask the employer such questions as:

- "Did you have options other than sacking the employee?"
- "Why didn't you choose one of those options?"

M. REDIRECT EXAMINATION

Following cross examination, you typically have a chance to conduct redirect examination. Redirect examination is an opportunity to respond to evidence elicited during cross examination. You cannot reprise a witness' entire direct examination testimony, nor can you use leading questions. And, unless the subject happens to fall within the scope of cross examination, you cannot use redirect to elicit information that you neglected to elicit on direct. However, a remedy may be available to you in this last situation. During redirect, ask the judge for permission to reopen direct examination for the purpose of eliciting evidence you forgot to ask about earlier. Judges will often grant the request, of course allowing opposing counsel to cross-examine as to any new evidence.

One typical purpose of redirect is to clarify a chronology already set out during direct examination if the chronology became muddled or was attacked during cross examination. For example, perhaps a cross examiner skipped back and forth in an effort to confuse a witness, and as a result might have confused the factfinder as to the time sequence of events. Redirect would be your opportunity to take your witness briefly through the proper sequence.

Another typical purpose of redirect is to offer explanations for inconsistencies that the cross examiner developed. For example, assume that on your direct as the prosecutor in a criminal case, an eyewitness identified the defendant as a robber. On cross, the cross examiner elicited evidence that right after the robbery, the eyewitness told the police, "I probably couldn't identify the robber—I didn't get a very good look." If the witness has an explanation, and you didn't elicit the explanation on direct while "taking the sting out of cross" (see Page 131), redirect is your opportunity to bring it out:

Q: Why did you tell the police that you probably couldn't identify the robber?

A: It was right after the robbery, I was really scared and my first reaction was not to get involved.

Q: Was that statement you made to the police accurate?

A: No. As I testified earlier, I got a full face view of the defendant for a couple of seconds.

Q: And why are you willing to identify the defendant here in court today?

A: I've thought about it, and I want to do what's right.

Q: Is there any doubt in your mind about the defendant's being the person who robbed the store?

A: None whatsoever.

Federal Rule of Evidence 611 gives judges discretion as to whether to allow redirect examination. Though judges normally allow redirect, you need not conduct it just because, like a mountain, "it's there." Particularly if you think that a witness held up better to cross examination than you expected, you may want to get the witness off the stand quickly and not allow opposing counsel another shot during recross.

N. HOUSEKEEPING TIPS

1. Elucidate Utilizing Prevalent Vernacular

Though lawyers are supposedly schooled in the arts of communication, many break out in legalese when they walk through courtroom doors. Instead of asking if "Jones got out of a car," they ask if "the individual then exited the vehicle." They do not ask if somebody went someplace; they ask if the person "had an occasion to proceed." Such formalities are unnecessary, and tend to detract from a story's impact. Remember, in the days before written language, storytellers used a variety of devices to make their stories more vivid and memorable. The largely oral (and aural) world of trial imposes some of the same communication needs on lawyers as preliterate societies imposed on their storytellers. Plain and simple language generally adds impact to questions and responses. And when a witness, for example an expert, uses a term that is uncommon, remember to ask the witness to explain it in every-day terms.

2. Watch the Witness

No, a witness is not likely to go away. But some-times, convinced that you have asked the greatest open question ever put to a witness, and that the witness has a dynamite response that will take awhile to deliver, you may use the time to scan your notes or prepare your closing argument. However, factfinders inevitably notice such behavior, and may infer that what the witness has to say isn't very important or has been thoroughly memorized. Also, even a well-prepared witness can give a surprise answer. If you are not paying attention, you may ask a follow-up question to the wrong testimony:

Q: What did you see next?

A: I don't remember anything else.

Q: What color was it?

Paying careful attention to witnesses and their an-swers can prevent such gaffes and add significantly to the impact of testimony.

3. Verbalize Gestures

Witnesses sometimes respond to questions with gestures or words that are meaningful only to some-

one watching the testimony. You both clarify the
record (e.g., for the benefit of appellate judges) and
emphasize testimony by converting such responses
to assertions. For example:

- You ask a "yes" or "no" question, and the
  witness responds by shaking her head up and
  down or sideways. The court reporter cannot
  record a non-verbal response, so you need to
  follow up with another question: "Please answer the question 'yes' or 'no' so the court
  reporter can take it down." or "Your answer is
  yes?" (As in the TV show "Jeopardy," better
  practice is to clarify the record in the form of a
  question to avoid a suggestion that you are
  testifying. However, judges will often permit
  you to clarify a non-verbal response yourself:
  "For the record, the witness answered yes.")

- You ask a "yes" or "no" question, and the
  witness responds with "uh huh" or "uh uh."
  This type of response is ambiguous, and you
  should clarify as if the witness had responded
  with a non-verbal head shake.

- You ask, "How far from Mr. Dumpty were you
  when he fell?" and the witness replies, "About
  from me to you." You might ask the witness to
  restate the distance verbally: "Can you tell us
  in feet approximately how far away you were?"
  However, witnesses are notoriously bad at distance estimates. To avoid creating a conflict
  between the verbal and non-verbal estimate,
  you might put your own estimate to the wit-

ness. In question form, you would ask: "Would you say that's a distance of about 10 feet?" More assertively, you might say, "Let the record reflect that the witness indicated a distance of about 10 feet." (You wouldn't be "leading" in either instance, because you're clarifying already-given testimony.) If the courtroom has a chart indicating the distance from the witness box to various points in the courtroom, another alternative is to ask the judge to refer to the chart and indicate for the record the distance referred to by the witness.

The problem of reducing gestures to verbal form becomes a bit stickier when a witness' gestures pertain to a "dynamic" activity. For example, assume that while physically describing a fight, a witness says things like, "She went like this, and he did this, then she put her arm up under here, and his head snapped back like this." Even the best play-by-play sports announcer couldn't paint a complete verbal picture of the fight. In such situations, consider a "freeze frame" approach. As the witness physically illustrates an event, stop the action at key points and verbally describe the witness' position at each point: "You're indicating now that the woman was standing almost directly behind the man; her right arm was around his neck, forcing his face upward at an angle of about 45 degrees, and her left hand was around the man's left wrist, and she was holding his left arm behind him bent at the elbow, in what you might call a half-nelson hold. Is that about right? Hey-were you playing Twister?"

4. Eliminate "Echoing," "I See" and Other Verbal Tics

Whether out of nervousness or a desire to give themselves time to think, some attorneys have a habit of preceding nearly every question with a verbal tic. Such tics include echoing part of a previous answer, or murmuring "I see", "uh-huh" or "thank you." A transcript might look like this:

Q: What happened next?

A: He huffed and he puffed.

Q: I see. And then what?

A: After a few minutes he blew the house down.

Q: Blew the house down. Could you describe. . . .

So annoying can such habits become that a factfinder may remember your tics more than the testimony. The court staff may even be tempted to start a pool, with entrants trying to guess the number of "I sees." Awareness of your own tendency towards verbal tics is a major step in eliminating them. Unlike radio personalities, you need not fill the courtroom air with constant verbiage. Silence is perfectly acceptable while you consider your next question.

O. LAYING COMMON FOUNDATIONS

As a trial advocate, you should look at evidence rules not as exclusionary, but in the way a chef looks at recipes-the rules tell you what ingredients are necessary for the introduction of evidence. These ingredients are "foundations," and this section describes foundational requirements that typically arise on direct examination.

1. Personal Knowledge

Before a lay witness (non-expert) can testify to a matter, you must lay a foundation showing that the witness has personal knowledge. (Federal Rule of Evidence 602) Examine this brief bit of testimony:

    1. Q: What did you see when you arrived at the scene?

    2. A: I saw the wolf laughing, and piles of straw laying all over the place.

    3. Q: Did the wolf say anything?

    4. A: Yes. The wolf said, "I huffed and I puffed and I blew the house down."

By asking about what the witness saw, Question No. 1 establishes a foundation of personal knowledge for the response (No. 2). However, you've not shown that the witness has personal knowledge of the wolf's statement. Perhaps someone else told the witness what the wolf said. To avoid a "lack of foundation" or "lack of personal knowledge" objection, include the personal knowledge basis of testimony in a question. For example, you might have phrased No. 3 as follows:

    3. Q: Did you hear the wolf say anything?

A witness' personal knowledge is often a natural by-product of scene-setting questions (see Page 107).

2. Conversations

Witnesses frequently testify to conversations, either that they have participated in or overheard. Many judges insist on a "where, when and whom" foundation for conversations. For example, consider this testimony:

Q: Did you have another meeting with Andre?

A: I did, we had dinner.

Q: Please tell us what was said during this meeting.

An adequate foundation is lacking for the dinner conversation. The appropriate foundational details might look like this:

Q: Did you have another meeting with Andre?

A: I did, we had dinner.

Q: When did this dinner meeting take place?

A: About two weeks later, in mid-June.

Q: Where did this mid-June meeting occur?

A: At Blassie's Bistro.

Q: Did anyone other than you and Andre participate in the meeting?

A: No, it was just the two of us.

Q: OK, now please tell us what was said during this meeting.

The Hearsay Trap Some advocates think they can avoid the hearsay rule if they don't ask "what was said" in a conversation. As a result they ask awkward questions such as, "What was the substance of the conversation?" or "After the conversation, what was you impression as to what happened to the truck?" Such questions are ineffective, both for providing accurate details and avoiding the hearsay rule. If a declarant's out of court statement is improper hearsay, so is a summary of the statement or an impression left by the statement. If you think an out of court assertion is admissible, ask for it directly and do not try to play games with the hearsay rule.

3. Refreshing Recollection

Despite your best preparation efforts, witnesses sometimes forget what they are supposed to say. You may use either leading questions or documents to refresh their recollection. You can use any type of document to refresh recollection; the document need not have been prepared by the witness nor be admissible in evidence. However, your adversary has the right to examine the document and introduce relevant portions of it. (Federal Rule of Evidence 612)

To refresh recollection with a document, ask a witness who claims a failure of recollection if looking at a document (e.g., "the police report," "your deposition") might refresh the witness' recollection. After showing the document to opposing counsel, hand the document to the witness and call the witness' attention to the relevant portion. Then remove the document and ask if the witness' recollection has been refreshed. If the answer is affirmative, re-ask the question. By way of illustration, assume that you've laid a proper foundation for testimony concerning what was said during a meeting. The following testimony then ensues:

Q: OK, now please tell us what was said during this meeting.

A: We talked about the frustration of trying to define objective reality in a postmodern world. Andre said that social groups wage a continuous battle for the dominance of their view of reality.

Q: Did Andre mention any groups in particular?

A: Yes, I'm sure he did, I just can't remember.

Q: Might it refresh your recollection if you looked at the book, "Postmodernity in a Nutshell?"

A: It might.

Q: Your Honor, I've marked for identification and shown to opposing counsel the book "Postmodernity in a Nutshell." (To witness:) Please look at pages 95–96 to see if that refreshes your recollection as to any particular social groups that Andre may have mentioned.

A: All right.

Q: (After removing the book) Is your memory now refreshed?

A: Yes, I remember now.

Q: Then I ask you again, what social group or groups did Andre mention as waging a continuous battle for the dominance of their version of reality?

A: Andre mentioned . . .

Had you chosen to refresh recollection with leading questions instead of with a document, the testimony might have looked like this:

1.   Q: Now please tell us what was said during this meeting.

2.   A: We talked about the frustration of trying to define objective reality in a postmodern world. Andre said that social groups wage a continuous battle for the dominance of their view of reality.

3.   Q: Did Andre mention any groups in particular?

4.   A: Yes, I'm sure he did, I just can't remember.

5.   Q: Well, did he refer to groups concerned with gambling?

6.   A: Oh, yes, he specifically said that lottery operators were trying to foist their view of reality on state governments.

Note that the leading question (No. 5) stops short of referring to the specific testimony you want the witness to give (No. 6). While you may be able to lead, you want the crucial evidence to come from the witness if at all possible. If in No. 6 the witness still were unable to remember, you might have had no choice other than to ask a more leading question: "Did he say that lottery operators were trying to foist their view of reality on state governments?"

You typically cannot refresh recollection when a witness gives a negative response. For example, assume that the testimony above had proceeded in this way:

1. Q: OK, now please tell us what was said during this meeting.

2. A: We talked about the frustration of trying to define objective reality in a postmodern world. Andre said that social groups wage a continuous battle for the dominance of their view of reality.

3. Q: Did Andre mention any groups in particular?

4. A: No, he didn't.

5. Q: Might it refresh your recollection if you looked at the book, "Postmodernity in a Nutshell?"

Judge: Counsel, the witness hasn't testified to an inability to recall. I will not permit you to refresh recollection. Please proceed.

Because you cannot refresh recollection, you'd have to impeach the witness pursuant to Federal Rule of Evidence 607. For example, you might offer into evidence the witness' inconsistent deposition testimony. Or, a judge might permit a leading question: "Isn't it true that Andre said that lottery operators were trying to foist their view of reality on state governments?"

To avoid having to impeach your own witness, you might include a reference to recollection in a question. That way, a judge is likely to interpret a "no" as a failure of recollection and permit you to refresh recollection with a document. For example, assume that Nos. 3 and 4 above were as follows:

3.   Q: *Do you recall* whether Andre mentioned any groups in particular?

4.   A: No, I don't.

Now the witness' "no" sounds like an inability to recall, and a judge should permit you to refresh recollection.

4.   Lay Witness Opinions

Lay witnesses can give opinions that are based on personal knowledge and are helpful to a clear understanding of testimony. (Federal Rule of Evidence 701) The latter portion of the rule expresses a preference for concrete observations, leaving the conclusions to be drawn from those observations to factfinders whenever possible.

For example, assume that Bonnie and Clyde are charged with murder. Bonnie fired the fatal shot, Clyde's responsibility is based on his having urged her to shoot. On direct examination by the prosecutor, a witness testifies as follows:

1.   Q: And how far from the scene of the shooting were you?

2.   A: No more than 15 feet.

3.   Q: What did you see?

4.   A: I heard the victim ask Bonnie a couple of times to hand over her gun, but Bonnie kept it pointed at the victim.

5. Q: Then what happened?

6. A: I heard Clyde, who was standing a few feet away, say, "Let him have it, Bonnie."

7. Q: And what did Clyde mean by this?

8. A: He meant that Bonnie should fire the gun.

9. Q: What happened after Clyde said "let him have it?"

10. A: Bonnie shot and killed the victim.

The opinion testimony (No. 8) is not supported by an adequate foundation. For one thing, the witness has not demonstrated sufficient personal knowledge to form an opinion about Clyde's meaning. At a minimum, an adequate foundation would probably include Clyde's tone of voice, any physical movements by Clyde accompanying the statement, and the expression on Clyde's face when he made the statement. Second, even with an expanded foundation a judge may conclude that the witness' opinion is not necessary to a clear understanding of the testimony. The judge or jury, apprised fully by the witness of the circumstances, may be just as capable as the witness of deciding whether Clyde meant "start shooting," "turn over the gun" or something else entirely when he said, "let him have it."

More common lay opinions, and typical foundational showings, are as follows:

● Opinion: Handwriting is that of a particular person. Foundation: Witness has personal knowledge of that person's handwriting. (Federal Rule of Evidence 901-b-2)

- Opinion: Speed of a car. Foundation: Witness is an experienced driver and observed speed of car long enough to form a reliable opinion.

- Opinion: A person was (or was not) intoxicated. Foundation: Witness is familiar with effects of alcohol and observed the individual long enough to form a reliable opinion.

In such situations, a foundation is adequate so long the proponent of the opinion offers sufficient evidence to sustain a finding of adequacy. (Federal Rule of Evidence 104-b)

CHAPTER 8

EXHIBITS

This chapter briefly reviews typical procedures for introducing exhibits into evidence, and sets forth examples of foundations for common types of exhibits. Be aware, however, that judges often have idiosyncratic methods of handling exhibits. Prior to your first trial before a judge, you should check with the judge's court clerk or other person who knows the judge's preferred methods of handling exhibits.

A. REAL VS. ILLUSTRATIVE EXHIBITS

Exhibits comprise a variety of tangible objects. Among the most common exhibits are:

- Real evidence, objects which are themselves sources of legal rights or liabilities. For example, real evidence might be a murder weapon, illegal drugs, a libelous pamphlet, or an obscene movie film (which would be "reel" evidence!).

- Illustrative (demonstrative) evidence, objects which attorneys often create for trial and which illuminate and clarify oral testimony. Typical illustrative exhibits include diagrams, photos of

154

the scenes of crimes and auto accidents, "Day in the Life" videos, and computer-generated re-enactments.

The distinction between "real" and "illustrative" exhibits often has little impact on foundational requirements. However, judges are more likely to allow jurors to take real than illustrative evidence into deliberation rooms.

Ethics note: The distinction between real and illustrative evidence may be crucial to an attorney's obligation to turn evidence over to the police. For example, assume that a client hands an attorney the weapon the client used in a murder, and a photo of the weapon. The attorney probably has to hand over the former to the police, but not the latter.

B. BENEFITS OF EXHIBITS

Except when the Original Writing Rule (Federal Rule of Evidence 1000) requires you to offer exhibits into evidence, the main reason to offer exhibits is to enhance a factfinder's understanding of testimony and add to the impact of testimony. Recall that people are primarily visual learners; about 85% of what people know is a result of visual learning. Thus, you "teach" more effectively when you supplement oral testimony with exhibits. One reason is that exhibits often add shelf life to testimony. Reviewed by factfinders during deliberations, exhibits may remind of testimony that otherwise might have been overlooked. As the old adage goes, a picture is worth four thousand words. (corrected for inflation)

Moreover, exhibits are less subject than witnesses to claims of error and incompleteness. For example, most of us would regard a photograph of the scene of an accident as more accurate than a witness' verbal description of the scene.

Exhibits also allow you to emphasize testimony through repetition. Often you can elicit evidence once verbally, and again in the context of an exhibit. For example, you may ask a witness who was struck by a boomerang to describe the boomerang orally. Then you can emphasize the key portions of the description when you offer the boomerang into evidence.

Finally, exhibits may simply meet jurors' expectations. Most jurors' notions of trial come from Hollywood. On television or in the movies, attorneys can go to prop rooms for exhibits and offer them into evidence by the carload. As a result, some jurors may expect you to dazzle them with tangible objects. For example, a juror may be leery of convicting a defendant when the prosecutor hasn't produced fingerprint exemplars. Or, a juror may expect you to produce the drafts and memoranda that preceded an agreement that you claim was made. While you can not offer irrelevant exhibits any more than you can offer irrelevant testimony, always consider what exhibits a factfinder may expect you to offer.

C. LAYING FOUNDATIONS
FOR EXHIBITS

Laying a foundation for the introduction of an exhibit into evidence normally is a three step process:

- Mark an exhibit and show it to opposing counsel.
- Elicit testimony authenticating the exhibit.
- Elicit testimony establishing the exhibit's admissibility.

Stipulations may allow you to sidestep all or some of these foundational requirements. For example, opposing counsel may stipulate to an exhibit's admissibility. Or, counsel may enter into a more limited stipulation that an exhibit is authentic and relevant, and dispute its admissibility on the ground that it is hearsay or unduly prejudicial. In the absence of stipulations, follow the general process set forth below.

1. Mark Exhibits

Marking an exhibit consists of tagging it with a number or letter so as to distinguish it from other exhibits. During trial, refer to a marked exhibit by its number or letter. Think of an appellate judge trying to understand testimony when a transcript reads, "Witness, did you ever see this letter? How about this one?" Contrast: "Did you ever see plaintiff's No. 1? How about plaintiff's No. 2?" Traditionally, plaintiffs' exhibits are numbered and defendants' are lettered. However, some judges prefer to number or letter all exhibits consecutively, regardless of which party offers them.

Until trial lawyers can convince manufacturers of objects likely to become exhibits to engrave little numbers or letters on them, the marking process will remain manual. Many judges prefer you simply to mark an exhibit when you first show it to a witness. Others want exhibits marked before trial, either during a pretrial conference or by the court clerk.

Example 1:

Q: What is the next thing you saw?

A: He pulled out a knife and started waving it around.

Q: Your Honor, I have here a knife and am putting the number 1 on the white evidence tag attached to the knife. I've shown the knife to defense counsel. May the knife be marked State's No. 1 for identification?

Judge: It may be so marked.

Q: May I show it to the witness?

Judge: You may.

Example 2:

Q: And what happened after that?

A: The car ended up in the tree. I guess then you could have called it an Oakmobile.

Q: Your Honor, I have here a photograph which the clerk has previously marked as Defense

"B." I've shown it to counsel for plaintiff. May I show it to the witness?

Judge: Yes, you may.

The marking process can be slightly more involved when you have more than one exhibit of the same type. When you have just one gun, it's fine to mark Exhibit No. 1 as a "gun." But what if you need to mark four letters, three photos, and two turtle doves? The record can no longer reflect that Exhibit No. 3 is a "letter" or a "photograph." You'll need an additional distinguishing characteristic. For example, you may mark one letter as a "letter dated June 28," and another as a "letter dated July 3." You have two letters dated June 28? Follow the same distinguishing characteristic principle: "Your Honor, I have two letters dated June 28. May the one addressed to Smith be marked Plaintiff's No. 4 and the one addressed to Wesson be marked Plaintiff's No. 5?"

When marking an exhibit, identify it by a neutral feature. For example, don't identify an exhibit as "a letter in which the defendant makes a full, callous and unambiguous admission of every element of our claim for relief."

2. Authenticate Exhibits

Authenticating means establishing that an exhibit is what you claim it to be. When authenticating an exhibit, try to get it into a witness' hands. Do not wave an exhibit in the air from counsel table. A witness will get very frustrated if you ask a witness to identify a needle from a distance of 30 feet.

Two questions are common to most authentications:

- To identify the exhibit: "Can you please tell us what Exhibit X is?"

- To establish a witness' personal knowledge: "How do you know?"

For example, after marking the photo of the car above, you might authenticate the photo as follows:

Q: Your Honor, may I approach the witness?

Judge: Yes you may, and you needn't continue to ask for permission.

Q: Handing you Defense "B," do you recognize what it depicts?

A: Yes. It shows the car after it landed in the old oak tree.

Q: How is it you recognize it as a photo of the car?

A: Well, I looked at it after the accident. That's what it looked like all right.

On many occasions you will need more of a foundation to establish a witness' personal knowledge. For example, witnesses may have to explain how they can identify mass-produced items. Consider how a witness might demonstrate personal knowledge in response to the question, "How do you know these are the scissors you saw?" The witness might respond:

- "I know these are the scissors I saw on the beach because I recognize the attached tag saying, 'Hilary's scissors; don't remove from room.' or

- "I know these are the scissors I saw on the beach because I initialed this tag and taped it to one of the blades."

When an exhibit is fungible or subject to decomposition or tampering, you may have to support a witness' personal knowledge with "chain of custody" testimony. To establish a chain of custody is to account for an exhibit's whereabouts prior to trial. For example, assume that an exhibit consists of a baggie of illegal drugs. The police officer who seized the baggie may have to establish how the officer recognizes the baggie as the one seized: "I put this little sticker on the baggie and marked it with the date and my initials." The officer may also have to offer evidence showing that the contents of the baggie are unlikely to have been tampered with: "I placed it in the police evidence locker and it's been there continuously except for when it was removed for testing by a police lab technician. It looks the same way now as it did when I seized it." To complete the chain, you may need further foundational testimony from the lab technician: "I removed the baggie from the police evidence locker and placed a sticker with the date and my initials on the baggie. The baggie was then in my evidence drawer in the police lab for two days. I tested the contents of the baggie and returned it to the police evidence locker, indicating on the sticker the date when I did so." The chain of custody testimony demonstrates that the exhibit is the same item that was seized and tested.

Chain of custody testimony doesn't have to be so exhaustive that no possibility of testimony of tampering or alteration exists. An exhibit is generally admissible so long as the evidence is sufficient to permit a factfinder to conclude that the exhibit is genuine (Federal Rule of Evidence 104–b).

"Lookalike" exhibits. If you can't get hold of the genuine article, you may authenticate an exhibit based on its "close resemblance" to the genuine article. For example, a witness may identify a boomerang as "nearly identical to the one that struck me." Of course, you'd have to show that the witness has personal knowledge of the appearance of the actual boomerang.

3. Establish an Exhibit's Admissibility

Once a witness authenticates an exhibit, you may need to demonstrate its admissibility. For example, you may need to elicit foundational testimony demonstrating that a written document qualifies under an exception to the hearsay rule, such as a business record (Federal Rule of Evidence 803 (6)) or a declaration against interest (Federal Rule of Evidence 804 (3)). Or, you may need to argue that the exhibit's relevance outweighs the risk of unfair prejudice (Federal Rule of Evidence 403). Sample foundations establishing the admissibility of common exhibits are set forth below.

Once you've established an exhibit's admissibility, you may move it into evidence. The usual magic words are, "Your Honor, I ask that Exhibit X be received in evidence." After giving opposing counsel a chance to object, the judge may utter the more magic words, "Exhibit X will be received in evidence."

4. Don't Take Exhibits Home With You

Once a judge has admitted an exhibit into evidence, you may be as uncomfortable with an exhibit as you may have been with your hands when you had to give a speech in the seventh grade. In either situation, the one rule to obey is the "in" rule. You shouldn't put your hands "in" your pocket when you make a speech, and you shouldn't put exhibits "in" your briefcase after they are in evidence. Exhibits generally remain court property until a judge orders their release. Unless you want the bailiff to treat you to an overnight stay "in" the local jail, leave admitted exhibits in the courtroom.

D. PUBLISHING EXHIBITS

Just as it's generally in your interest to communicate arguments throughout trial, you usually want jurors to understand the contents of an exhibit as soon as it's admitted into evidence. Obviously, you needn't do anything special to familiarize jurors with large physical exhibits, such as shovels and football linebackers. But if your exhibit is a letter or a photograph, and it goes from you to the judge to the witness to the court clerk, you'll need to take an extra step to "publish" it, or inform jurors of its contents.

With a written document, you might ask a witness to read a key portion to the jury. Doing so wouldn't violate the Original Writing Rule, because the document is already in evidence. A second method is to hire a professional exhibit preparation company to make an enlargement which you can display on an easel. A third method is to ask a judge for permission for jurors to physically examine an exhibit. For instance, you may ask a judge to allow the jurors to examine the photograph you've just offered into evidence.

A judge may be reluctant to grant the last request, because testimony has to halt while each juror pores over an exhibit. A frequent judicial rejoinder to this type of request is, "They'll have it during deliberations. Let's move on." Two steps that can help you achieve a favorable response are:

- Support the request with an argument as to why the jurors need to see the exhibit immediately: "Your Honor, if I might be heard on my request. This witness will be testifying to an incident that took place in several rooms in a house. Unless the jurors see the photographs of the rooms, they will be unable to understand the testimony."

- Minimize the delay by having a separate copy of an exhibit for each juror.

E. FOUNDATIONS FOR COMMON EXHIBITS

1. Photographs

The typical foundation for a photograph is testimony from a witness with personal knowledge that "the photo fairly and accurately depicts" its contents. For example, return to the witness who authenticated a photo of a car that landed in an old oak tree. The foundational testimony might go as follows:

Q: Handing you Defense "B," do you recognize what it depicts?

A: Yes. It shows the car after it landed in the old oak tree.

Q: How is it you recognize it as a photo of the car?

A: Well, I looked at it after the accident. That's what it looked like all right.

Q: Does the photo fairly and accurately depict the condition and location of the car immediately following the accident?

A: It does.

Q: Your Honor, I move Defense "B" into evidence.

Judge: Any objection? Hearing none, the exhibit will be received into evidence.

When a witness has personal knowledge of whatever is depicted in a photo, you needn't identify who took a photo or the type of camera or film used to take it. Even the date a photo was taken is often unimportant. For example, even if the photo of the car had been taken months after the accident, it's likely to be admissible so long as the witness testifies that it fairly and accurately depicts the condition of the car right after the accident.

The most common objection to photos is that they are misleading or unfairly prejudicial (Federal Rule of Evidence 403). For example, such an objection may be made if you offer into evidence:

- a photo of the scene of a crime or an accident, and the scene changed significantly between the time of the events and the taking of the photo.

- a series of gory autopsy photos in a wrongful death case.

- a photo of a movie star without makeup.

2. Diagrams

A diagram is a schematic drawing, typically of a scene of important events in a story. As a visual object which jurors can take with them when they deliberate (at least if you prepare it on paper, rather than on a blackboard), diagrams share the advantages of other exhibits. In addition, diagrams can enhance a witness' credibility. Many witnesses who nervously answer questions while rooted to a witness chair testify with confidence when they can stand and mark up a diagram. Too, diagrams may allow you to emphasize important testimony, as you can sometimes elicit evidence once orally, and then again as a witness marks a diagram. Finally, as compared to exotic exhibits such as videotaped or computer-generated re-creations of traffic accidents, diagrams are usually cheap. A diagram can be yours for the price of paper and pen, and even that you may be able to cadge from the court.

Though professional attorney services will be delighted to prepare diagrams for you, often you can simply meet with a witness prior to trial and prepare a skeletal diagram. In court, the witness can identify the scene depicted in the skeleton, and as practiced in your office before testifying, fill in people, objects and their movement during testimony.

A diagram generally is not, and need not be, a photographically accurate representation of a locale. Hence, diagrams tend not to be effective for depicting abstract conditions, such as the adequacy of lighting. Nor are they helpful for depicting precise details. For example, unless your witness happens to be the top student at the Matchbook School of Art, a diagram could not exactly trace a witness' physical movements during an argument.

The following diagram lends visual context to this verbal discussion of effective use of diagrams. Assume that you and a witness have prepared the following diagram prior to trial:

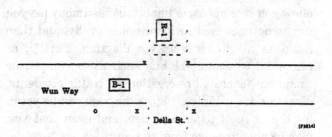

Wun Way   B-1

Della St.

[F3014]

As you see, the diagram can serve only to illustrate a witness' testimony. Without a witness, you
cannot tell if it pertains to the scene of a crime or a
traffic accident, or to an application for a zoning
variance. In this case, the foundational testimony
may go as follows:

1. Q: Calling your attention to the diagram
marked "Exhibit A," do you recognize what that
is?

2. A: Yes, it's a diagram of the intersection
where the accident took place.

3. Q: Do you know how the diagram was
prepared?

4. A: Yes. I prepared it the day before yester-
day, in your office.

5. Q: What location does the diagram depict?

6. A: It's Wun Way, at the point where Wun
intersects Della St. in the Hampstead Garden
section of the city. Wun is an east-west street,
and Della runs basically north-south at that
point.

7.   Q: Did you personally place the markings on the diagram?

8.   A: Yes.

9.   Q: I notice two rectangles on the diagram. What do they represent?

10.   A: The rectangle on Wun is a blue car that was approaching Della, signalling to make a left turn. The other rectangle is the red car that was going south on Della.

11.   Q: All right. Please place a "B–1" in the rectangle that represents the blue car, and an "R–1" in the rectangle that represents the red car. Also, perhaps you can place an arrow behind each rectangle to show in what directions the cars were headed when you first noticed them.

12.   A: Ok.

13.   Q: Looking at the diagram, I also notice four "x" marks and an "o." Could you please explain what those markings represent?

14.   A: Yes. The "x" marks are traffic signals on each corner at that intersection. The "o" is where I was standing when I saw the accident.

15.   Q: And the pair of dotted lines that crosses Della St., just to the north of the intersection with Wun?

16.   A: That's a crosswalk.

17.   Q: What were you doing when you were standing at the point marked "o?"

18. A: I was waiting for Aura David to meet me. She's my partner in the interior designer business, and we were going to make a presentation to the law firm of Cooper & Berg, whose offices are there on Wun.

19. Q: Did you continue to watch the cars you've identified as B–1 and R–1?

20. A: Not continuously. I heard a horn, and I thought it might be Aura, so I looked away to my left for a moment or two. I saw it wasn't her, so I glanced toward the intersection again.

21. Q: The intersection of Della and Wun?

22. A: That's right.

23. Q: Did you notice the cars you've labeled B–1 and R–1 after you turned back to look at the intersection?

24. A: Yes.

25. Q: Please place another rectangle on the diagram at the approximate position of the blue car when you saw it for the second time, and label that rectangle "B–2." Do the same for the red car, and label that rectangle "R–2."

26. A: Okay.

27. Q: When the cars were at positions B–2 and R–2, were you still at the position you've marked

28. A: Yes, I was.

29. Q: What is the approximate distance from point "o" to "B–2?"

30.   A: I'd say about 40 feet.

31.   Q: And the approximate distance between the cars when they are at points "B–2" and "R–2?"

32.   A: Pretty close. Maybe about 20 feet.

33.   Q: How fast would you say the blue car was going when it was at the point you've marked "B–2?"

34.   A: I'd say . . .

Here, you begin by asking the witness to identify the skeletal diagram (Nos. 1–16). As the story emerges, you ask the witness to add to the diagram by showing a change in location (No. 25). Having a witness mark only key changes prevents a diagram from resembling an aerial map of the New York Subway system. The markings enable you to clarify a chronology by providing a basis for witness estimates of such matters as distance (No. 30) and speed (No. 34).

As this short example implies, using a diagram can consume substantial time. A witness who provides too many details is likely to tax a factfinder's patience and credulity. Hence, confine pursuit of detail to crucial events.

As you may recall, one way to verbalize a witness' physical gestures is to say something like, "Let the record reflect that the witness indicated. . . ." (See Chapter 7, Page 141). By contrast, you generally needn't verbalize a witness' diagram markings. For example, the witness in the example above testified that the approximate distance between the cars at points "B–2" and "R–2" was about 20 feet. You needn't indicate "for the record that the distance between B–2 and R–2 is about 20 feet." The witness' testimony makes that evidence already a matter of record.

Because diagrams tend to be informal, they are often susceptible to an objection that they are misleading or unfairly prejudicial (Federal Rule of Evidence 403). For example, opposing counsel might argue that a diagram inaccurately shows the location of obstacles that were in a witness' line of vision, or the length of skidmarks. Your general response should be that the diagram is illustrative of testimony, not precisely accurate, and that the adversary can bring out such considerations during cross examination. Under Federal Rule of Evidence 104–b, a diagram is usually admissible so long as the witness has sufficient personal knowledge to prepare the diagram.

3. Signed or Handwritten Documents

To offer a handwritten exhibit into evidence, you need to introduce foundational evidence connecting the exhibit to the person you claim is its author. Such a foundation is necessary even for a signed document-suspicious beasts that they are, evidence rules don't assume that a document signed by "John Hancock" was actually written by John Hancock. However, myriads of ways of offering foundational evidence "sufficient to sustain a finding" (Federal Rule of Evidence 104–b) that a person authored a document exist. For example, under Federal Rule of Evidence 901 you may elicit evidence from a person who saw the document prepared or who is familiar with a person's handwriting. You may even argue that a document's contents are sufficient to support a finding that your claimed author wrote it.

4. Printed or Fax Documents, Form Letters, Brochures

You can lay the foundation for a printed document through the testimony of a witness who knows how it was prepared. Usually, however, the foundations for printed documents lie in the documents themselves. For example, printed documents typically emanate from businesses, and a business inscription is itself an adequate foundation (Federal Rule of Evidence 902 (7)). You can often connect a faxed document to its author with the telephone number that a fax machine usually prints on the document. The contents of a printed document are often sufficient to link it to the person or organization you claim to be the author (Federal Rule of Evidence 901 (4)). Finally, in civil cases, foundations are generally established during the discovery process, particularly through "Requests for Admission." A party is likely to prefer admitting authenticity in response to a Request for Admission to paying the expenses of proving authenticity (See Federal Rule of Civil Procedure 37–c–2).

5. Hearsay Foundations

An assertion in a document is just as susceptible to hearsay objections as an oral assertion. Thus, all "communicative" exhibits raise potential hearsay issues. The foundational showing necessary to obviate a hearsay objection varies with the document.

For example, to qualify an exhibit as a business record you'll need to offer evidence that it was prepared in the course of a regularly conducted business activity (Federal Rule of Evidence 803 (6)). The person or persons who prepared a business record do not have to testify. A "custodian of records" or other witness familiar with a business' procedures can normally lay the foundation and demonstrate a record's trustworthiness.

To qualify an exhibit as an admission, you'll need to offer evidence that it was prepared or authorized by a party-opponent (Federal Rule of Evidence 801–d–2).

Of course, many exhibits are not hearsay at all because they are offered for purposes other than their truth. For instance, a contract or a warning notice often is not hearsay because its contents are relevant without regard to their truth.

6. Professional Exhibits

Technological advances in professional exhibit preparation make informal diagrams seem as old-fashioned as buggy whips. When a trial involves a jury and a large pot of money or a celebrity party, you may want to turn to a professional exhibit company. (If you've never used one before and don't know of an attorney who has, consult the ads in magazines for litigators.) These companies specialize in graphic designs that make your key evidence vivid and understandable.

Depending on a client's budget, companies can produce exhibits such as:

- Enlargements of pages from depositions or contracts, with key language "pulled out" and color-highlighted.

- Accurate diagrams, color-coded and magnetized to allow the easy movement of objects.

- Enlargements of locations with overlays, each overlay showing how the location changed over time.

- "Day in the Life" videos, depicting an injured person's daily activities.

- Computer re-enactments of accidents, the process by which a product was developed and marketed, etc.

Like any other exhibits, professionally-prepared exhibits must be marked and authenticated, and meet evidentiary requirements. The most common objection to such illustrative exhibits is that their probative value is outweighed by the dangers of unfair prejudice or misleading the jury (Federal Rule of Evidence 403). For example, an opponent may claim that whatever is depicted in an exhibit is not supported by evidence in the record. Or, an adversary may claim that a "Day in the Life" video distorts an injured person's condition by showing the person trying to perform one activity after another with no rest in between.

Judges consider such objections very carefully. Since a professional may even colorize an exhibit in such a way as to maximize its psychological impact, judges are wary of the danger that professionally-prepared exhibits will mislead jurors. Whenever you think it possible that a judge will exclude a professional exhibit, ask a company to prepare at least two versions of an exhibit, one less extreme than the other. Clients are not fond of spending big money for exhibits which never see the light of admissibility.

When hiring a professional to prepare exhibits, think of the professional as an expert witness. Just as you ordinarily rely on an expert to identify significant evidence, so should you look to an exhibit preparation professional to advise you on what to put in an exhibit and how to make the exhibit effective. For example, simple exhibits usually have more impact than complex ones, and a professional is likely to know better than you how to convey key evidence clearly and vividly.

CHAPTER 9

CROSS EXAMINATION

Unlike direct examination, which is usually "witness-centered" (see Chapter 7), cross examination should be almost entirely "attorney-centered." Instead of providing a story and asking witnesses to describe events in their own words, during cross examination you typically seek to extract specific items of evidence that advance your arguments. And the choice of words is up to you, not the witness. What direct and cross examination have in common is that during both you seek to illustrate your arguments.

A. THE MYSTIQUE OF CROSS EXAMINATION

Cross examination carries a mystique that may induce you to view cross as a boxer who possesses both a tremendous knockout punch and a glass jaw. One question if asked will produce triumph, whereas another will inevitably bring shattering defeat. Part of the reason is that movies and TV often focus on the glory or the agony awaiting cross examiners. For example, Perry Mason routinely saved his clients with cross examinations wrenching confessions from witnesses or even jurors. On the other

177

hand, prosecutor Claude Dancer's final cross examination comes to a disastrous end in the classic courtroom film, "Anatomy of a Murder."

Moreover, stories about Great Trial Lawyers often revolve around their cross examination exploits. For example, one oft-told tale concerns the "Triangle Shirtwaist Fire" case. Company officials who operated a New York sweatshop were charged with criminal negligence after a fire broke out and killed numerous employees. Trampling on the Received Wisdom against letting a witness retell a story on cross examination, the cross examiner repeatedly asked the key prosecution eyewitness to "Please tell us again what happened." Each time, the witness told the story using identical words. The cross convinced the jurors that the eyewitness had simply memorized a story, and the officials were acquitted.

Academics too have contributed to the mystique of cross. The great evidence scholar John Henry Wigmore (who of course never cross examined a witness in court in his life) wrote that cross examination was "the greatest legal engine for the discovery of truth ever invented." The late Professor Irving Younger often threatened to haunt any trial lawyer who asked a non-leading cross examination question before trying 25 cases. Finally, textbooks are filled with "rules" of cross which, if violated, will surely produce disaster.

For example, the "nose story" illustrates the doom awaiting the cross examiner who asks "one question too many." The story involves a defendant who allegedly bit off his victim's nose. A prosecution eyewitness testified that the defendant did the dastardly deed. Up steps the cross examiner, and the cross proceeds in essence as follows:

Q: Where did the fight take place?

A: In the middle of the field.

Q: Where were you?

A: On the edge of the field, about 50 yards away.

Q: What were you doing there?

A: Just looking at the trees.

Q: You had your back to the fight?

A: Yes.

Q: The first you knew there was a fight was when you heard the alleged victim scream, right?

A: That's true.

Q: You didn't turn around until after the alleged victim screamed, correct?

A: Correct.

Q: How can you say, then, that my client bit off the person's nose?

A: Because I saw him spit it out.

The last question, of course, is the dreaded "one too many." Until that point, the cross had eliminated the eyewitness' ability to observe. However, stories such as these should not cause you to dread cross examination. After all, had the cross examiner not asked it, surely the evidence would have come out on redirect. Indeed, in most situations the testimony would already have been elicited during direct examination. The point is that cross examination is rarely as critical as it is often made to appear.

For example, consider this situation that arose early in the author's career. Representing on appeal a client who had been convicted of setting seven grass fires, the author moved for bail pending appeal. At the hearing on the motion, three witnesses testified in support of the bail request. (Strange but true, all three witnesses were members of the jury that had voted to convict!) The prosecutor responded with a surprise witness-the county Fire Marshal. The Marshal testified that in the weeks prior to the defendant's arrest, 40 fires had been set in various parts of the community; and that none had been set since the defendant had been in jail. The author wasted no time asking a question to which he did not know the answer:

> "Did you have any information connecting my client to these 33 other fires?"

Of course, the answer was a disastrous "yes," just as the Received Wisdom suggested it would be. Nevertheless, the mistake was not fatal-the judge granted the motion.

This section is not an invitation to reckless cross examination. By all means, do not encourage adverse witnesses to describe events in their own words, or ask questions whose answers you cannot anticipate. Rarely, however, does a single cross examination question "make or break" a case. Typically, a "poor" cross simply rehashes a witness' direct testimony, whereas a "successful" cross develops some additional evidentiary support for an argument you already planned to make.

Nevertheless, the mystique of cross examination has the potential to undermine your efforts. A belief that you're supposed to win every case on cross may goad you into fierce but pointless combat with every adverse witness. Or, a fear that one question will prove fatal may cause you to forsake judgment and inspiration in favor of slavish adherence to "rules."

B. GENERAL PRINCIPLES

Effective cross examinations generally adhere to the principles set forth below.

1. Argument–Driven Questioning

Cross examination should illustrate your arguments by juxtaposing items of evidence pertaining to the same argument. Moreover, probe topics because they are important to arguments, not simply because they are part of a story testified to during direct examination. If you try to take issue with everything said by an adverse witness, you'll probably allow the witness to rehash the entire story. (And if the story didn't persuade the factfinder the first time, the second time might do it!) Moreover, the factfinder may not recognize the significance of whatever helpful information you do elicit because it is dwarfed by the retold story.

The following example suggests how you might illustrate an inferential argument during cross examination. Assume that you represent a plaintiff in an automobile personal injury case. One of your factual propositions is that the defendant was driving in excess of the speed limit. You've developed an argument based on evidence that the defendant was 20 minutes late for a meeting at the time of the accident. The argument looks like this:

"People who are 20 minutes late to a meeting are likely to drive in excess of the speed limit, especially when . . .

- they've arranged the meeting themselves.

- the meeting is with a potential new customer.

- they cannot inform the potential new customer that they will be late.

- the potential new customer has cancelled two previous meetings."

On cross examination of the defendant, you might illustrate this argument as follows:

Q: At the time of the accident you were 20 minutes late for a meeting, correct?

A: That's true.

Q: This was a meeting you had personally arranged?

A: Yes.

Q: And this was a pretty important meeting, wasn't it?

A: More or less like other business meetings,
I'd say.

Q: Well, the meeting was with someone you
hoped would become a customer of yours, right?

A: Yes.

Q: This customer had already cancelled two
previous meetings?

A: I think so.

Q: Your answer is yes?

A: Yes.

Q: And you had no way to tell the customer
that you were running late, did you?

A: No.

This cross marshals all the evidence supporting
the "late for a meeting argument." By illustrating
the argument in this way, you hope to affect the
factfinder's "mind set" (see Page 89) by helping the
factfinder recognize the significance of the evidence
at the time you introduce it. By contrast, eliciting
events according to chronology might mask the
significance of some of the evidence. For example,
in following a chronological order you would have
elicited evidence that the defendant personally arranged the meeting well before you focus on the
accident itself. As a result, the factfinder might not
recognize a connection between that evidence and
the argument that the defendant was speeding.

2. Leading Questions.

Leading questions are the key to targeting evidence to arguments. As you recall from Chapter 7,

leading questions are essentially assertions in question form. Use of leading questions allows you and not a witness to determine the content of testimony. Moreover, you prevent witnesses from retelling their stories by limiting witnesses to confirming or denying your assertions.

For example, assume that you want to establish that after Jack fell down and broke his crown, "Jill came tumbling after." You might ask:

- An open question: "What happened after Jack broke his crown?"

- A leading question: "After Jack broke his crown, Jill came tumbling after, correct?"

The witness can respond to the open question in a number of ways. For instance, the witness might testify to Jack's crying, to Jack's physical appearance, or to what the witness said after seeing Jack's crown break. If the witness does mention Jill, the witness may not use your preferred words: "Jill slipped on the hill a bit later." The leading question, by contrast, allows you to determine both the content and the scope of the testimony.

Don't overexaggerate the power of leading questions. A witness will not automatically agree with an assertion just because you put it in the form of a leading question. A dialogue such as this will never happen:

Q: On direct, you testified that the light was green, correct?

A: Yes, I said that.

Q: And during your marriage vows, you stated that the light was green, did you not?

A: Yes, that's right.

Q: You swore to your religious leader that the light was green?

A: I did.

Q: Now, the light was actually red, wasn't it?

A: Yes, the light was red, I admit it. Wow, leading questions are really powerful.

In real life, truth is multi-dimensional. For example, an employer asked to testify about an employee's job performance could discuss numerous topics truthfully. To control the content and scope of cross examination, you have to ask leading questions that elicit the aspects of the truth that support your arguments.

3. One–Item Questions

Limit leading questions to one assertion. One-item questions tend to increase a factfinder's comprehension, add persuasiveness and discourage lengthy responses and explanations. Compare the sequence of one-item questions below with the complex question that follows it:

Q: "You walked into your supervisor's office, correct?"

Q: "You told her that you didn't care what she wanted you to do?"

Q: "Then you called her a sorry excuse for a manager?"

Q: "And you walked out of the office?"

Q: "You slammed the door?"

————

Q: "When you walked into your supervisor's office, you told her that you didn't care what she wanted you to do, called her a sorry excuse for a manager, walked out of the office and slammed the door, isn't that right?"

The second question covers the entire event with a single question. Compared with to the first series of questions, the latter is more likely to produce a lengthy, explanation-filled answer. Moreover, the latter is more likely to draw an "argumentative" or "compound" objection, further diluting the impact of your desired information.

One-item questions also allow you to provide emphasis by stringing together a series of favorable responses. For example, a series of "yes" answers to the sequence of questions above is likely to have greater impact than a single "yes" in response to the second question.

Tone of Voice: To paraphrase ancient parental wisdom, it's not just what you ask but how you ask it that counts. Use a firm tone of voice that conveys your expectation that the witness answer only "yes" or "no" to a leading question. (The movie lawyer technique of yelling questions from two inches away is firm, but improper.)

4. Safe Questions

A final general principle of effective cross examinations is that you plan for cross according to the following Safety Model:

Cross Examination Safety Model

- Highly Safe Questions
  - Witness' Provable Prior Statement
  - Consistency with Established Facts
- Medium Safe Questions
  - Consistency with Everyday Experience
  - Assumed Testimony of Unavailable Witness
- Unsafe Questions
  - Fishing

The Safety Model assumes that your arguments have identified the evidence which you hope to elicit from a witness. The Safety Model is a method of evaluating the likelihood that an adverse witness' answers will advance your arguments regardless of what those answers are. For example, defending a robbery case, you want a prosecution eyewitness to admit to being extremely nervous at the time of the robbery. The safer a question, the stronger the likelihood that the witness either will admit to being extremely nervous, or you can contradict an unfavorable answer. Thus, the Model focuses attention on what you can prove, not on the uncertainty surrounding what an adverse witness may say. The Model does not say, "Ask only safe questions." You may decide to ask unsafe questions-to fish-but should understand when you are doing so to increase your chances of a successful catch.

As you can see, the Safety Model above carries forward some of the elements of the Credibility Model (see Page 25). The Credibility Model indicates factors affecting credibility; the Safety Model indicates the likelihood that you'll be able to elicit evidence to support those factors.

C. CROSS EXAMINATION SAFETY MODEL: HIGHLY SAFE QUESTIONS

1. Witness' Provable Prior Statement

A question is highly safe if your desired answer is consistent with a witness' provable prior statement. A prior statement is "provable" if you can offer the prior statement into evidence as a prior inconsistent statement if the witness' story changes. For example, a prior inconsistent statement might be provable because a witness made it during a deposition, or to another person who you can call as a witness. The question is safe because either the witness will confirm the prior statement, or you can impeach a changed story with the prior statement. (Under Federal Rule of Evidence 801–d–1–A, the prior statement is admissible as substantive evidence only if it was made under oath, as in a deposition. Otherwise, it is admissible only to impeach the changed story.)

For example, assume that you represent an injured plaintiff in a medical malpractice case. On cross examination of the defendant doctor, an anesthesiologist, you want to offer evidence that the doctor knew that the plaintiff had eaten a meal within one hour of surgery. This evidence would support an argument that the doctor carelessly used the wrong anesthetic. Your question would be something like:

Q: Doctor, at the time you administered anesthetic you knew that the plaintiff had eaten a meal within the preceding hour, correct?

This question is highly safe if:

- At the doctor's deposition, the doctor testified, "I knew that the patient had eaten a meal within an hour of the surgery."

- The doctor mentioned to a colleague who is available to you as a witness, "I knew that the patient had eaten a meal within an hour of the surgery."

Both questions are highly safe because either the doctor provides your desired answer, or you later contradict an unfavorable answer by reading from the doctor's deposition or calling the colleague as a witness.

Note that your highly safe question makes no mention of its source. Your question would have been improper had you asked, "Doctor, according to what you said in your deposition (or told your colleague), at the time you administered anesthetic you knew that the plaintiff had eaten a meal within the preceding hour, correct?" The fact that the witness made the earlier statement is hearsay and irrelevant unless and until the witness contradicts the earlier statement at trial.

Working backwards, note how your ability to ask highly safe questions at trial often depends on your deposition techniques. To serve as the basis of a highly safe question, a prior statement must leave a witness without "wriggle room" to explain away a seeming inconsistency. The more vague or imprecise a former statement, the less useful it is as the basis of a highly safe question. Often, of course, you have no control over the content of a prior statement. You are stuck with whatever a witness wrote in a memo, shouted to a neighbor, or said in a banner attached the back of a blimp. But when you do have control, as during deposition questioning, try to pin witnesses down to the exact statements you would like them to repeat in court.

For example, assume that you represent Bud Porter, a consumer who allegedly was defrauded into buying a set of encyclopedia. Your contention is that the salesperson intentionally concealed the fact that the set Porter was buying consisted only of volumes beginning with letters that could be part of diphthongs. A portion of the salesperson's deposition testimony was as follows:

Q: When you first met Mr. Porter, did you show him what he'd be buying?

A: "No, I didn't actually show Porter the set of encyclopedias."

On cross, this questioning ensues:

Q: You never actually showed the set of encyclopedias to Mr. Porter, did you?

A: Yes, I did.

Q: At your deposition, you testified, did you not, "I didn't actually show Porter the set of encyclopedias."

A: I did say that. But if you'll notice, your deposition question asked only about my initial meeting with Mr. Porter. Now you asked if I ever showed him the set of encyclopedias, and I did. I came back the next day, and showed it to him.

Here, the question is not highly safe because the cross examination question does not precisely track the deposition testimony.

2. Consistency With Established Facts

A cross examination question is also highly safe if your desired answer is consistent with "established facts." "Established facts" are those which in your judgment a factfinder is nearly certain to accept as accurate. For example, the source of "established facts" may consist of an assertion in a document which has been or can be offered in evidence, or testimony by another witness that you are confident the factfinder will believe. In such situations, if the witness fails to provide your desired answer, you argue for the accuracy of your version of events based on the established facts.

For example, a factfinder is likely to regard an almanac as authoritative as to the phases of the moon. Therefore, if supported by an almanac, this

question would be highly safe: "The moon had set
an hour before you claimed to have seen the defendant by moonlight, isn't that right?" Either the
witness provides your desired answer, or you offer
that portion of the almanac into evidence. (Before
he became President, Abraham Lincoln won a case
by doing just that.)

Similarly, a factfinder is likely to regard a parish
priest as authoritative as to when Mass was celebrated on a given evening. Therefore, based on
what a priest has told you, the following question to
another witness would be highly safe: "The actual
time that Mass was celebrated at St. Swithens that
night was 10:00, correct?"

D. CROSS EXAMINATION SAFETY MODEL: MEDIUM SAFE QUESTIONS

1. Consistency With Everyday Experience

Questions are medium safe if your desired answers are consistent with everyday experience. If a
witness does not give your desired answer, you
argue that the factfinder should disbelieve the answer because it conflicts with everyday experience
(it is implausible). Questions in this category are
only medium safe because a factfinder may evaluate
everyday experience differently than do you, and
because witnesses often offer explanations that viti-
ate seeming implausibilities.

For example, assume that you represent the defendant in an auto accident case. Gail Lawton, a

witness for the plaintiff, testified on direct that she
was stopped at a red light when she saw the defendant make a left turn at an unsafe speed and bear
down on the plaintiff, who was in the crosswalk.
Lawton did not see the actual impact, however,
because moments before she turned away to check
on the color of the light. You contend that the
plaintiff never was in the crosswalk, and that the
accident happened past the intersection when the
plaintiff dashed out suddenly from between two
parked cars. A portion of your cross of Lawton is as
follows:

1. Q: You noticed a car making a left turn?

2. A: Yes.

3. Q: And this car was speeding?

4. A: Correct.

5. Q: You also knew that the plaintiff was in
the crosswalk, in the path of the car?

6. A: That's right.

7. Q: You must have immediately feared for
the plaintiff's safety?

8. A: Yes.

9. Q: You immediately realized that the plaintiff was in danger of being hit by the car?

10. A: Yes.

11. Q: That must have been frightening?

12. A: It was horrible.

13. Q: You realized that the collision was imminent?

14. A: I did.

15. Q: Yet you must have been hoping that somehow the plaintiff would escape injury?

16. A: Yes.

17. Q: You were very concerned about what would happen to the plaintiff?

18. A: I was.

19. Q: Yet at that moment you turned away to check on the color of the light?

20. A: Well, yes.

Here, everyday experience is the source of questions about how an individual is likely to react when a collision is imminent. Either the witness will agree that, e.g., she was concerned for the plaintiff's safety (No. 17), or you will argue that her denial is implausible. The questions support your argument that the plaintiff was not in the crosswalk, else the witness would not have turned away.

Testimony from the first trial of Eric and Lyle Menendez provides another example of cross examination based on consistency with everyday experience. In a widely-publicized case, the Menendez brothers were charged with murder after admittedly killing their wealthy parents. The brothers' defense was a form of self-defense. They contended that they genuinely (though mistakenly) believed that their parents were about to kill them following years of sexual abuse. Their first trial resulted in a hung jury; the second produced two murder convictions.

In the first trial, a key item of defense evidence was Eric's testimony that he was shocked when shortly before the killings, he saw his mother pull off Lyle's toupee. To rebut Eric's testimony that he didn't know until then that Lyle wore a toupee, the prosecution called Lyle's ex-girlfriend who testified that some months earlier, Eric had told her that Lyle wore a toupee. The defense cross examination of the ex-girlfriend was substantially as follows:

Q: Tell me about the time when you had this conversation with Eric. What day of the week was it?

A: It was a long time ago, I don't remember the exact date.

Q: You don't even remember the month, is that right?

A: I remember approximately the time I was out there.

Q: What's the approximate time?

A: It could have been in the spring, I don't know-January, February, March, April.

Q: What were you doing this day that you say you had this conversation with Eric Menendez?

A: Just talking to Eric.

Q: The whole day?

A: No.

Q: So what did you do the rest of the day?

A: I don't recall, it was a long time ago.

Q: What else did you talk about with Eric?

A: I don't remember.

This cross examination was the basis of an argument attacking the ex-girlfriend's credibility. The defense argument was addressed to what it hoped was the factfinder's everyday experience that people who are telling the truth about an event can remember more than a single isolated remark.

2. Assumed Testimony of Unavailable Witness

Questions can also be medium safe when you have favorable information, but can only offer the information during cross of an adverse witness. For example, perhaps you cannot locate the only other person who can supply the information, or perhaps the other person claims an inability to recall the information. In such a situation, confront the adverse witness with the circumstances concerning your desired information. If you demonstrate that you are fully aware of those circumstances, and imply that you can contradict an undesired answer, the witness may provide your desired information.

For example, assume that as the prosecutor in a murder case you want to establish that at least five seconds elapsed between a pair of shots. Bobbie, who witnessed the shooting, gave this information to your investigator but is unavailable to testify. You hope to elicit the information during cross examination of defense witness Asimow, who also witnessed the shooting. Your cross might go as follows:

Q: You were seated at the bar when the shots were fired, correct?

A: That's right.

Q: Other people were in the bar as well?

A: Sure, a few others.

Q: Do you recollect that a young woman, with dark hair and wearing a blue dress, was also in the bar?

A: I think I remember someone like that. I wasn't paying close attention to other customers.

Q: Well, she was seated about five seats from you, near the tasteful moosehead on the wall?

A: That seems right.

Q: And you spoke to her briefly about the kind of beer she was drinking?

A: Maybe, I don't really recall.

Q: Well, would you know if the woman's name was Bobbie?

A: No. she didn't tell me her name.

Q: But she was sitting about 10 feet from you?

A: About.

Q: And you had no trouble hearing the shots?

A: None at all.

Q: They were loud, like firecrackers?

A: I'd say so.

Q: Then it's safe to assume that Bobbie was near enough to have heard the shots also?

Opp: Objection, Your Honor. Calls for a conclusion.

Judge: It's close, but the author gets to make the rulings. I'll allow it. You may answer.

A: I suppose so.

Q: Now, there was a five second interval between the shots, right?

A: ...

The questions concerning the circumstances of the shooting and Bobbie's location may convince Asimow that Bobbie can contradict an inaccurate answer, motivating Asimow to provide your desired information. Of course, the technique might fail utterly if an adverse witness realizes that the rebuttal witness is unavailable. Here, for example, you shouldn't refer in a question to "Bobbie, the woman whose current whereabouts are a complete mystery to me."

You can use this same technique when the evidence you hope to elicit is based on the witness' own prior statement. If you cannot independently prove up the prior statement (e.g., the witness to whom the statement was made is unavailable), consider asking questions reminding the witness of the circumstances surrounding the making of the prior statement. For example, assume that in the example above, Bobbie had told you that Asimow had told her that five seconds elapsed between the shots. Bobbie, however, is unavailable to testify. When you ask Asimow about the time that elapsed between the shots, Asimow replies, "I don't recall exactly." The following types of questions might elicit your desired information:

Q: Do you recall speaking to a young woman in the bar?

A: Vaguely. I talked to a lot of people that night.

Q: Yes, but I'm referring to a woman you talked to about a minute after the shots were fired. Do you recall that?

A: It's all pretty hazy.

Q: She was wearing a blue dress, and she asked you if you were OK?

A: I remember something like that.

Q: You said you were fine, and said something about your experience in the army?

A: It's possible.

Q: And didn't you tell this woman that at least five seconds elapsed between the shots?

A: . . .

E. CROSS EXAMINATION SAFETY MODEL: UNSAFE QUESTIONS ("FISHING")

Generally, unsafe questions are those whose answers you cannot rebut. You hope to uncover favorable evidence, but must "take the answer" if it is unfavorable.

When safe questions are lacking, "no questions" may be a reasonable alternative to fishing. (See Page 217) However, fishing is sometimes necessary. For example, perhaps you represent a criminal defendant who will neither testify nor present evidence, so you have to cross examine even in the absence of safe questions. Or, you may choose to fish based on an intuitive judgment about a witness' vulnerability.

Fishing is the type of cross examination which is most likely to result in a rehash of evidence given on direct examination. The following suggestions may help you avoid that result:

- Ask open rather than leading questions. For example, if you want to know whether anything might have impaired a witness' ability to observe an event, consider asking a questions such as, "Describe your activities in the hour preceding the event." One reason to ask open questions is a tactical one: witnesses who describe events in their own words sometimes unwittingly provide helpful information. A second reason is legal: evidence and ethical rules generally forbid you to suggest information in the absence of a good-faith belief that the information is accurate. For example, without a good-faith belief, you could not ask, "Did you ingest cocaine in the hour preceding the event?"

• Use an "if what you say is true, what else would be true" approach. Using this approach, you probe surrounding details and avoid frontal assaults on testimony. Witnesses rarely recant on cross what they said on direct. As in this example, witnesses almost always stick to their stories:

Q: On direct, you testified that my client said, "I mean the Peerless ship that is painted red," correct?

A: Right.

Q: Are you sure my client said that?

A: I am.

Q: Really, really sure?.

A: Yes, I was right there.

Q: Gee, my client says different. Are you sure you're sure?

A. . . .

Here, you are doing more than fishing. You are sitting idly in a boat waiting for fish to jump in, and it rarely happens. Instead, ask about details surrounding important events that a witness should be aware of if the witness' testimony were accurate. If the witness cannot testify to the details, you have a basis for arguing that the important evidence is inaccurate. To identify the surrounding details about which you might inquire, ask yourself, "If what this witness says is true, what else is also likely to be true?" For example, assume that you are to cross examine a witness whose direct testimony is, "I am a former high jump champion." If what the witness says is true, you would expect the witness to recall the year of the championship, the winning height, etc. If the witness cannot recall such surrounding circumstances, you've undermined the witness' credibility:

Q: What year did you win the championship?

A: I don't remember.

Q: What was your winning height?

A: I'm not sure.

Q: Where did you win the championship?

A: Don't remember that either.

(For another example of a cross that probes surrounding circumstances, see the "Menendez" example on Page 195.)

- Conduct a "probe for details" cross. As the name implies, a "probing for details" cross asks for additional information about events to which a witness has already testified. If the witness is able to recall few details, or purports to remember an unbelievable number of details, you've undermined the witness' credibility. Example: Some time ago, the author was involved in a trial in which an important event concerned lunch conversations which had taken place a decade before the trial. A witness lost credibility by claiming to be able to recall not only what was said, but the precise order in which topics arose, in numerous different conversations. (Since infinite details accompany every happening, judges may limit your questioning pursuant to Federal Rule of Evidence 403, on the ground that it's consuming undue time.)

Probing for details can be especially effective when inquiries concern measurable quantities such as time and distance. People are notoriously poor judges of such things, and often create conflicts in their testimony. For example, a witness who says he had a "good view" of an event might estimate the distance as "50 yards." Similarly, students in the author's Trial Advocacy class have estimated the length of a 300 foot law school hallway anywhere from 75 to 450 feet!

• Use a "Hop, Skip and Jump" questioning pattern. This does not require you to engage in calisthenics in the middle of trial. Instead, you intentionally probe events non-sequentially. Some witnesses can testify believably only if they stick to a memorized chronology. Non-sequential probing may demonstrate the dearth of their actual recall. A brief example of "hop, skip and jump" questions is as follows:

Q: After the lunch meeting, you and Mr. Even met twice more, first a week later, and then two weeks later?

A: Yes.

Q: At the lunch meeting, you discussed the quality of cotton fiber that was to be shipped on the Peerless?

A: Yes,

Q: And he said it would be Surat cotton, of middling fair quality?

A: Yes.

Q: He mentioned this again during the third meeting?

A: I'm not sure, I think so.

Q: How about during the second meeting?

A: I can't recall now.

Q: In the third meeting, you never asked Mr. Even to clarify what he meant by "middling fair quality, right?"

A: The third meeting? I don't remember.

Q: And during the initial lunch meeting?

A: Maybe, I think so.

Here, the non-sequential questioning may suggest uncertainties that didn't appear on direct examination. However, be aware that a judge may consider rapid topical shifts to be argumentative. Moreover, a factfinder may empathize with a witness and attribute any confusion to what the factfinder considers an unfair questioning technique. Finally, you may succeed in confusing yourself as much as a witness.

- Be sensitive during direct examination to topics that an adversary avoids or that seem problematic for a witness. Those may be topics that you can profitably probe. You run a small risk that an adversary is "sandbagging-" omitting a topic intentionally with the expectation that you will barge in and elicit damning evidence yourself. If so, right after the trial consider sandbagging the adversary's lawyer yourself-literally!

F. IMPEACHMENT WITH PRIOR INCONSISTENT STATEMENTS

This section examines techniques for demonstrating that an adverse witness' trial testimony is inconsistent with a witness' previous statement. This is a common form of impeachment because factfinders often distrust witnesses who "blow hot and cold," and because when you can offer the previous statement into evidence this is a highly safe form of cross examination.

1. Evidentiary Rules

Under Federal Rule of Evidence 801–d–1–A, you can offer a witness' inconsistent statement into evidence for its truth if the inconsistent statement was made under oath. If the inconsistent statement was not made under oath, it is admissible only to cast doubt on the accuracy of the testimony with which it is inconsistent. For example, assume that on direct a witness testifies, "The light was green." On cross, the witness admits to saying two months before trial that "The light was red." If the earlier statement was made under oath (e.g., during a deposition), the statement is substantive evidence that the light was red. Otherwise, the factfinder can consider the earlier statement only on the witness' credibility. (In a few jurisdictions, such as California, a prior inconsistent statement is admissible as substantive evidence regardless of whether it was made under oath.)

When you are prepared to impeach a witness with a prior inconsistent statement, you may either:

- A. Offer evidence of the prior inconsistent statement during cross examination; or

- B. Forgo cross with respect to the prior statement, and instead offer the statement into evidence when it is next your turn to present evidence. You may also offer a prior inconsistent statement into evidence if you follow Option A, and a witness denies making the prior statement.

Option B is subject to two limitations: (1) the so-called "collateral evidence rule" (see below); and (2) you must not excuse a witness from giving further testimony, allowing the adversary to recall the witness after you've offered the prior inconsistent statement into evidence. (Federal Rule of Evidence 613–b)

Option A carries an "impact" advantage. When you confront a witness with a prior statement on cross, the inconsistency is apparent to a factfinder. By contrast, a factfinder may fail to recognize the inconsistency if you follow Option B and have to wait hours or days to offer a prior inconsistent statement into evidence. On the other hand, Option B avoids the danger of an immediate explanation that may undercut the force of the impeachment.

("I did once say that the light was red. But that's because your client was holding a gun to my head.")

The "collateral evidence rule" is addressed to a judge's discretion under Federal Rule of Evidence 352. The rule defines those situations in which cross examination is your only chance to offer a prior inconsistent statement into evidence. If you fail to do so, or attempt to and the witness denies making the earlier statement, you may not offer the earlier statement into evidence. A prior statement's "collateralness" depends on a judge's determination of the importance of the matter to the issues in a case. If a judge thinks that a prior statement relates to an unimportant matter, the judge is supposed to deem it collateral and limit you to cross examination.

A frequent issue is whether you can impeach an "I don't remember" answer with a prior statement. The issue arises this way:

Q: The light was red, correct?

A: I don't remember.

Assume that on a prior occasion, the witness had said that the light was red. Traditional doctrine would not allow you to offer the prior statement into evidence for the reason that it is not inconsistent for a witness to forget information. However, other options may be open to you:

- If the witness is a party, offer the prior statement as an admission. (Federal Rule of Evidence 801–d–2).

- If the statement was made under oath, ask that the witness be deemed unavailable and offer the statement as "former testimony." (Federal Rule of Evidence 804)

- Argue that the inability to recall is feigned and an equivalent to a denial. If the judge agrees, you can offer the prior statement as inconsistent.

2. Impeachment Techniques

You may follow a three-step process to impeach testimony with a prior inconsistent statement:

- Pin down the in-court testimony. By asking a witness to repeat the testimony you plan to impeach, you emphasize the inconsistency and prevent the witness from claiming that "I misspoke on direct."

- Enhance the credibility of the prior statement, especially when the prior statement is admissible as substantive evidence that advances your argument.

- Offer evidence of the prior statement and MOVE ON. When you harp on an inconsistency, you invite an explanation and risk a ruling that you are argumentative.

The following example demonstrates how you might impeach a witness with a prior inconsistent deposition statement:

1. Q: The light was green when you first saw the car, correct?

2.   A: Yes.

3.   Q: You had your deposition taken in this case, did you not?

4.   A: Yes, I did.

5.   Q: And when you testified at your deposition you took an oath to tell the truth, correct?

6.   A: Yes.

7.   Q: You took the same oath you took today?

8.   A: Yes.

9.   Q: I take it that your memory of events was better at the time of your deposition that it is now?

10.   A: Maybe, it was almost a year ago.

11.   Q: And you were told that you could look over your deposition before signing it, correct?

12.   A: Yes, but I didn't ...

13.   Q: Excuse me, I'll repeat the question. You were told that you could look over your deposition before signing it, correct?

14.   A: Yes.

15.   Q: Your Honor, I'd like to read from Page 64, lines 7–11 of what has been previously identified as the witness' deposition.

16.   Judge: You may proceed.

17.   Q: Question. What color was the light when you first saw the car? Answer. It was red. Were you asked that question and did you give that answer?

18. A: Yes.

19. Q: Now let's turn ...

Here, you first pin down the witness' direct examination testimony (No. 1). Alternatively, some attorneys prefer to include the phrase, *"You testified during direct examination that* the light was green when you first saw the car, correct?" Next, you elicit evidence about the circumstances under which the prior statement was made that may enhance its credibility (Nos. 5–14). Many of these questions are taken from the standard deposition "preamble." Finally, you read the inconsistent statement into evidence (No. 17). Alternatively, you might have read the statement into evidence at No. 5, before you enhanced credibility. The direct juxtaposition of the inconsistent statements may magnify the impeachment's effect.

If the prior inconsistent statement had been in a letter or report written by the witness, you'd have to authenticate the exhibit before reading from it:

1. Q: The light was green when you first saw the car, correct?

2. A: Yes.

3. Q: May I approach the witness, Your Honor? I am showing you a document marked Exhibit 22 for identification. Do you recognize it?

4. A: Yes, that's a report I prepared after the accident.

5. Q: That's your signature at the bottom of page 2?

6. A: Yes.

7. Q: And you prepared the report only two days following the accident?

8. A: Let me check. Yes.

9. Q: I take it that you wanted the report to be as accurate as possible?

10. A: Yes.

11. Q: Your Honor, I'd like to read from Page 2, the second paragraph of Exhibit 22. "The light was red when I first saw the car." That's what you wrote in this report, correct?

12. A: Yes.

13. Q: Now let's turn …

Again, you repeat the direct testimony (No. 1), enhance the prior statement's credibility (Nos. 7–10), and then offer the statement (No. 11). As before, you might have offered the prior statement into evidence before enhancing its credibility. Note that Question 9 is based on everyday experience, and therefore is "medium safe." However, a witness is unlikely to dispute the point.

In each of the above examples, you adhere to the advice to MOVE ON after the impeachment is complete. When you impeach, bells don't ring, the judge doesn't applaud and the adversary doesn't write out an immediate check. To make up for this lack of drama, you might be tempted to push further: "So you lied on direct when you testified that the light was green?" or, "Why have you changed your story?" Restrain yourself. The first question is argumentative; the answer to the second will probably elicit an explanation that adds your name to the author's as unfortunate developers of the "mystique of cross."

A few other suggestions for smooth impeachments:

- When you pin down a witness' testimony, parrot it exactly. If you paraphrase, a witness may balk, opposing counsel may object that you are misquoting the witness, and the force of impeachment may be diluted.

- If you plan to impeach two or three bits of testimony with prior statements, pin down each one before proceeding with impeachment.

- Remember that you cannot impeach one witness with the statement of a different witness. For example, if adverse witness Jerry testifies, "The light was green," you cannot cross examine him by asking, "Louise says that the light was red, correct?"

G. EMPHASIS TECHNIQUE: "NO, NO, NO"

In general, emphasis is a natural byproduct of cross examination principles. That is, emphasis results from juxtaposing the evidence supporting your arguments via one-item leading questions. However, the "no, no, no" emphasis technique is as useful on cross as on direct examination. A string of negative responses can add emphasis to your affirmative version of events. For example, to emphasize that it was a bear and not some other critter that went over the mountain, you might ask:

Q: It was a bear that went over the mountain, wasn't it?

A: Yes.

Q: It was not a person?

A: No.

Q: Or a gorilla?

A: No.

Q: Or a deer?

A: No.

Q: It was a bear?

A: Yes.

H. EMPHASIS TECHNIQUE: ULTIMATE CONCLUSION QUESTIONS

You illustrate an argument when you marshal the evidentiary items pertaining to that argument. To further emphasize your desired inference, consider asking an "ultimate conclusion" question. For example, examine the questions below, based on a cross examination in the media-frenzy rape trial of William Kennedy Smith. On direct examination, prosecution witness Ann Mercer testified that she was a friend of Patty Bowman, who Kennedy Smith allegedly raped. Mercer also testified that Bowman called Mercer and asked her to hurry to the Kennedy estate, where Bowman told Mercer of the rape. A portion of the defense attorney's cross examination of Ann Mercer was substantially as follows:

Q: Ms. Mercer, after receiving the phone call from Ms. Bowman you immediately drove to the Kennedy estate, correct?

A: That's right.

Q: And when you got there she told you that she had been raped?

A: Correct.

Q: But you didn't take her immediately to the hospital, did you?

A: Not immediately, no.

Q: And you didn't immediately call the police, did you?

A: No.

Q: Instead, you walked around the estate with Mr. Smith looking for Ms. Bowman's shoes, right?

A: That's right, she wanted her shoes.

Q: You walked through a dark house with a man you had just been told was a rapist?

A: Yes I did.

Q: And you walked alone with this alleged rapist down to the beach?

A: Yes.

Q: And it was dark where you were walking, correct?

A: Yes.

Q: Ms. Mercer, isn't it true that the reason you were alone with Mr. Smith and didn't call the police right away is that Ms. Bowman never told you that she had been raped?

A: That's not right. She told me exactly what I testified to.

The last is the "ultimate conclusion" question. You do not expect a favorable answer, for that would be tantamount to an admission of perjury. Rather you might ask it to emphasize the conclusion that you want the factfinder to reach based on the witness' implausible behavior: that Bowman did not in fact tell her that Kennedy Smith was a rapist (and therefore that no rape occurred).

Do not routinely ask "ultimate conclusion" questions. For one thing, judges often regard them as argumentative. Second, you may weaken an argument in the mind of a factfinder who is unwilling to accept your specific inference. For example, Mercer's testimony might lack credibility for any of a number of reasons, and a juror might resist the single one you identify (that Bowman did not tell Mercer that Bowman had been raped). Finally, ultimate conclusion questions often provoke witnesses into rebuttal, leaving an adverse witness with the last word.

I. OPEN QUESTIONS

As you know, you should generally avoid open questions during cross examination. However, open questions can be desirable and even sometimes necessary. For example, a string of leading questions may give a factfinder the impression that you are a verbal bully afraid of what an adverse witness will say if given a chance. Hence, look for safe opportunities for open questions. For example, you might have asked Ann Mercer, the witness in the Kennedy Smith example above, to "please describe the beach" where she and the defendant walked. Since any description of the beach furthers your argument that Mercer did not rush for assistance and therefore had not been told by Bowman that a rape had occurred, the open question is safe.

Open questions may be necessary when you "fish." It is hard to lead when you do not know where you are going. Also, open questions encourage witnesses to talk, and may increase the chance that a witness will disclose favorable information.

J. ORDER OF QUESTIONING

On cross, your typical goal is to elicit specific evidence that advances your arguments. Since you are rarely interested in establishing a chronology, on cross you will usually follow a "topical" format. That is, you often pursue topics without regard to chronology. Factors to consider when choosing an order of topics include:

- When you hope both to elicit new favorable information from a witness and to impeach testimony that the witness has already given, do the former first. Once you attack a witness' credibility, the witness may become wary and qualify whatever favorable information you do elicit.

- Begin on a topic that advances your strongest argument.

- Alternatively, begin with a topic that allows you to ask the safest questions. Even if the argument is not your strongest, the early success may boost your confidence and detract from the witness' overall credibility.

- Begin cross with whatever topic direct finishes. Like the bull who makes a dramatic entrance by charging directly at the matador, you leap into the fray by taking up right where direct left off. This tactic takes advantage both of primacy and recency: the direct examiner's final topic is your first one.

K. FORGOING CROSS EXAMINATION

Throwing a witness to a cross examiner is akin to leaving a teenager alone with the keys to a sports car. Neither can resist the temptation to take action. However, "no questions" can often be your best option. If you cross examine and accomplish nothing, you've probably boosted an adversary's case even if you do not elicit additional harmful evidence. Unlike with love, it can be worse to have crossed and lost than not to have crossed at all.

One common situation for forgoing cross arises when you rely on normative arguments. For example, assume that you represent a parent charged with child abuse for leaving a baby unattended in a car for a short period of time. Your client admits to leaving the child alone, but argues that it was "reasonable" to do so under the circumstances. If you try to develop factual disputes during cross examination, you might divert the factfinder's attention from your normative argument. The factfinder might reason that if the adverse witness is credible, you lose.

A second situation in which you might reasonably forgo cross arises when a witness' testimony relates to an issue you don't dispute. For example, if you represent a defendant who is only contesting damages, you might forgo cross of a "liability" witness.

Beyond categories, you will have to rely on judgment when deciding whether to forgo cross. For example, if a factfinder seems impressed by an adverse witness, all cross may do is extend the positive impression. Whenever you cross examine, you implicitly promise to elicit favorable information. If you fail to live up to your promise, you damage a case even if you reveal no new damaging evidence.

L. SILENT ARGUMENTS

You may address silent arguments during cross as well as during direct examination. As you recall from Chapter 5, silent arguments arise when evidence gives rise to possible inferences that may not be explicitly asserted.

To understand how evidence elicited during cross examination might give rise to silent arguments, consider another example from the first trial of Eric and Lyle Menendez. The brothers were on trial for murdering their parents. A prosecution witness testified that Eric had told her months before the killings that he knew that his brother wore a toupee. (This testimony tended to undermine the brothers' "imperfect self-defense" argument.) On cross, the defense attorney attacked the witness' ability to recall Eric's remark. (See Page 195) The cross then continued substantially as follows:

Q: Why were you talking to Eric on that occasion?

A: I was visiting the house, so I stopped by his room to say hi.

Q: Did you stay in the house?

A: No, I stayed in the guesthouse.

Q: You stayed in the guesthouse with Lyle, correct?

A: Yes.

Q: You didn't always stay in the guesthouse?

A: No, I just stayed with Lyle sometimes.

Q: So you weren't in the house talking to Eric because you were sleeping there?

A: No.

This defense cross examination suggests that the witness is untrustworthy because she "sleeps around." The defense attorney could not argue this explicitly, so could not offer the evidence as "relevant to the silent argument." However, the evidence comes in (subject to Federal Rule of Evidence 403) as relevant to the defense argument that the conversation never took place at all.

M. RESPONDING TO EVASIVE ANSWERS

Though you frame the most leading question in your most assertive tone a voice, witnesses often respond evasively or non-responsively. Though such responses may detract from a witnesses' credibility, they may also prevent you from eliciting your desired response. Consider this dialogue:

Q: The bear then went over the mountain, correct?

A: Where else could it have gone?

The answer is not responsive. Though the witness seems to tacitly concede that the bear went over the mountain, you are entitled to an unambiguous response. The techniques described below should enable you to insist on an answer while emphasizing a witness' evasiveness.

1. Repeat the Question

The simplest technique is to simply repeat the question:

Q: The bear then went over the mountain, correct?

A: That bear was always getting loose.

Q: But the bear did go over the mountain, correct?

An alternative to personally repeating a question is for a court reporter to reread it. Do not yourself instruct a court reporter to reread a question; ask the judge to do so. To save time, however, most judges will prefer that you repeat a question.

2. "I Didn't Ask X, I Asked Y"

A slight variation perhaps gives greater emphasis to an evasive response. You proceed as follows:

Q: The bear then went over the mountain, correct?

A: That bear was always getting loose.

Q: I didn't ask you whether the bear was always getting loose. I asked you if the bear then went over the mountain.

3. Repeat and Move to Strike

A more aggressive response is to combine a repeated question with a motion to strike the non-responsive one. For example:

Q: The bear then went over the mountain, correct?

A: That bear was always getting loose.

Q: Your Honor, I move to strike the witness' answer as non-responsive.

Judge: Motion granted. I instruct the jurors to disregard the witness' last answer.

Q: All right, I'll ask you again. The bear then went over the mountain, correct?

4. Ask Judge to Instruct a Witness to Answer

Especially when a witness is evasive on more than one occasion, ask the judge to instruct the witness to answer. In front of a jury, such an instruction may appear to ally the judge with your client. You should simply ask the judge for an instruction, rather than launch into an oral law review article on the harm done by evasive witnesses:

Q: The bear then went over the mountain, correct?

A: That bear was always getting loose.

Q: Your Honor, will the court please instruct the witness to answer the question.

Judge: Witness, please answer counsel's question.

Q: All right, I'll ask you again. The bear then went over the mountain, correct?

Some judges may allow you personally to instruct a witness to answer. However, unless a judge explicitly authorizes you to do so, make your request through the judge.

5. Avoid Arguing With a Witness

No matter what you think of an adverse witness, your courtroom behavior must show respect to the court and the institution of trial. One aspect of this is to refrain from arguing with witnesses or answering their questions. You can subtly point out that if witnesses want to ask questions, they will first have to go to law school:

Q: You leaped without looking, correct?

A: What would you have done in that situation?

Q: What I would have done is not the issue, and I am not under oath. You did leap without looking, correct?

In the heat of battle, you may well be tempted to reply: "Glad that you asked. I would have...." However, as you are not a witness, save such ripostes for negotiation or closing argument.

6. Don't Settle for "May" and "Might"

"May" and "might" are two classic weasel words which may deceive you into thinking that a witness has given your desired response. Consider this exchange:

Q: The chicken reached the other side, correct?

A: It may have.

The answer is neither a denial nor a positive response. Thus, you should press for a further response:

Q: Colonel Campbell, isn't it a fact that the chicken did reach the other side?

A: Yes.

N. RESPONDING TO EXPLANATIONS

Attacking a witness' credibility runs an inevitable risk of explanation. Witnesses may try to explain seeming implausibilities, or explain why they made inconsistent statements. You cannot prevent an adversary from eliciting an explanation on redirect. However, it is generally in your interest to prevent a witness from offering an explanation during cross. This section examines techniques that may help you do so.

1. Don't Invite Explanations

Witnesses sometimes ask if they can explain an answer. You should usually politely deny permission, unless you know what the explanation is and can contradict it. Consider this example:

Q: You never saw him holding the gun, right?

A: May I explain?

Q: Please just answer the question. Your attorney will have a chance to question you after I finish. You never saw him holding the gun, right?

A: That's right.

Here, the witness asks for permission to explain, and you properly keep control of the testimony.

2. Repeat Your Question

Witnesses don't always ask for permission to explain answers. Instead, they may blurt out explanations before you can stop them from doing so. In such situations, one alternative is for you to ignore an explanation and emphasize the witness' evasiveness by repeating your question:

Q: You never saw him holding the gun, right?

A: Correct, but I saw it on the ground less than a foot away from him after I heard the shot.

Q: I'll ask you again. You never saw him holding the gun, correct?

This technique allows you to emphasize evidence supporting an argument without arguing with a witness.

3.   Interrupt an Explanation

A second way to defend against an unexpected explanation is to cut it off in mid-response. Do not shout down or talk over a witness. Stand (if you are sitting), perhaps hold out your hand in a "stop" position, and signal with a phrase like "Excuse me" that the witness is not to say more. Then ask your next question. The testimony may unfold as follows:

Q: You never saw him holding the gun, right?

A: Correct, but I . . .

Q: Excuse me, but you've answered the question. Now let me ask you . . .

4.   Move to Strike an Explanation

If you're cross examining the World's Fastest Blurter or are a bit slow on the objection switch, you may be unable to prevent the factfinder from hearing an explanation. Your fall-back position is then to object to the explanation, move to strike it and ask the judge to instruct the jury (if one is present) to disregard the answer. The usual ground for objection is that an explanation is "non-responsive," though of course an explanation may also be objectionable as hearsay, irrelevant or some other evidentiary sin. The testimony may go as follows:

Q: You never saw him holding the gun, right?

A: Correct, but I saw it on the ground less than a foot away from him after I heard the shot.

Q: Your Honor, I move to strike everything after "correct" as non-responsive and ask that you instruct the jury to disregard it.

Judge: Granted. Jurors ...

Judges will not necessarily sustain such an objection, especially when they believe that an answer would be misleading without the explanation. However, often judges will grant the request and leave it to opposing counsel to elicit the explanation on redirect examination.

5.   Pursue an Implausible Explanation

Don't be so poised to prevent or strike explanations that you fail to recognize implausible ones. Often, witnesses impeached with inconsistent statements or implausible actions offer explanations that only further detract from their credibility. In such situations, you may emphasize an explanation's implausibility:

Q: Now, you testified on direct that the robber had a scar, is that correct?

A: Yes.

Q: Do you recall talking to Officer Fox, just a short time after the robbery?

A: Yes.

Q: And Officer Fox asked you some questions about the robbery?

A: That's right.

Q: And he asked you for a description of the robber?

A: Yes.

Q: You wanted to be as accurate as possible in your description, correct?

A: Of course.

Q: And your memory of the robbery was fresher when you spoke to Officer Fox than it is now, correct?

A: I guess so.

Q: Didn't you tell Officer Fox that the robber had no distinguishing marks?

A: Yes, but you've got to understand that I was really nervous when I spoke to the Officer.

Q: That's understandable. But you're nervousness did not prevent you from telling the Officer that the robber was about 6' tall, did it?

A: No.

Q: And you still stand by that statement, correct?

A: Yes.

Q: And you're nervousness didn't prevent you from telling the Officer that the robber weighed about 180 pounds?

A: No.

Q: Your nervousness only prevented you from failing to tell the Officer that the robber had a scar?

A: I guess so.

These questions suggest the implausibility of the witness' "nervousness" explanation. While witnesses will not always cooperate by offering implausible explanations, think twice before moving to strike an explanation.

6. Pre–instructing Witnesses

Aware of a witness' propensity to explain answers, you might consider preceding a question with an instruction such as, "Please just answer this question yes or no." However, some judges consider such comments to be an improper attempt to intimidate a witness. A subtler and more allowable alternative is to phrase an instruction as a question: "If you can fairly answer my next question yes or no, will you do so?"

7. Anticipating Explanations: "Close the Door"

If you cannot entirely tame the beast of Sudden Explanation, you may at least try to anticipate it. Think of the reasonable explanations that witnesses may offer for implausible behavior or prior inconsistent statements. Then "close the door" by negating a likely explanation before pursuing impeachment.

If a witness provides an explanation that would
negate the value of your planned impeachment, you
may abandon the impeachment. For example, your
cross of the robbery eyewitness in the subsection
above might have gone as follows:

Q: Do you recall talking to Officer Fox just a
short time after the robbery?

A: Yes.

Q: And Officer Fox asked you some questions
about the robbery?

A: That's right.

Q: You were able to remember the robbery
and had no difficulty telling the Officer what you
had seen, correct?

A: That's right.

Q: Now, you testified on direct that the robber had a scar, is that correct?

A: Yes.

Q: (proceed as above)

Here, you anticipate that the witness might explain away a prior inconsistent statement by citing
nervousness or a similar problem. You "close the
door" on such explanations before eliciting evidence
of the inconsistency. And if the witness nevertheless
offers the "nervousness" explanation, you can point
out that the explanation is inconsistent with the
"closing the door" evidence!

O. "CROSS" EXAMINATION?

Dramas often offer a quite literal picture of "cross" examination. Cross examiners are routinely portrayed as snarly megalomaniacs to whom Attila the Hun would find it hard to relate. Some clients may even prefer such a combative style, concluding that "my attorney was really in there battling for me."

Factfinders, however, may not be so receptive. If jurors perceive you as taking unfair advantage of your power to pose questions, they may empathize with witnesses regardless of whether you extract some favorable testimony. Even snide remarks can bring judicial opprobrium and juror hostility:

Q: You arrived there about 3 P.M.?

A: I'm not sure.

Q: You're not sure of much, even the time.

Judge: Counsel, I'm striking that remark from the record. Confine yourself to asking questions or you'll have me to deal with.

By all means ask questions firmly and when appropriate insist on answers in a professional manner. But stepping over the line into nastiness usually does more harm than good.

P. "YOUR STORY" CROSS EXAMINATION

A "your story" cross consists of confronting adverse witnesses with the version of events to which your witnesses will testify. For example, assume an assault prosecution in which each party claims that the other "started it." As the defense lawyer, you might conduct "your story" cross as follows:

Q: Mr. Rogers, what really happened is that you started the argument by calling my client a pusillaneous tetrahedron, correct?

A: No I did not.

Q: Didn't you pick up a bottle and walk towards my client with it?

A: That's not what happened.

Q: etc.

As with "ultimate conclusion" questions (see Page 213), you do not expect a "your story" cross to produce favorable answers. After all, witnesses rarely answer the implied question, "Aren't you an abject liar?" affirmatively. Nevertheless, the benefits of this form of cross include:

• You avoid fishing.

• A factfinder may perceive you as fair for giving an adverse party a chance to respond to your version of events.

• As a defense attorney, you may offset some of the plaintiff's "mind set" advantage by reminding a factfinder during the plaintiff's case-in-chief of your version of events.

• In a criminal case in which the defendant will not testify and will call no witnesses, a "your story" cross is the only way to put a competing version of events before a factfinder.

- Often, parties to a dispute agree to at least certain events. To the extent that an adverse witness agrees with "your story" questions, the witness accredits your client's version.

- Note: English criminal procedure sometimes requires defendants who want to present a defense version of events to first put "your story" questions to prosecution witnesses.

Q. CHARACTER EVIDENCE IMPEACHMENT

Federal Rules of Evidence 608 and 609 define the circumstances under which you can attack a witness' credibility with character evidence. (Though not defined in the Federal Rules of evidence, character evidence attacking credibility generally consists of evidence of conduct unrelated to the facts in a case from which a factfinder can infer that a witness has a propensity to be untruthful.) Generally, you can attack a witness' character for truthtelling with evidence that:

- a witness has been convicted of any crime involving dishonesty or false statement.

- subject to Rule 403, a witness has been convicted of a felony.

- subject to Rule 403, a witness has engaged in conduct not resulting in a conviction from which an inference of untruthfulness can be drawn. Extrinsic evidence of the conduct is inadmissible; you must "take the answer" on cross examination.

- the witness has a reputation for untruthfulness;

- a witness' opinion is that another witness is untruthful.

Improperly-admitted character evidence can be highly prejudicial. To save your client the time and expense of a mistrial, in a jury trial you should normally seek an advance judicial ruling concerning the admissibility of character evidence.

R. PROTECTING YOUR WITNESSES

This section examines the common types of improper questioning in which your adversary may engage during cross examination, and sets forth appropriate objections you may make. These issues are addressed largely to judges' discretion under Federal Rule of Evidence 611.

1. Argumentative Questions

An argumentative question is one which forces a witness to respond to opposing counsel's argument. Typical examples include:

- "Which is true-what you told your neighbor or what you testified to on direct?"

- "How do expect the jury to believe that?"

- "Can you explain why the police officer disagrees with your account of what happened?"

The proper objection is "Objection, argumentative."

2. Rapid–Fire Questioning

Rapid-fire questioning occurs when an adversary fires off a new question at the first indication that a witness has answered a previous one. Overly-aggressive cross examiners may even interrupt witnesses in mid-answer. Just as hearing "Flight of the Bumblebee" may cause a slow diner to become flustered and eat too fast, so may rapid-fire questions cause witnesses to respond too quickly and make careless mistakes. Overly-rapid responses may also prevent you from objecting to improper questions.

This tactic is not what the Constitution means by a "speedy trial." Advise witnesses during pre-trial preparation (see Chapter 11) to pause before answering cross examination questions. During trial, you may object that counsel's tactics are argumentative, constitute harassment of a witness, do not allow a witness to complete an answer, or do not allow you sufficient time to object.

3. Misquoting a Witness

When an adversary asks a witness about previously-given testimony, be sure that the adversary quotes testimony accurately. For example, assume that on direct your witness testifies, "I was staring at him through the open window for at least five seconds." On cross, the adversary asks this question:

Q: Now, when you got this pretty good look at him, did you ...

This question misquotes the witness. Moreover, whether "staring through an open window for five seconds" constitutes a "pretty good look" is for a factfinder to determine, not for an adversary to characterize during questioning. Protect the record and your witness by objecting that, "the question misquotes the witness."

CHAPTER 10

CLOSING ARGUMENT

In dramas, the importance of closing argument is often so magnified that a trial seems similar to a game of professional basketball: all is prelude to the final moments, when the contest is won or lost. However, the "mind set" phenomenon is a reminder that judges and jurors don't store away evidence for later digestion as squirrels do nuts. Typically, factfinders evaluate and are influenced by evidence as they hear it. By the time of final summation, factfinders often have reached tentative decisions. That is why this book stresses the need to illustrate arguments throughout a trial. Closing argument is an opportunity to underscore those arguments and demonstrate how and why they justify a favorable verdict.

Thus, a closer sporting analogy to closing argument is a football coach's game plan. Like a game plan is often evident in a team's play, your arguments should be apparent to a factfinder from the testimony that you elicit. A judge or juror should be aware of your principal arguments before you begin to speak. However, you have a couple of advantages over football coaches. They usually cannot talk about game plans until after a game is over; discussion of your "game plan" during final summation gives you a chance to influence the outcome. Also, when discussing your game plan you do not have to wear funny-looking sweaters.

A. CLOSING ARGUMENTS REFLECT INDIVIDUAL STYLE

If you follow the advice of earlier chapters, your direct examinations will typically unfold as chronologies, with witnesses describing many events in their own words. Your cross examinations will typically eschew chronology, as you rely primarily on leading questions to elicit evidence supporting your arguments. By contrast, closing argument is harder to "typecast" than direct or cross examination. Your closing arguments are likely to be more reflective of your individual personality and experiences than your direct or cross examinations. Two factors contribute to the individual uniqueness of closing arguments:

- Closing argument is subject to far less judicial control than other phases of trial. The relaxed evidentiary standards are exemplified by the judge's response that often follows objections to remarks made during closing argument: "Overruled, it's only argument." (For a discussion of the most important evidentiary rules that do apply to closing argument, see Page 276.)

- The scope of closing argument is far broader than that of direct and cross examination. During direct and cross, you are generally limited to eliciting factual information. During closing, you can not only discuss this information, but can also incorporate such matters as substantive and procedural rules of law, the generalizations underlying your arguments, and your desired result.

Fortunately, the effectiveness of closing argument is not tied to a particular style or personality. You can deliver effective summations whether you are quiet and methodical or (like many lawyers of the past) given to a bit of bombast. Nevertheless, the looser structure of closing argument does not equate to a total lack of direction. For example, many recipes for Caesar salad dressing may exist. Each recipe will probably consist of ingredients that are essential to a Caesar salad (e.g., olive oil, parmesan cheese and garlic) and optional ingredients (e.g., eggs). Similarly, this chapter examines ingredients that you may want to put into a closing argument. Which are essential to a particular argument, however, depends on your best professional judgment about the circumstances of each case.

B. INTRODUCTORY REMARKS

A closing argument is a species of public oratory, and like most speeches often benefits from introductory remarks. In an introduction you may:

● thank jurors for their attention and stress the importance of their deliberations to both parties. The trial has probably inconvenienced many of them, so this gesture is both socially

polite and a useful way to demonstrate your
fairness and belief in the adversary system.

• refer to your desired result. Early disclosure of
a "bottom line" can help a factfinder realis-
tically evaluate your arguments. For example, a
factfinder in a criminal case who understands
at the outset that your desired defense verdict
is conviction of a lesser included offense rather
than a not guilty verdict might give your arguments greater credence. For further discussion
of how to argue a result, see Page 266.

• when the complexity of a case merits, provide a
roadmap to the remainder of the argument. For
example, you might say something like, "This
case boils down to two issues-did my client rely
on the defendant's statements, and was that
reliance reasonable? I'll talk to you first about
reliance, and then the reasonableness of that
reliance. At the conclusion, I'll ask you to return a verdict in favor of the plaintiff in the
amount of ... " Referring back to a roadmap as
an argument proceeds is an effective way of
providing organization.

• briefly describe the legal elements and the factual propositions which satisfy those elements.
For example, in a fraud case you might say
something like, "The judge will shortly instruct
you that one issue we have to prove is that Ms.
Woods relied on the bank's statement. As I'll
discuss, the evidence clearly shows that Ms.
Woods relied on the bank's offer of construc-

tion financing when she purchased the land for a miniature golf course."

- refer to the burden of proof. This may be especially important if you represent a defendant in a criminal case, but even on behalf of a civil plaintiff you may say something like, "The judge will also shortly instruct you that as the plaintiff we have the burden of convincing you that fraud took place by clear and convincing evidence. I'll discuss what that means in a few minutes. I'm confident that you'll find that we've more than met this burden."

C. ORDER OF ARGUMENTS

Once past any introductory remarks, the organization of a closing argument is within your absolute discretion. The following general suggestions may help your planning:

- In civil cases, normally you should discuss liability issues before damages.

- Put your affirmative foot forward. If you have tried to establish a factual proposition's accuracy, argue its accuracy before attacking the adversary's position.

- Frontload arguments that pertain to the issues that a factfinder is likely to see as the most important. Base your judgment on such factors as which issues dominated questioning, what questions a judge asked, and jurors' physical reactions to testimony. (e.g., Did jurors seem more intent whenever a particular issue arose?)

- When two or more arguments support the same issue, make the argument you consider stronger first. Don't fall into the "last, and most importantly," syndrome. First, studies suggest that the order of arguments affects their persuasiveness, and that unlike dessert, your best arguments should come first. Second, and most importantly ...

D. EVIDENCE REVIEW

An evidence review is a recapitulation of evidence. You may summarize just your client's version of events, or you may also point out where the adversary's version is the same or different. Sometimes, you may want to summarize all the important evidence before delivering any of your arguments. Perhaps more often, you may want to summarize the evidence on a particular issue before delivering an argument which centers on that issue (e.g., "Let's first get straight what all the witnesses had to say about the fingerprint.") The benefits of an evidence review include helping a factfinder:

- understand complex or technical evidence. Hearing evidence for a second time may switch on a factfinder's light of understanding.

- remember the evidence in an extended trial (e.g., two days of testimony extended over eight trial days because of annual "Vasco de Gama Days" holiday celebrations). In such situations, consider a witness-by-witness review of evidence: "Let me briefly review the testimony of the witnesses who testified on the plaintiff's behalf. They were Sonny Boulevard, Max Avenue V, Della Street and Rocky Road, all of whose names are synonymous with many of the byways of our community. Sonny testified.... Max attended that same meeting, and he stated ... Della met with the defendant the next day. She described that meeting by telling us ... Finally, Rocky, the wholesaler who is the defendant's main supplier, told us...."

• arrange events in chronological order. Blending witnesses' individual stories into a single overall story may be especially important when order has become scrambled during the testimony.

• recognize the strong emotional impact of your client's version. (As the famous scholar Karl Llewellyn wrote about appellate briefs, how you summarize facts can greatly influence a factfinder's reactions.)

Nevertheless, evidence reviews have a variety of potential downsides. They can be tedious. A factfinder may tune out when you refer to testimony during an evidence review and then again in the context of an argument. Moreover, adding an evidence review layer to arguments may de-emphasize the arguments. Finally, if you fail to mention unfavorable evidence, the adversary may argue that your summary was misleading.

E. EXPLICITNESS OF ARGUMENTS

One of your primary closing argument decisions concerns the explicitness of your arguments. For example, assume that you want to argue in an auto accident case that a building contractor was driving carelessly because moments before the accident, the contractor had received a car phone call informing the contractor of a problem on a job site. You might make a highly implicit argument:

> "What does the phone call evidence suggest about whether the contractor was paying enough attention to the road?"

Usually, however, you'll want to follow the suggestions below and make a much more explicit argument. Among other qualities, in an explicit form of argument you might marshal evidence, specify your desired inference, refer to and illustrate underlying generalizations, and explain why the factfinder should accept your argument.

Explicitness is of course a matter of degree; few arguments are fully implicit or fully explicit. Moreover, explicitness is not the only measure of an argument's effectiveness:

- Some studies suggest that people hold more firmly to conclusions when they arrive at conclusions on their own rather than having the conclusions pointed out for them.

- Certain arguments, such as silent arguments, cannot be made explicitly. (See Chapter 5) For example, you probably can't argue explicitly

that a factfinder should believe a witness because the witness is deeply religious. (Federal
Rule of Evidence 610) However, assuming that
evidence of the witness' religiousness was properly admitted, you might make an implicit silent argument by reminding the factfinder of
that evidence. (For a further discussion of silent arguments, see Page 267.)

- Specifying a particular inference risks alienating jurors who may accept a consistent but
  different inference. For instance, if you argue
  explicitly that an adverse witness lied, you may
  alienate a juror who has some doubts about a
  witness' credibility but who is unwilling to conclude that the witness lied.

- The more explicit an argument the longer it is,
  and judges can be quite explicit at times about
  the length of argument!

Nevertheless, this section emphasizes techniques
for making arguments explicit because no matter
how effectively you marshal evidence around arguments during testimony, closing argument is often
your only chance to explain the reasoning process a
factfinder should follow and disclose your desired
conclusions. For example, assume that as a prosecutor you want a jury to infer from a defendant's
actions at a crime scene that the defendant was
trying to escape. Your direct examination of an
eyewitness was as follows:

    Q: How much time elapsed between the time
    you heard the gunshot and saw the defendant go
    past you?

A: No more than a couple of seconds.

Q: Can you describe what the defendant was doing when the defendant went by you?

A: Yes, I'd say the defendant was running quickly.

Q: In which direction?

A: Well, away from where it sounded like the gunshot came from.

Q: Did the defendant turn while running past you?

A: I noticed the defendant turn around in the direction of the gunshot while running past me.

No matter how extensive the questioning, the "opinion rule" (Federal Rule of Evidence 701) would probably prevent the witness from testifying to an opinion that the defendant was trying to escape. During closing argument, however, you could urge this conclusion on the factfinder and explain the connection between "escape" and "guilt."

Another reason for the emphasis on explicitness is that if you are like many people you will tend to make implicit arguments. Our culture has a ready label for fully explicit people-bores! To convince a factfinder in the face of an adversary, you will generally have to be more explicit than when you tell a friend about a film or your most recent dental work. The examples below suggest techniques for making arguments explicit.

1. Explicit Inferential Arguments

Begin with an inferential argument you might have developed on behalf of the plaintiff in an auto accident case. You contend that a building contractor is liable in negligence for injuring a pedestrian because the contractor was inattentive to the road. One of your arguments is based on what you consider to be important evidence that moments before the accident, the contractor received a car phone call informing the contractor of a problem on a remodeling job site. With your marshaled "especially whens" (see Chapter 4), your argument is as follows:

Building contractors who receive a car phone call informing them of a problem with one of their remodeling jobs are likely to be inattentive to the road, especially when....

• the problem has to be dealt with before the project can continue.

• the problem is a large one.

• the contractor is the owner of the company.

• the contractor is in the vicinity of the job site.

• the contractor decides to go immediately to the job site.

An explicit version of this argument may go as follows:

"As I mentioned earlier, one of the issues you must decide is whether the contractor was inattentive to the road just before the contractor

struck the plaintiff. Remember that the defendant admitted on cross examination that just
moments before the collision, the defendant received a car phone call from the office informing
the defendant of a problem on a remodeling job
site. Isn't it likely that building contractors such
as the defendant who hear of a problem on a job
site are going to be thinking about the problem as
they drive? That's especially likely to be true
when, as in this case, the contractor is in the
vicinity of the job site when the call comes
through and the problem is a large one that
requires the contractor's immediate attention. We
know that the problem required the defendant's
immediate attention because, as the defendant
also admitted, the problem had to be dealt with
before the project could continue and the defendant immediately changed course to head for the
job site. Moreover, as the president of the company, it was the defendant who had the most to lose
if work was delayed. So the defendant had lots of
reasons to be thinking about the problem, and as
a result was not paying attention to the road
when the plaintiff was struck."

This argument portion is fairly explicit. You identify the issue to which the argument pertains, refer
to the important evidence and the "especially
whens," assert the generalization underlying your
desired inference ("building contractors such as the
defendant who hear of a problem on a job site are
going to be thinking about the problem as they
drive"), and conclude with your desired conclusion.

You can make the argument even more explicit by analogizing portions of the argument to the factfinder's own experiences. (See Page 256 for more on using analogies.) For example, the generalization portion of the above argument might go as follows:

"Isn't it likely that building contractors such as the defendant who hear of a problem on a job site are going to be thinking about the problem as they drive? I know that none of you are building contractors, but you can probably all think back to a time when you've been driving in your car and heard some distressing news on the radio. Wasn't your instinctive reaction to think about the bad news and how it might affect you personally? That's a common type of reaction, it's something we all do. And that's especially likely to be true when, as in this case . . ."

Similarly, a more explicit version of the argument might analogize to the factfinder's financial experience:

"Moreover, as the president of the company, the defendant had the most to lose if work was delayed. Think back to how you and people you've known have reacted when they are in danger of losing a substantial sum of money. Don't we all think about how to eliminate or minimize the problem so we can limit our losses?"

2. Explicit Credibility Arguments

In an effort to be explicit about how to deliver explicit arguments, this section illustrates techniques for explicit credibility arguments. Assume that you continue to represent the plaintiff in the auto accident case, and that one of your witnesses observed the collision and testified that the plaintiff was in the crosswalk at the time of the accident. The defendant disputes this witness' testimony, contending that the plaintiff suddenly ran out from between two parked cars some distance down the road from the crosswalk. Thus, based on the Credibility Model (see Page 25) you have developed an argument supporting the credibility of your witness' account of the plaintiff's location. That argument is that the witness' testimony is credible because:

- The witness had the physical ability to observe the plaintiff's location. The witness was in a car next to the crosswalk, it was daylight and the witness' view of the crosswalk was unobstructed.

- The witness had a reason to observe the plaintiff because the plaintiff was wearing the same shirt that the witness had recently bought.

- The witness is unbiased and has no financial stake in the case's outcome.

An very implicit form of an argument supporting the witness' credibility would be:

"Remember the witness who was in the car right next to the crosswalk. Can you doubt her credibility?"

A more explicit version of this argument, including references to the factfinder's experiences, might go as follows:

"As you remember, a witness testified on the plaintiff's behalf that the plaintiff was in the crosswalk in the moments just prior to being struck. If you look at the evidence, you'll see that this witness is correct and that the defendant's account of the plaintiff's location is not to be trusted. First, look at the witness' location, in a car right next to the crosswalk waiting for the light to change. Right here, where the witness placed an "x" on the diagram. The witness had no trouble seeing the plaintiff in the crosswalk-it was broad daylight and the witness had an unobstructed view. And like we all do when we're stopped at an intersection waiting for a light to change, the witness looked around. Maybe we don't always pay attention to what we're looking at, but in this case the witness had a particular reason to notice the plaintiff-the plaintiff was wearing a shirt that the witness had just purchased. Think back to your own experiences-don't we all pay special attention when we notice someone wearing the same clothes that we're wearing or have just bought? Finally, remember that the witness has nothing to gain by testifying-the witness is neutral and unbiased, and came in here and told you exactly what happened. Every shred of evidence tells us that the witness is correct when the witness says that the plaintiff was in the crosswalk moments before being struck."

Again, maximum explicitness is not always a virtue, and you have a variety of explicitness options. For example, you can make an explicit inferential argument less so by omitting mention of a generalization, and can add an implicit tone by concluding an argument with a question rather than an assertion. For instance, you might have concluded the above argument with a remark such as,

"Isn't it apparent that the witness is correct when the witness says that the plaintiff was in the crosswalk moments before being struck?"

Moreover, you will often deliver multiple arguments, and can make some more explicit than others. Whatever your judgment, to be persuasive your courtroom arguments will often have to be more explicit than in your social conversations.

F. TWO–SIDED ARGUMENTS

Even if your formal factfinding has been limited to sorting out which child is telling the truth when both say, "he hit me first," you understand that an effective argument often describes both why one side is correct and the other is not. Hence, you typically need to make two-sided arguments which not only advance your desired outcome, but also attack an adversary's claims.

1. Responding to an Adversary's Arguments

Two-sided arguments are of two types. A two-sided argument may:

- Attack an adversary's arguments. For example, you may attack an adversary's inferential argument with "except whens," and attack the accuracy of an adversary's version of events with Credibility Model factors.

• Respond to an adversary's attack on your arguments. For example, you may describe why your inferential argument is valid despite the adversary's "except whens," and why the adversary's credibility attacks on your witnesses do not undermine the accuracy of your version of events.

Consider first an example of attacking an adversary's arguments. Assume that you represent the pedestrian who was allegedly struck in a crosswalk by a truck negligently driven by a contractor. The defendant contractor has made an inferential argument asking the factfinder to infer from circumstantial evidence that the contractor was carrying expensive kitchen cabinets in the back of the truck that the contractor was being especially attentive to the road. The generalization underlying the adversary's argument is something like, "People are especially likely to drive carefully when they are carrying valuable objects." During cross examination of the contractor, you elicited "except whens:" the accident occurred late in the afternoon, and the contractor had been driving around with the cabinets in the back of the truck all day. Based on these "except whens," you might make the following two-sided inferential argument:

"The defendant argues that people are especially likely to drive carefully when they are carrying valuable objects. But recall that this accident

occurred late in the afternoon, and that the defendant admitted that those cabinets had been in
the back of the truck all day. This evidence
proves that those cabinets had no effect on how
the defendant was driving. You know from your
own experience that the longer people carry objects in their cars and trucks, the less attention
they tend to pay to them. Having driven around
with those cabinets all day, it's highly unlikely
that the defendant was thinking of them just
before striking the plaintiff."

Consider next an example of responding to an
adversary's attack on your arguments. Assume that
in the personal injury case, your witness testified on
the pedestrian's behalf that the defendant contractor was speeding just before striking the pedestrian.
The defense has attacked the credibility of this
witness based on an argument that the witness and
the pedestrian have become personal friends since
the accident. Your response to this argument may
proceed as follows:

"The defendant asks you to conclude that the fact
that the witness and the pedestrian have become
friends since the accident means that you
shouldn't believe the witness. This argument has
no merit. The witness and the pedestrian were
not friends when the accident took place, and
they weren't friends an hour later when the witness told the investigating police officer exactly
what the witness told you on the stand. Their
friendship had no impact on the witness' obligation to give truthful and accurate testimony.

Their friendship thus should play no part in your deliberations."

2. Preempting an Adversary's Arguments

Preemption means anticipating and responding to an adversary's argument before the adversary has a chance to make it. For example, you may tell a factfinder that the adversary will attack your witness' credibility based on the witness' friendship with the pedestrian before the adversary actually makes this argument.

Preemption is a familiar argument technique, one you have probably used often. For example, perhaps as a teenager you made an argument such as,

"Dad, I really ought to be allowed to borrow the car tonight. I haven't borrowed it in three weeks. I know you don't like me driving at night, but I'll be with Hilary and Kevin and they are both really experienced and careful drivers."

Here, you anticipate and respond to your father's "no night driving" argument.

Preemption is often even more necessary in trials. If you argue first and will not have a chance to respond, preemption can be your only opportunity to counter an adversary's arguments. For example, if you want a factfinder to understand why the witness' friendship with the pedestrian in no way undermines the witness' credibility, you may have to first articulate this possible argument. You may do so either by:

- Attributing the argument to the adversary: "Now, the defendant will undoubtedly argue that the fact that the witness and the pedestrian have become friends since the accident means that you shouldn't believe the witness. This argument has no merit ..."

- Attributing the argument to the factfinder. As when responding to silent arguments (which an adversary can't make explicitly; see Page 267), you may want to preempt arguments that you think a factfinder may come up with: "Now, you may be wondering whether the fact that the witness and the pedestrian have become friends since the accident has any effect on the witness' believability. It does not ..."

Exercise care when deciding to preempt. You do not want to spend too much time talking about an adversary's potential arguments, nor do you want to risk suggesting convincing arguments that neither the adversary nor the factfinder would have thought of!

3. Inoculation

Inoculation is a technique in which you acknowledge the validity of an argument while pointing out why it should not dictate the outcome of a case. Somewhat akin to "giving the devil his due," inoculation tells a factfinder that a successful outcome does not require the factfinder to resolve every argument in your client's favor.

For example, assume that you represent a defendant in a criminal matter. One of your arguments is that the arresting officer lied when the officer testified that your client confessed. To inoculate against the prosecution's argument that a police officer would not commit perjury to secure a conviction, you might make the following argument:

"The prosecution correctly says that police officers are generally honest and wouldn't lie just to get a confession. Our justice system works because most police officers behave honestly. But the question you have to decide isn't how most police officers usually behave. The question is how a single police officer behaved in this specific case. And when you examine the evidence, you'll see why in this particular case the officer did not testify truthfully . . ."

This argument acknowledges the general validity of the prosecution's argument, but explains why its general validity does not dictate the outcome of the specific case.

G. ANALOGIES

Analogies are powerful legal reasoning tools, fundamental to common law development. For example, in his famous *Palsgraf v. Long Island Railway* opinion, Justice Cardozo decided that a railroad was not liable when a platform guard negligently dislodged a package which exploded and the explosion caused a scale to fall over, injuring a person on the platform. Cardozo analogized the unique platform events to a situation in which one person jostles another in a crowd and causes a bomb to fall and explode. Because for Cardozo liability would not exist in the second situation, neither should it exist for the railroad.

1. Developing Analogies

Analogies are equally powerful in closing arguments. An analogy between some aspect of a lawsuit and everyday life can help persuade a factfinder that your version of events is accurate. If a factfinder accepts the analogy and agrees with your everyday illustration, the factfinder is likely to find your argument persuasive. To develop persuasive analogies, follow a two-step process:

- Consider the general category of which a case-specific event is but an example; then,

- Identify a familiar example of the general category.

You can use analogies to illustrate and add vividness to any aspect of a case. For instance, assume that you seek damages on behalf of a plaintiff who because of a congenital back defect suffered severe injuries in a minor fender-bender type collision. You seek damages under the "take the plaintiff as you find her" legal principle. You might use an analogy to help explain the meaning of this principle to a jury. The specific rule is part of the general category of rules that in law and fairness make us liable for the injuries that we inflict through negligence. Finding an everyday illustration of this general category might produce an argument along these lines:

> "What does the law mean when it says that you take the plaintiff as you find her? Suppose you had three dolls, each of identical size and each dressed exactly alike. However, one doll is made of steel, another is made of wood, and the third is made of glass. If someone comes along and negligently knocks down and breaks the glass doll, you would want that person to pay for it. You wouldn't let the person avoid payment by claiming that no damage would have been done had the steel doll been knocked down. Paying for the harm you actually cause that is the meaning of the principle that you take the plaintiff as you find her."

This analogy draws on people's everyday experiences with recompensing people for broken objects. The analogy thus helps a juror adopt a favorable attitude towards the rule that underlies your argument. Other familiar analogies for legal principles include:

- The Burden of Proof: "The judge will instruct you that we have to prove our case by a preponderance of the evidence. What does this mean? Assume that you have a balance scale and you place all our evidence on one side of the scale and all of the defendant's evidence on the other side. If our side of the scale is heavier even by the weight of a single feather, we have proved our case by a preponderance of the evidence."

- Use of Common Sense: "The judge will instruct
  you that you can use your common sense when
  evaluating the evidence. To understand what
  this means, suppose that you saw someone
  walk into the courtroom wearing a wet rain-
  coat. Your common sense would tell you that it
  was raining outside. No one needs to tell you
  that it was raining, your common sense allows
  you to draw an inference. And it is perfectly
  proper for you to draw such common sense
  inferences from the testimony you heard in this
  case."

- Effect of Inconsistent Statements: "The judge
  will instruct you that in considering the defendant's credibility, you may consider any inconsistent statements made by the defendant.
  What does this mean? Assume that you were
  planning on taking your family to a museum,
  and wanted to know if it would open on Sun-
  day. You call the museum, and the receptionist
  assures you that the museum will be open. The
  next day you call back, and the same receptionist tells you that it will be closed. This inconsistency would so destroy your trust in the receptionist that you would not know whether to go
  to the museum."

As Cardozo did in *Palsgraf*, you may also use
analogies to influence a factfinder's evaluation of
evidence. For example, assume that you represent
the defendant contractor in the auto accident case.
The defendant testified, "I was driving extra carefully because I was carrying expensive kitchen cabi-

nets in the back of my truck." Generalizing, you
might see this as an example of how "People drive
carefully when they are transporting valuables." To
provide a familiar analogy, you might argue:

> "You can well understand how carefully my client
> was driving. Perhaps you're not a contractor, and
> you've never carried kitchen cabinets in the back
> of a truck. But undoubtedly you've driven with a
> small child in your car, or perhaps an expensive
> glass figure you had just gotten as a gift or a
> carton of eggs on the seat. You know that you
> instinctively drive more carefully when you are
> carrying children or valuable and breakable ob-
> jects."

A few suggestions for developing persuasive analogies:

- Never use analogies which put a factfinder in
  an unfavorable light: "We have all had the
  experience of stealing candy from a baby."

- As a general rule, the shorter an analogy the
  better. Lengthy analogies-e.g., a description of
  the labors of Hercules-are confusing and tend
  to deflect a factfinder's attention from the
  point you were trying to make in the first
  place.

- Determine familiarity according to a factfinder's likely background, not your own. An analogy to "the feel of moonrock between your
  toes" is unlikely to strike a responsive chord.
  While you may draw analogies from the Bible,

the sports page, or television, make sure they will be familiar to your factfinder.

- Develop "stock" analogies, particularly for legal principles such as the burden of proof that arise repeatedly. However, you'll need to adjust if you appear more than once before the same factfinder and you notice the factfinder mouthing an analogy along with you.

The persuasive power of an analogy that is "right on" was perhaps nowhere better illustrated than during the 1976 Republican Convention, on national television. Convention delegates favoring the nomination of Ronald Reagan wanted the delegates to adopt a rule requiring potential presidential nominees to name their vice presidential choices before the balloting for the presidential candidate began. Delegates favoring the nomination of Gerald Ford were opposed to the idea. During the debate, a convention delegate used the following analogy to illustrate her argument that it was unfair to change rules in the middle of the convention:

"In South Carolina we have two sets of rules for the playing of checkers. Under one rule you must jump your opponent if you have the opportunity. Under the other, jumping the opponent is optional. However, there is one further rule that we always apply no matter which of the first two rules is being used. You can't change the rule about whether or not you have to jump in the middle of the game."

Perhaps aided by this analogy, Ford's followers defeated the proposal.

2. Responding to an Adversary's Analogy

Using an adversary's analogy against the adversary can be a dramatic and effective rebuttal technique. One rebuttal method is to attack an analogy's factual similarity. For example, if you represent the defendant in the "three dolls fenderbender case," you may use the same analogy to make the point that your primary defense is the plaintiff's own negligence:

> "Counsel used the example of the three dolls to try to convince you that the defendant should pay for the plaintiff's injuries. We agree that if a person throws a rock against a piece of glass, he should pay for it. But that is not what happened here. Here, the piece of glass was thrown against the rock, and the person holding the rock is not responsible for that."

A second rebuttal method is to accept the adversary analogy's factual fit, but use it to draw a different inference:

> "Counsel talked about how people drive more carefully when they are carrying valuable cargo like children or fancy glass objects. If you think about it, counsel's own example explains exactly why the defendant drove carelessly-the defendant was so focused on those cabinets that the defendant was concentrating on the cabinets instead of on the road."

Pointing out that an analogy (like circumstantial evidence) can "cut both ways" is an effective method of deflating an adversary's argument.

H. CREDIBILITY ARGUMENTS

This section discusses two concerns that potentially arise whenever you attack the credibility of an adversary's version of events.

1. Lying or Mistaken?

When attacking credibility, your desired inference may be either that an adverse witness is lying, or that the witness is mistaken. As a general rule, factfinders are more willing to conclude that a witness is mistaken than that a witness is lying. Thus, "mistake" should be your desired inference whenever it is a reasonable one. Such credibility arguments proceed generally along these lines:

"You can place no faith in Mr. Whittington's testimony. His inability to remember anything that happened prior to their turning onto Manchester, and his conflicting statements to the police officer, render his testimony plainly unreliable. As to his claim that the light in the defendant's direction was green, you must remember that as her husband, he is naturally biased. When a loved one is involved, we often unintentionally remember things the way we wish they were, not the way they actually occurred. You'll see this when you compare Mr. Whittington's testimony with that of Ms. Stockport ..."

This argument's "bottom line" is that Whittington is mistaken, and therefore his testimony is unreliable. Such an argument is likely to be more persuasive than one which requires a factfinder to conclude that Whittington lied.

On occasion, the only inference you can reasonably ask a factfinder to accept is that an adverse witness lied. For instance, as a prosecutor you may be unable to argue sensibly that an alibi witness was mistaken about having been out of town with the defendant when a crime was committed. In such situations, you should explicitly acknowledge the "lying" inference.

2. "Falsus in Uno, Falsus in Omnibus?"

A second issue concerns the range of a credibility attack. To what extent can you argue that an inconsistency or implausibility affects an adversary's entire story? To persuade a factfinder that an adverse witness' story (or an adversary's overall story) is unworthy of belief, you generally need to stress the significance of the implausibility or inconsistency.

For example, assume that you are the defense attorney in the rape prosecution of William Kennedy Smith. The rape allegedly took place in the Kennedy Palm Beach estate. Prosecution witness Ann Mercer testified that her friend, the woman allegedly raped by Smith, told Mercer minutes after the attack that a rape had occurred. Cross examining Mercer, you elicited evidence that after hearing about the alleged rape, Mercer accompanied Smith throughout the dark house and grounds of the

Kennedy estate, looking for the shoes of the woman who had allegedly been raped. You think that this portion of the story is implausible, and based on this implausibility want to urge the factfinder to disregard the entire rape story. You might argue as follows:

"Ms. Mercer's testimony about what happened that night just doesn't make sense. Supposedly, as soon as Ms. Mercer arrives at the Kennedy estate, her friend tells Ms. Mercer about the rape. But Ms. Mercer admits that after hearing this, she went into the house with Mr. Smith searching for her friend's shoes. When they couldn't find the shoes in the house, she and Mr. Smith walked all over the dark grounds to the beach, looking for them.

"Ms. Mercer's story just doesn't make sense. Would she have walked all over a dark house and estate with Mr. Smith if she had just been told that Mr. Smith had raped her friend? Rape is an extremely traumatic experience. Wouldn't Ms. Mercer have wanted to get her friend away from the place where it happened as soon as possible? Use your common sense-do people leave friends alone at the scene of a rape while they go off in the dark to look for a pair of shoes with the alleged rapist? Moreover, wouldn't Ms. Mercer want to seek medical attention for her friend as soon as possible, and report the crime to the police?

"The only sensible conclusion you can reach is that the prosecution's case is a fiction. Her friend did not tell Ms. Mercer that she had been raped. Change this one fact, and everything makes sense. If Ann Mercer hadn't been told that a rape had occurred, it is perfectly reasonable for her to have gone off with Mr. Smith in search of her friend's shoes. Ms. Mercer would not have been in fear of Mr. Smith, nor would she have wanted to remove her friend from the house as soon as possible. Ms. Mercer's actions speak far louder than her words, and they tell you that no rape occurred. What is true is exactly what Mr. Smith told you: the intercourse was consensual."

By emphasizing the significance of the alleged implausibility, this defense argument gives the fact-finder a basis for disbelieving the prosecution's overall story.

I. THE RESULT

You generally don't want to leave a factfinder confused about your desired result. Thus, an effective closing argument generally explicitly sets forth a desired result. For example, as a prosecutor you may state that "The evidence requires that you return a verdict of first degree burglary." As a criminal defense attorney, you might assert that "The prosecution has failed to prove its case beyond a reasonable doubt, and you should return a verdict of not guilty." If you want to preserve the possibility of a not guilty verdict while being realistic about conviction of a lesser included offense, you might state your desired result in the alternative: "You should find the defendant not guilty of assault with a deadly weapon. At most the prosecution's evidence might support simple assault." (Note: many defense attorneys believe it a mistake to concede the possibility of conviction even on lesser charges.)

In civil cases, some jurisdictions forbid plaintiffs from making explicit arguments about the amount of damages for pain and suffering. In jurisdictions where you can mention specific numbers, you may not want to do so for fear of aiming too low. Even so, you can be fairly explicit about your desired result:

"Thus, the evidence amply demonstrates that the defendant fraudulently promised to produce a limited edition series of Great Law Professors trading cards. You should assess general damages in the sum of at least $175,000, and to punish the defendant for its fraudulent conduct impose punitive damages in the amount of at least $500,000."

J. SILENT ARGUMENTS

You may recall from Chapter 5 that silent arguments often affect factfinding. For example, a jury's verdict may be influenced by a party's ethnicity or economic status. Such arguments usually cannot be made explicitly because they are more a product of emotion and bias than of reason. However, during closing argument you may try to undermine a silent argument when you believe that your client is its likely victim. For example, assume that you fear that a factfinder will disbelieve an important witness who testified on your behalf, because of the witness' low socio-economic status. To counter such an "argument," you might say something along these lines:

"The plaintiff might argue that you shouldn't believe Sara's testimony, because Sara doesn't use two dollar words or wear fancy clothes. But we all know the old saying, 'you can't judge a book by its cover.' Use your common sense and think about what Sara said, not her speaking skills or the clothes she wore, and you will realize that her testimony is 100% accurate."

Note how in the course of countering the silent argument, you can cleverly imply that it is the nasty adversary who would stoop so low as to rely on such an inappropriate argument.

Silent arguments often grow out of a factfinder's emotional reaction to evidence. A good way to respond is to acknowledge the emotion and try to distance your client from it. For example, assume that your client is charged with committing multiple child molestations. You may acknowledge the factfinder's understandable emotional feelings as you caution against their influence:

"You have heard the testimony of children who have been subjected to brutal, repulsive acts. It has been at least as difficult and painful for my client Mr. Genghis to listen to as I am sure it has been for you. We do not in any way minimize the severity of their injuries. But please do not let your feelings for the children override your consideration of the evidence that Mr. Genghis was not the person responsible for these terrible acts."

K. NORMATIVE AND "PSEUDO–NORMATIVE" ARGUMENTS

Recall from Chapter 5 that normative legal elements require factfinders to evaluate conduct according to community norms or standards. That is, to determine whether a party behaved "unreasonably" or whether a breach of contract was "material," a factfinder implicitly evaluates facts according to the factfinder's beliefs about what behavior is normal and how much deviance to permit. An explicit normative argument may explore the fairness or justness of a party's conduct, the consequences that flowed from that conduct and the possibility of alternative behavior. For example, you might argue that a police officer's use of a baton to subdue an arrestee was not reasonable because the arrestee wound up with a fractured skull, and because the officer could have called for backup help before making the arrest.

"Pseudo-normative" arguments appeal to a factfinder's sense of community values even when the factual dispute is purely historical. For example, assume that you contend that a defendant made a false statement or committed a murder. These are historical propositions. A factfinder needn't make a normative judgment to decide either issue. Nevertheless, judges and jurors generally bring into the courtroom community values such as fairness, and a "pseudo-normative" argument tells a factfinder why a historical outcome is fair and just.

For example, assume that in a personal injury case you have made a historical argument about the damages caused by a defendant's negligent conduct. Your pseudo-normative argument might go on to discuss the fairness of adequate compensation and the value that people should pay for the harms they cause. Similarly, in a copyright case you might argue that the public would be deprived of creative ideas if a few resemblances in stories constituted infringement.

L. ARGUING LEGAL PRINCIPLES

When you deliver a closing argument, in a jury trial a judge will have already instructed the jury, or you will know the instructions that the judge will give after the arguments. In either case, explaining critical instructions and demonstrating how your arguments connect between abstract legal principles and factual stories are usually important parts of a final summation.

1. The Burden of Proof

Some reference to the burden of proof is standard in nearly every argument, even during introductory remarks. You may use analogies to illustrate its meaning (see Page 258), and defense attorneys frequently remind a factfinder of the plaintiff's burden at the beginning (see Page 240) and the end of an argument. In addition, you may integrate references to the burden of proof into specific arguments.

For example, return to the auto accident case involving a building contractor's alleged careless driving. Page 246 sets out the plaintiff's inferential argument based on evidence that shortly before the accident, the defendant received a car phone call advising the defendant of a job site problem. Integrating the burden of proof into that argument might produce the following analysis:

"As I mentioned earlier, one of the issues you must decide is whether the contractor was inattentive to the road just before the contractor struck the plaintiff. Remember that the defendant admitted on cross examination that just moments before the collision, the defendant received a car phone call from the office telling the defendant about a problem on a remodeling job site. Isn't it likely that building contractors such as the defendant who hear of a problem on a job site are going to be thinking about the problem as they drive? That's especially likely to be true when, as in this case, the contractor is in the vicinity of the job site when the call comes through and the problem is a large one that requires the contractor's immediate attention. We know that the problem required the defendant's immediate attention because, as the defendant also admitted, the problem had to be handled before the project could continue and the defendant immediately changed course to head for the job site. Moreover, as the president of the company, the defendant had the most to lose if work was delayed. *Remember, this is a civil case, and to hold the defendant liable you only have to conclude that it is more probable than not that this phone call, together with all the other evidence, establishes that the defendant drove carelessly.* The defendant had lots of reasons to be thinking about the job site problem, and as a result was not paying attention to the road when the plaintiff was struck."

Reminding jurors of the burden of proof is especially important when, as in the example above, you represent a civil plaintiff. Jurors who hear the words "burden of proof" often automatically think of the criminal standard of "beyond a reasonable doubt." Thus, an effective civil plaintiff's argument often explicitly and common-sensically explains the difference between the civil and criminal burdens.

2. Other Jury Instructions

Jury instructions would be a strong contender in any "Least Effective Form of Communication" contest. Voluminous, often abstract and read by judges with the enthusiasm of a dental patient reading a report recommending a root canal, jury instructions are more likely to confound than enlighten. Therefore, you typically should explain important instructions and relate them to your arguments.

For example, judges typically instruct jurors that circumstantial evidence is evidence from which an inference can be drawn. These words may mean little to visually-oriented jurors, who have never seen an inference let alone drawn one. Thus, when relying on an inferential argument you may want to explain the instruction and its application. For example, a portion of the inferential argument on Page 271 might go as follows:

"Remember that the defendant admitted on cross examination that just moments before the collision, the defendant received a car phone call from the office informing the defendant of a problem on a remodeling job site. Now, Her Honor will shortly instruct you, and I paraphrase, that circumstantial evidence is evidence from which you can draw an inference. The term may be unfamiliar to you, but drawing inferences is perfectly proper and something we do all the time in daily life. An inference is simply a conclusion you reach based on information. For example, if you hear a report that an accident has occurred at midday on a main road, you will no doubt infer that it produced a traffic jam. This is exactly the kind of common sense reasoning you should use to infer that receiving the car phone call caused the defendant to drive carelessly. Isn't it likely that building contractors such as the defendant who hear of a problem on a job site are going to be thinking about the problem as they drive? That's especially likely to be true when, as in this case . . ."

You should explain critical substantive rules as well as procedural rules like the burden of proof and inferential reasoning. For example, in a suit involving the sale of goods, you might discuss an instruction concerning damages as follows:

"The Judge will shortly instruct you that defendant GlueAll's breach of warranty caused Ms. Taylor's loss if that breach was a substantial factor in bringing about the loss. In other words, we must prove that GlueAll's mistakenly filling the tube with cake icing instead of adhesive was a substantial factor in causing Ms. Taylor's house to collapse. The term 'substantial factor' is critical. It means that for you to award damages to Ms. Taylor, we do not need to prove that GlueAll's mistake was the entire cause of the building's collapse, or even that it was the most important cause. As long as GlueAll's mistake was an important reason for the collapse, so long as it was more than a minor cause, more than an insubstantial factor, the law compels you to award damages to Ms. Taylor."

As you can see, explaining and illustrating jury instructions can be time-consuming. Therefore, you'll typically have to limit discussion to the most important instructions.

M. EFFECTIVE COMMUNICATION TECHNIQUES

Think back to the teachers and speakers who have impressed you as credible and knowledgeable. Those same characteristics are likely to impress a factfinder. This section summarizes effective oral

communication skills. (Wearing a toga while standing over a slain despot in front of a crowd at the
Roman Forum is an effective technique, but not one
generally available to trial lawyers.)

One key to effective communication is to talk
directly to a factfinder. Don't read a closing argument. A closing argument that is read always
sounds stilted. Moreover, if you read an argument
you'll inevitably lose eye contact with a factfinder
and talk too fast, often causing a factfinder to miss
part of what you're saying. (In a public forum such
as a courtroom, you should speak intentionally
slower than you do when you speak with friends in
social settings.) Certainly you can prepare and refer
to notes or an outline of your argument. You may
even read a jury instruction or a critical section of
testimony verbatim to give it added emphasis. In
general, however, you cannot project sincerity and
confidence if you read a closing argument.

Second, don't speak in a monotone; try to vary
the pitch and pacing of an argument.

Third, use simple sentences and ordinary words.
Explain complex terms, especially when one of your
experts used them during testimony or in a report
that was received into evidence.

Finally, look for opportunities to refer to exhibits
and other visual aids. For example, during opening
statement you might have referred to a chart summarizing your expected evidence. (See Chapter 6) If
so, bring back that same chart during closing argu-

ment to demonstrate that you lived up to your promises.

These techniques are consistent with every speaking style, whether you be quiet or energetic. You need not take acting lessons or be a gifted orator to deliver an effective closing argument.

N. RULES OF CLOSING ARGUMENT

This section examines the evidentiary principles that commonly come into play during closing argument.

1. Confine Argument to the Record

The most fundamental rule of closing argument is that you cannot argue "facts outside the record." The most frequent ways of violating this rule include:

- Referring to non-existent evidence: "What? The tenant did not confess to being an axe murderer when talking to the landlord about the rent? I take it back."

- Referring to evidence admitted for a limited purpose for a different purpose: A hearsay statement was admitted as evidence of the declarant's state of mind, and you argue as though the statement had been admitted for its truth.

Usually, arguing facts outside the record draws an objection and a judge's admonishment to a jury to disregard your remark. However, a severe misstatement or repeated misstatements can result in a mistrial and sanctions.

The corresponding rule that you can draw reasonable inferences from evidence in the record can make application of the "confine argument to the record" rule less than obvious. For example, assume that you represent the plaintiff in the case of the auto accident in which a contractor struck a pedestrian. You have offered evidence that just before the accident, the contractor received a car phone call advising the contractor of a job site problem. You can draw your desired inference for the factfinder, arguing that "the defendant was so upset by the call that the defendant was not paying adequate attention to the road." But what if you argue, "For the defendant to have changed direction after receiving the phone call, the problem must have threatened the financial solvency of the defendant's contracting business." Is this a reasonable inference, or a reference to facts outside the record? Such rulings are within a judge's discretion, but judges often overrule objections that "Counsel is misstating the record" with the statement, "It's only argument."

If in a jury trial a judge sustains an objection that you have misstated the record, an effective response is to assure the jurors that you are attempting to be accurate, and remind them that in any event they are the ultimate authority regarding the evidence.

If you are uncertain whether an adversary's remark amounts to a misstatement of the record, especially in a jury trial you should be reluctant to object. If the judge overrules your objection, jurors may take that as a judicial endorsement of the adversary's argument. If you will have a chance to argue after your adversary finishes, the better alternative to objecting is often pointing out that while your adversary may have made a splendid argument, it was not based on the evidence:

> "Opposing counsel misled you with the argument that Jack accompanied Jill up the hill. A witness testified only that both Jack and Jill went up the hill. No witness testified that they did so simultaneously. Moreover, their friend Hansel testified that Jack left the house at least 20 minutes before Jill, making it likely that they did not climb the hill together. Now, when you look at the evidence that was actually introduced, you'll see . . . ."

Moreover, the rule against arguing facts outside the record does not prevent you from referring to generalizations based on everyday experience. Factfinders are supposed to bring their experiences and common sense into the courtroom, and you can refer to the generalizations underlying your desired inferences during argument. For example, a prosecutor trying to explain a robbery victim's initial refusal to identify the culprit could argue that "fear of retaliation often makes people afraid to cooperate with the police." On the other hand, citing specific research underlying a generalization might be improper if unsupported by the record. For example, assume that the prosecutor had argued that, "according to a recent study by the National Justice Committee, 25% of crime victims initially refuse to cooperate with the police." Without support in the record, the argument is probably improper.

2. Puffing

"Puffing" is a sales technique by which sellers and advertisers make exaggerated claims to induce customers to do business. The technique is generally acceptable in the marketplace, in part on the theory that few consumers would seriously believe that "wearing our toe plaster makes you feel like you're walking on air."

A trial is not a commercial venture, and puffing may be less effective a seller of inferences than of toe plasters. Nevertheless, puffing is generally acceptable during closing argument. For example, you may state that "Nelson's credibility is above reproach" or "liability couldn't be clearer" even if Nelson's credibility and liability are in doubt. Puffing is tolerated because an occasional excess of zeal is inherent in the adversary system, and because the line between proper and improper inferences is often difficult to discern. Moreover, we expect factfinders to have sufficient common sense not to be misled by puffing.

Puffing becomes unacceptable if it amounts to misstatement of evidence or if your appeal is likely to lead a factfinder to substitute emotion for reason. For example, assume that a prosecutor argues that a defendant acted like "a wild animal, a rotten beast." Such an argument appeals so strongly to a jury's emotions that a judge is likely to deem it improper.

3. Stating Personal Opinions ("Vouching")

A seemingly settled rule of argument warns you against stating your personal opinion. However, consider this common form of argument:

> "Jack would have you believe that he went up the hill to fetch a pail of water. However, as Jill testified, and as you might expect, the well was located at the bottom of the hill. I think that Jack was not telling the truth, and that Jill's testimony shows that Jack went up there for another purpose entirely. I think that purpose will become clear if you look at Hansel's testimony ..."

Though you refer throughout to your personal opinion, this type of argument is common and proper. You can give your opinion about the credibility or the probative value of evidence. Generally, if you can mentally substitute the phrase, "I submit that the evidence shows ..." for "I think ... ," your argument is proper.

The real thrust of the "no personal opinion" rule is to prevent counsel from personally vouching for a desired outcome. That is, you should not ask a factfinder to evaluate evidence based on your personal credibility or integrity. For example, consider these arguments:

- "Never in my 32 years of practice have I represented a client who has been so careful to rectify errors in shipments promptly."

- "Their defense is preposterous. But defense counsel has no scruples against putting out unmeritorious claims."

- "I have never cross examined a witness who told as many lies as did Lem Bezzle."

Each of these arguments improperly puts counsel's personal credibility or integrity in issue. Here as in other areas, the law rewards subtlety. If you want to sway a factfinder with your personal qualities, you'll have to do it implicitly through such silent argument methods as your courtroom professionalism and shoe styles.

4. "Send a Message" Arguments

It is generally improper to argue the effects of a verdict on the community at large. For example, a prosecutor cannot argue that a guilty verdict "will send a message to drug dealers that they are not wanted." The argument's vice is that it deflects the factfinder's attention from the evidence, as a guilty verdict would send the prosecutor's desired message regardless of the defendant's guilt or innocence.

5. "Theory of the Case" Arguments

While a settled definition of "theory of the case" is non-existent, one popular meaning is that it consists of an explanation for why events occurred as you contend. Because people tend to believe in cause-and-effect, a factfinder is more likely to accept your version of events if you offer an explanation for why those events took place. For example, a factfinder may be more likely to convict a defendant of a crime if it believes that the defendant was motivated by jealousy or greed.

"Theory of the case" arguments are proper if you base them on evidence in the record, or if they constitute reasonable inferences from evidence in the record. For example, if you've offered evidence that an alleged murderer stood to inherit the victim's estate, you may argue that "this was a crime of greed." However, you could not ask the factfinder to infer that "the defendant wanted the money right away to start an illegal drug trafficking ring" unless you could base the inference on evidence in the record.

O. ARGUMENTS IN BENCH TRIALS

To what extent should you modify a closing argument in bench trials? You generally need not modify arguments' factual content. These arguments pertain to unique historical events, and a judge's legal sophistication doesn't necessarily imbue a judge with insights into historical interpretation. Thus, explicitness, preemption, analogies and the other techniques described above are typically as appropriate in bench as in jury trials. On the other hand, in bench trials you would not generally need to explain the meaning of procedural and substantive rules, unless you want to give an Olympics-hopeful judge practice in the Gavel Throw.

In bench trials, a judge's comments and questions often allow you to tailor arguments to the judge's specific concerns. In jury trials, few jurisdictions allow jurors to pose questions, even in writing through the judge. Thus, you are typically left to your judgment as to which issues jurors consider most significant.

P. ARGUMENT EXCERPTS: "PEOPLE VS. O. J. SIMPSON"

In 1995, actor and former football hero O. J. Simpson was prosecuted for murdering his ex-wife Nicole Brown Simpson and her friend, Ron Goldman. Simpson was found not guilty in a nine month long "trial of the century" that was broadcast live on television to much of the world. (In a separate and non-televised 1997 civil trial, Simpson was found liable for the wrongful death of the two victims; the jury awarded millions of dollars in damages to their families.) Excerpts from the arguments in the criminal trial will serve to illustrate many of the techniques described in this chapter.

1. Introduction

Prosecutor Marcia Clark introduced her argument with such remarks as, "I'm sorry if I say things that you don't need to hear or ... are already clear to you. Please bear with me because I am not a mindreader and I don't know. First I want to take the opportunity to thank you ... from the bottom of my heart.... You have made a tremendous sacrifice. You haven't seen your children enough.... I apologize for that.... But at the conclusion of all of our arguments, when you open up the windows and let the cool air blow out the

smokescreen that has been created by the defense
... you will see that the defendant has been proven
guilty easily beyond a reasonable doubt.... Now, I
would like to start with the evidence...."

Defense attorney Johnnie Cochran Jr. began by
telling the jurors that, "I'm not going to argue with
you ... what I'm going to do is to try and discuss
the reasonable inferences which I feel can be drawn
from this evidence. At the outset, let me join with
the others in thanking you for the service that
you've rendered. You are truly a marvelous jury,
the longest serving jury in Los Angeles County ...
the final test of your service as jurors will not lie in
the fact that you've stayed here more than a year,
but will lie in the quality of the verdict that you
render ... one other group I should thank are our
marvelous court reporters .. I want to tell you right
at the outset that ... Simpson, like all defendants,
is presumed to be innocent.... As he sits over
there now, he's cloaked in a presumption of innocence."

2. Use Exhibits

For her closing argument, prosecutor Clark prepared and referred to continuously a timeline chart
depicting the prosecution's version of how events
unfolded. Responding to the prosecution's claim
that a dark knit cap offered into evidence was part
of Simpson's disguise, defense attorney Cochran put
on the knit cap while arguing that "O. J. Simpson
in a knit cap from two blocks away is still O. J.
Simpson. It's no disguise."

3. Puffing

The defense accused police officer Mark Fuhrman of planting evidence and offered evidence that he had lied about not referring to African–Americans as "niggers." During closing argument, defense attorney Cochran called Fuhrman "a lying, perjuring, genocidal racist." Cochran also called Fuhrman the "personification of evil" and compared him to Hitler, "another man not too long ago in the world who had those same views."

4. Silent Arguments

The defense could not reasonably argue that "celebrity sports heroes don't commit murder." However, addressing jurors who might adopt a silent argument that someone of Simpson's stature would not commit murder, prosecutor Clark argued that "it's really kind of hard to believe that the man we saw in the movies and commercials could do this. But he did. And the fact that he did doesn't mean that he wasn't a great football player. It doesn't mean that he never did a good thing in his life. Nothing takes that away. That's still here. It will always be here. But so will the fact that he committed these murders."

Responding to a possible silent argument that a verdict of acquittal was tantamount to a vote against the police force, defense attorney Cochran argued: "This case is not-let me state it at the outset-about attacking the Los Angeles Police Department. We're not anti-police in making these statements. You're not anti-police. We all need the police ...But ... what all of us should have are honest, effective, nonbiased police officers."

5. Remind Factfinder of Unkept Opening Statement Promises

Prosecutor Darden told the jurors that during opening statement, defense attorney Cochran had promised but failed to elicit the following evidence:

- evidence of an alibi.

- evidence that four people, none of them Simpson, had been seen running from the crime scene.

- evidence that the defendant was at home practicing golf at the time of the murders.

- expert evidence that Simpson was not a wife batterer.

6. Analogies

Providing an analogy for how the jurors should go about their fact-finding task, prosecutor Clark said that "it is up to you, the jury, to weed out the distractions, weed out the side shows, and determine what evidence is it that really helps me answer this question (of who the killer was). And it is kind of like the artist, the sculptor. Someone went to him and said how do you make an angel. Well, I take a piece of marble and I remove everything that is not an angel. That is what you have to do."

Prosecutor Clark, arguing that reasonable doubt doesn't require that every possibility be accounted for: "I compare it to a jig-saw puzzle ... To know what a jig-saw puzzle is depicting, if you're missing a couple of pieces of the sky, you still have the picture ... So I kind of compare a jury trial to that because it often happens that there are things that are not shown to you.... But those are like pieces of the sky, you don't need them."

The prosecution offered evidence of DNA analysis of blood found at the crime scene and in Simpson's car and home to tie Simpson to the murders. The defense claimed that some blood samples were planted by the police, while other samples were contaminated by faulty police methods. Defense attorney Barry Scheck analogized the police laboratory to "a black hole," and used an analogy to illustrate the argument that problems with blood taken from a pair of socks justified the jurors' ignoring all the blood evidence: "If you find a cockroach in a bowl of spaghetti, do you then take every strand of that bowl of spaghetti to look for more cockroaches or do you just throw it away and eat no more?"

Defense attorney Cochran, implicitly warning the jurors against "mind set:" "In America you have to wait until you hear all the evidence.... People are not making up their minds at the beginning. You don't decide a baseball game or a football game at halftime. You wait until the end."

7. Responding to an Adversary's Analogy

Defense attorney Cochran, responding to prosecutor Darden's theory of the case "fuse" analogy (see subsection 10 below): "This fuse he kept talking about kept going out. It never blew up, never exploded. There was no triggering mechanism ... it was a nice analogy ... let's look at this photograph (taken hours before the murders) ... if you want to see how he looks while he is in this murderous rage, while this fuse is going on ... where is the fuse now?"

8. Falsus in Uno, Falsus in Omnibus

The defense offered evidence that a police officer who testified for the prosecution had made a false statement in a search warrant to search Simpson's home. Defense attorney Cochran argued, "You can't trust him. You can't believe anything he says, because it goes to the core of this case. When you are lying at the beginning you will be lying at the end. The Book of Luke talks about that. If you are untruthful in small things you should be disbelieved in big things."

9. Inoculation

Police officer Mark Fuhrman was shown to have lied when he testified that he hadn't used the term "nigger." Acknowledging the legitimacy of the defense attack on Fuhrman's credibility while arguing that it shouldn't control the outcome, prosecutor Clark argued, "Just so it is clear. Did he (Fuhrman) lie when he testified here in this courtroom saying that he did not use racial epithets in the last 10 years? Yes. Is he a racist? Yes. Is he the worst the LAPD has to offer? Yes. ... In fact, do we wish that there were no such person on the planet? Yes. But the fact that Mark Fuhrman is a racist and lied about it on the witness stand does not mean that we haven't proven the defendant guilty beyond a reasonable doubt, and it would be a tragedy if ... you found the defendant not guilty in spite of all that (evidence) because of the racist attitudes of one police officer."

10. Theory of the Case

Defense attorney Cochran: "It seems to us that the evidence shows that professional police work took a backseat right at the beginning. Untrained officers trampled, they traipsed through the evidence ...they allowed this investigation to be infected by a dishonest and corrupt detective. We think if they had done their jobs as we have done, Mr. Simpson would have been eliminated early on ... That's what this case is about, not following the rules."

Prosecutor Clark: "And defense would say, no motive, no motive. It's one of the oldest motives ever known ... anger, fear of abandonment, jealousy, loss of control of Nicole and himself." Prosecutor Darden amplified on this, talking about previous domestic violence: "This relationship, it is like a time bomb, ticking away ... a bomb with a long fuse ... as each incident occurred, that fuse got shorter ...at some point, this bomb is going to explode."

11. Explain Jury Instructions

Prosecutor Clark: "This is a real important instruction ... because it is the burden of proof that

the People have.... now, to tell you about reasonable doubt, it is kind of a funny definition because it
talks to you about reasonable doubt in very negative terms ...so I'm going to go through it pieces at
a time to try and give you a little hand here."

12. Two–Sided Argument

Prosecutor Clark: "The defense ... hint that the
blood was planted .. that multiple other blood-
stains were contaminated and that somehow all the
contamination only occurred where it would consistently prove that the defendant was guilty ... If
what they are saying is true then ... why is it that
the samples of blood they took from her pool of
blood didn't come up with the defendant's blood
type?"

13. Preemption

As evidence of Simpson's anger toward and motive to kill his ex-wife, the prosecution offered evidence of Simpson's earlier violent behavior towards
his ex-wife. Prosecutor Darden: "I'm sure the defense is going to get up here at some point and say,
that domestic violence evidence, it's irrelevant.
They may say just because this defendant had some
violence in his marriage, that it doesn't prove anything. Well ...it's because when you look at all of
that, it points to him."

14. The Result

Defense attorney Cochran: "Soon it will be your
turn. You have the keys to his future ... We believe

you will do the right thing, and the right thing is to find this man not guilty on both of these charges."

15. Pseudo–Normative Argument

Defense attorney Cochran: "If we as the people don't continue to hold a mirror up to the face of America and say this is what you promised, this is what you delivered, if you don't speak out, if you don't stand up, if you didn't do what's right, this kind of (police mis-) conduct will continue on forever and we will never have an ideal society, one that lives out the true meaning of the creed of the Constitution or of life, liberty and justice for all."

CHAPTER 11

ODDS AND ENDS

Intertwined with testimony and argument are the myriads of procedures that constitute the rituals of trial. This chapter describes the most important of these procedures. However, the chapter does not reveal which procedures are "odds" and which are "ends." Life must have some mystery!

Some of the procedures, such as voir dire and introduction of expert testimony, tend to be regulated through statutes, court rules and appellate decisions. Others, such as when and where you stand and how you address the court and opposing counsel, are largely products of custom and practice. The latter sets of procedures especially are likely to vary from courtroom to courtroom. For example, in one courtroom stepping into "the well" (the floor area between counsel table and the judge's bench) may be perfectly acceptable; in another, you may get a quicker hook than a bad vaudevillian. Thus, seek advice regarding a judge's procedural preferences from the court clerk or another attorney, or observe a judge in action before your case is scheduled. Otherwise, when you try a case you may end up feeling like the party guest who wonders why nobody else is in costume.

A. EXCLUDING (SEQUESTERING) WITNESSES

Sequestration orders aim at preventing witnesses from influencing each other's testimony. (See Federal Rule of Evidence 615) Sequestration orders typically:

- bar potential witnesses from the courtroom during trial to prevent them from hearing the testimony of other witnesses; and

- instruct potential witnesses not to discuss a case with other witnesses.

Some judges make sequestration orders on their own motion. If not, you can make an oral request at the outset of a trial. Before celebrating a successful request, remember that the order will apply to both sides' witnesses.

Where do excluded witnesses go? In short trials, to the corridor, or at least no further than the cafeteria. In longer trials, most jurisdictions have "on call" subpoena procedures, which allow witnesses to carry on their affairs outside the courthouse as long as they can appear in court on short notice.

Sequestration orders do not apply to parties. They may be paying dearly for their day in court, and should not have to miss a moment of it. Parties can derive some benefit from this privilege. By opting to testify last, parties can first hear what the other witnesses have to say. Attorneys who represent abstract entities, such as prosecutors, usually can designate a representative (e.g, an investigating police officer) to remain in court throughout testimony, even though that representative will testify.

B. STIPULATIONS

Stipulations are agreements between counsel. Apart from conferring on a court powers that it does not have ("we stipulate that if convicted, the defendant can be tarred and feathered"), you can stipulate to nearly any legal or factual issue. For example, you can stipulate to the admissibility of evidence, to an expert's qualifications, or to the content of a witness' testimony.

Typically, you'll arrive at a stipulation out of court. During trial, inform the judge of the stipulation at the time it becomes relevant. For example, you may advise the court of a stipulation to an expert's qualifications when the expert is about to testify. Similarly, you may advise the court of a stipulation that a document qualifies as a business record when the document is marked for identification.

To protect against an adversary's sharp practices, insist on reducing stipulations to writing. In court, some attorneys may try to back out of oral stipulations by finding subtle ambiguities: "Your Honor, I did agree to stipulate that the animal on the premises had four legs, a tail, and barked. But I certainly did not intend to stipulate that it was a dog." If an unexpected disagreement prevents you from entering a stipulation into the record, you may suddenly find yourself in the middle of trial unprepared to prove a fact which you thought would be resolved by stipulation.

Typical stipulations include:

- Qualifications of an Expert. You may stipulate that, e.g., "Dr. Lipkis is qualified to render a medical opinion." Indeed, when an adversary's expert is abundantly qualified, offering to stipulate to the expert's qualifications may prevent the adversary from parading the expert's honors and achievements before a jury. Judges, cognizant of time pressures, often try to persuade attorneys to accept such stipulations. However, you may want to resist an adversary's offer to stipulate to your expert's abundant qualifications. In such situations, you may argue that the impressive foundational information goes to the weight and not merely the admissibility of an expert's testimony, or that the information has particular relevance to the factual propositions to which the expert's opinion relates.

- Accuracy of a Fact. You may stipulate that a fact or group of facts is true. For example, you may stipulate that, "All of the king's horses were at the wall," or that, "The chicken came first." Such stipulations are binding for the purposes of the litigation. For example, you cannot attack the credibility of evidence whose accuracy has been stipulated to. Of course, you can question the inference that a factfinder

might draw from a stipulated fact: "We did
stipulate that all the king's horses were at the
wall. But that in no way undermines our contention that the king was negligent. First, consider ... "

● Content of Testimony. You may stipulate to the
content of testimony without agreeing to its
accuracy. For example, you may stipulate that,
"If called and sworn, Ptolemy would testify
that the sun and all the planets revolve around
the earth." Even after that stipulation is made
on the record, you could attack the credibility
of Ptolemy and the opinion.

You might ask an adversary to enter into such a
stipulation to save time, to avoid having to ask for a
continuance if a witness suddenly becomes unavailable, and perhaps to prevent inconsistencies that
might appear if you called the various observers of
an event as witnesses. You might accede to an
adversary's request for such a stipulation to save
time and to keep a very credible witness off the
stand.

● Admissibility of Evidence. Beyond stipulations
to an expert's qualifications suggest, stipulations can obviate almost every foundational
showing. For example, with respect to exhibits,
attorneys often offer to "stipulate to yours if
you stipulate to mine." Attorneys may also
stipulate that an oral hearsay statement qualifies as a "spontaneous exclamation," or that a
witness has personal knowledge. When you

don't seriously contest a foundation, stipulating to admissibility is a useful way to save valuable court time.

C.   MAKING OBJECTIONS

An objection should be a product of two components:

- realizing (perhaps with faint echoes of your Evidence instructor) that an evidentiary rule has been violated; and

- a tactical reason to object.

Since you may have less time to object than the time interval between a traffic light turning green and the cabbie behind you honking, objections decisions may seem a daunting task. However, take solace in realizing that the danger that you will lose a case because you fail to make an objection is negligible. You will almost always know about and consider the admissibility of critical evidence before it's offered, so you are rarely faced with a sudden decision.

1.   Motions in Limine

A "motion in limine" is a request for a pretrial admissibility ruling. While the motion can be made by a party seeking a ruling that evidence is admissible, more typically a party makes a motion in limine to ask a judge to rule that an adversary's evidence is inadmissible. Motions in limine are often oral, though you may file a written motion accompanied by a trial brief.

Compared to resolving admissibility issues in mid-trial, motions in limine have a number of advantages. For example, if a judge grants your pretrial motion excluding evidence, your adversary cannot refer to the evidence during trial, and must instruct witnesses not to refer to it. By comparison, even if the judge sustains your mid-trial objection, jurors may hear the improper evidence. (Judges routinely admonish jurors to disregard improper evidence, but the effect of such admonishments is uncertain.) Moreover, you can plan more effectively for opening statement and testimony if a judge has already ruled with respect to important evidence. Finally, judges often delay ruling on motions in limine, hoping to make a more educated decision during trial. However, the fact that you made a motion in limine may add force to your objection when you renew it in mid-trial.

2. Tactical and Ethical Considerations

Especially in jury trials, objections can backfire even if they are sustained. Jurors often feel that an attorney who objects too much is attempting to conceal damaging information. Prosecutors are particularly wary of such adverse inferences, and often are reluctant to object.

Moreover, you have an ethical responsibility to object only in good faith. You may not object in order to rattle a witness, pay back an obstreperous opposing counsel, or demonstrate your expertise by making an objection that allows you to cite a footnote in an obscure 19th century Paraguayan opinion.

As a result, you should in general object only when evidence is both improper and in some way damaging. This is a judgment you will have to make on a case-by-case basis. For example, you may choose to let an occasional leading question or mention of irrelevant evidence go by without objection. On the other hand, if you suspect (perhaps based on behavior at a deposition) that opposing counsel is prone to rely repeatedly on improper leading questions, or that a witness is given to extemporaneous irrelevant answers, you may want to object from the outset of trial to each impropriety.

A difficult tactical and ethical question can arise when you object in the hope that opposing counsel is unaware of an exception that you know exists. For example, you might object to hearsay in the hope that opposing counsel does not realize that the assertion qualifies as a declaration against interest. (Federal Rule of Evidence 804–b–3) Many attorneys would forgo objecting in these circumstances, unless objecting forces the adversary to offer evidence for a limited purpose. For instance, you might make a hearsay objection to an out-of-court assertion if you thereby force opposing counsel to offer it for the limited purpose of "effect on the hearer."

Finally, recognize that an objection may serve only to educate your adversary. For example, assume that you successfully object when an adversary constantly asks improper leading questions. All you may accomplish is to force the adversary into an open questioning style which enhances the credibility of the adversary's witness.

3. Objections Procedures

Objections should usually consist of nothing more than the word "objection" followed by the concise ground for objecting. For example, you might state, "Objection, hearsay;" or, "Objection, the question calls for a narrative response." Most judges view "speaking" objections the same way they view speaking demurrers: with contempt. Thus, do not combine an objection with a lecture on, e.g., the importance of the hearsay rule to the democratic way of life. If a judge wants elaboration, count on the judge to ask for it.

Technically, a judge may overrule an objection if you state the wrong ground, or neglect to state any ground. (For example, "Objection, the question calls for inadmissible information" is an improper objection.) In practice, however, a judge may sustain an obvious objection before you get it fully out of your mouth. A judge may even sustain an objection for which, in the judge's opinion, you have chosen the wrong ground: "Well, I don't think it's irrelevant, but it's hearsay under the reasoning of an obscure 19th century Paraguayan opinion. I'll sustain it on that ground."

The general rule is that you must object as soon as the ground for objection is apparent. Thus, you should:

- Object to an improper question after it is asked and before it is answered.

- Object to an improper answer as soon as you can, even if you have to interrupt a witness to do so. If the judge sustains (upholds) your objection, move to strike the improper testimony. For example, consider the following sequence:

Q: When did Jenni arrive?

A: At eight o'clock, just after she knocked all the cookies a Girl Scout troop was trying to sell off the table.

Here, the ground for objection first appears in the answer. Depending on your reflexes, at some point after "o'clock" you would object that the remaining portion of the answer is "non-responsive" or "irrelevant." For the sake of the court reporter, first get the witness to stop talking (Stand up and say, "Excuse me"), then state your objection. If the judge sustains your objection, then "move to strike everything after eight o'clock" and ask the judge to instruct the jury to disregard the stricken testimony. Unless it is formally stricken, a factfinder can consider improper evidence. Do not conclude by thanking the judge. Many attorneys habitually thank more people than the winner of a Best Picture Academy Award when a judge sustains an objection. "Thank you" is improper because it implies that the judge is doing a favor rather than making a ruling required by law.

If your objection is overruled (denied), in earlier days you would have had to "take exception" to preserve an objection for appeal. "Taking exception" was the legal equivalent of, "Oh, yeah?" Now, objections themselves preserve evidentiary points for appeal; you need not take "exception" to adverse rulings.

Do not immediately argue with a judge who you believe has improperly overruled your objection. Ask for permission to argue by asking "to be heard further."

Finally, don't whine when making objections. Some attorneys object in voices that make it seem like their entire lives have been dogged by improper evidence. Object in a professional and dignified tone of voice, as when you question witnesses or make final argument.

4. Continuing Objections

You may make a "continuing" objection when a judge has overruled an objection that pertains to a whole line of inquiry. If the judge allows a continuing objection, you can forgo objecting to the entire area of inquiry without running the risk that an appellate court will rule that you "waived the objection" by failing to object every time the area was raised.

For example, assume that you contend that all events that occurred after March 31 are irrelevant. This dialogue ensues:

Q: Turning your attention to April 1, where were you?

You: Objection, irrelevant.

Judge: Overruled.

Rather than having to object to every question pertaining to events taking place after March 31, you may request a "continuing objection." Thus, this dialogue may ensue after the above ruling:

You: Your Honor, might I have a continuing objection to all questions and responses pertaining to events that occurred after March 31?

Judge: You may.

In addition to preserving the point for appeal, continuing objections save you from alienating a factfinder with constant objections.

5. Offers of Proof

You can ask for an offer of proof when you are unclear about what a witness will say. Generally, an offer of proof is an attorney's summary of a witness' expected testimony. For example, an adversary asks, "Please tell us what was said in the June 8 conversation." You have little information about this conversation, and don't know whether the testimony will be objectionable. You would prefer to prevent a jury from hearing improper evidence in the first place rather than objecting to evidence the jury has already heard. Make a request for opposing counsel to make an offer of proof at the bench. If the judge grants the request, opposing counsel will briefly summarize the witness' expected testimony out of the jury's hearing. If the evidence is objectionable, you can make the objection at the bench.

6. Beyond Objections

Objections are not always sufficient to protect your client from unfair prejudice. For example, a witness may repeatedly refer to improper evidence, and an opposing counsel may barrage you with groundless objections or constantly ask improper leading questions. In such situations, consider asking the judge for remedies beyond sustaining an individual objection. For example, you may ask the judge:

- To instruct a runaway witness to confine answers to the questions. In an extreme situation, you may ask the judge to strike a witness' entire testimony.

- To warn obstreperous opposing counsel that continuing groundless objections will be dealt with by sanctions, including awarding of a mistrial and costs and possible referral for disciplinary action.

- To strike testimony which opposing counsel repeatedly and improperly tries to suggest through leading questions.

7. Common Grounds for Objection

Objections go either to the content of testimony or to the forms of questions. Common substantive objections include:

- "Irrelevant" (Federal Rule of Evidence 402). Irrelevant information wastes court time and is not logically connected to factual propositions.

  Example: Houston is charged with petty theft. The prosecutor asks the store security guard, "Do people often try to steal merchandise?" The question is irrelevant because the actions of other people have no logical connection to Houston's guilt or innocence.

Sometimes, an adversary's argument as to why evidence is relevant can allow the adversary to preview a closing argument in front of the jury. Therefore, you may want to approach the bench to make an "irrelevant" objection.

- "Probative Value Substantially Outweighed by Unfair Prejudice" (Federal Rule of Evidence 403). The typical vice of evidence made inadmissible by Rule 403 is that its emotional impact is likely to override a factfinder's rational faculties.

  Examples: (1) A personal injury plaintiff offers a severed left leg into evidence. (2) A criminal defendant's prior conviction is likely to unduly influence the jury's determination of whether the defendant committed the charged crime.

- "Hearsay" (Federal Rule of Evidence 801). Hearsay is an out-of-court assertion offered for the truth of its contents. The usual vice of hearsay is that the factfinder cannot evaluate the credibility of the declarant.

Example: To prove that Felice ran a red light, the plaintiff offers into evidence a phone caller's assertion a few days after the accident, "I saw what happened and Felice ran the red light."

- "Speculation" or "Improper Opinion" (Federal Rule of Evidence 701); "Lack of Personal Knowledge" (Federal Rule of Evidence 602). Testimony concerning hypothetical situations or describing matters beyond a witness' ability to perceive is unreliable and invades the factfinder's province.

  Examples: (1) "Why did the bear go over the mountain?" (A witness can only speculate as to the reason for another's actions.) (2) "If you knew what the spleen looked like, would you have removed it?"

A "lack of personal knowledge" objection is also appropriate when you think that a witness is testifying based on hearsay. If in response to a lack of personal knowledge objection a witness admits that testimony is based on another person's out-of-court assertion, then you may make a hearsay objection.

- "Lack of foundation" (Federal Rule of Evidence 104). Evidence which fails to meet foundational requirements is unreliable. Since all evidence is subject to one kind of foundation or another, an objection based on "lack of foundation" is almost always a proper ground of objection.

Example: Jordan offers a company document into evidence, but cannot show that it was prepared in the ordinary course of business, thus it fails as a business record.

- "Improper character evidence" (Federal Rule of Evidence 404). Evidence is generally improper when its relevance depends on an inference concerning a party's propensity to engage in conduct.

  Examples: (1) To prove that Larry was speeding, the adversary seeks to elicit Darryl's opinion that Larry tends to drive over the speed limit. (2) To prove that Andrea robbed a bank, the prosecution offers evidence that Andrea has committed two burglaries.

"Form" objections typically are addressed to a judge's discretion under Federal Rule of Evidence 611. Common "form" objections include:

- "Vague," "Unintelligible," "Ambiguous." A question is improper when its scope is so broad or uncertain that you cannot understand it or anticipate a witness' answer.

  Examples: (1) "Please describe the nature of the event." (2) "When did you first become aware, with reference to the three meetings, that circumstances had changed but which on further reflection turned out to be mistaken?"

- "Compound." A compound question consists of multiple parts, leaving you uncertain of which a witness might answer. The problem usually arises during direct examination.

Example: "Please describe what happened during this meeting and then tell us what actions were taken afterwards."

- "Calls for a Narrative Response." Testimony is supposed to emerge in question-answer format in large part to allow attorneys to anticipate and object to improper testimony. Questions that are framed so broadly that they invite witnesses to describe large chunks of information can therefore be improper. The problem usually arises during direct examination.

Example: "Please describe the events culminating in the invention of the hula hoop."

Note: Witnesses sometimes launch into narrative responses to proper questions. When that occurs, you can interrupt a witness' answer to object that "the witness is narrating" or that "no question is pending."

- "Asked and Answered." Attorneys who rehash testimony with the same witness waste court time. On direct examination multiple questions seeking the same evidence can also constitute an improper method of emphasizing portions of a story. And on cross examination, multiple questions on the same topic may constitute argumentative "badgering." However, judges often allow cross examiners to go over already plowed ground when witnesses are evasive.

Examples: Direct examination-"Ruth, please tell us again what happened when the robber came into the store." Cross examination-"You just said a moment ago that the first cup of porridge was too cold, right?"

- "Assumes facts not in evidence." A question is improper when an attorney makes an assertion as a precursor to a question. The form of the question does not allow a witness to respond to the attorney's assertion. The problem most commonly occurs during cross examination.

  Example: "Doctor, with spiral fractures so readily apparent on x-rays, how come you didn't notice this one?"

- "Argumentative." Questions are argumentative when instead of asking for information they confront witnesses with an attorney's argument or ask witnesses to give opinions about other witnesses' testimony. The problem almost always arises on cross examination.

  Examples: (1) "Why shouldn't the judge believe the two other witnesses who saw things differently?" (2) "You don't want the jurors to infer from the fact that you were late for a meeting that you were speeding, do you?"

- "Leading." Leading questions are improper because they allow attorneys to testify through the mouths of friendly witnesses, right? However, even on direct examination (when the impropriety normally arises), judges sometimes permit leading questions. (See Chapter 7)

- "Misquotes the witness." When an attorney incorporates previous testimony in a new question, even subtle variations can alter a factfinder's perception of the testimony. The problem normally arises during cross examination. As with questions that assume facts not in evidence, the form of questions that misquote witnesses generally doesn't allow a witness to point out the alteration.

  Example: On direct, a witness testified that he had just awakened and was "a bit groggy" when he heard a shot and saw the defendant run past his window. The cross examiner asks, "Now, when you're in your bedroom pretty much out of it, how much time goes by between the time you heard the shot and someone ran past your window?"

- "The witness failed to order the salad dressing on the side." Actually, this is not a common ground of objection outside California.

- Summary of Common Objections (to bring to court or parties)

Substantive objections

  "Irrelevant" (Federal Rule of Evidence 802)

  "Probative Value Substantially Outweighed by Unfair Prejudice" (Federal Rule of Evidence 403)

  "Hearsay" (Federal Rule of Evidence 801)

  "Speculation" or "Improper Opinion" (Federal Rule of Evidence 701); "Lack of Personal Knowledge" (Federal Rule of Evidence 602)

"Lack of foundation" (Federal Rule of Evidence 104).

"Improper character evidence" (Federal Rule of Evidence 404).

Form objections (Federal Rule of Evidence 611)

"Vague," "Unintelligible," "Ambiguous"

"Compound"

"Calls for a Narrative Response"

"Asked and Answered"

"Assumes facts not in evidence"

"Argumentative"

"Leading"

"Misquotes the witness"

D. RESPONDING TO AN ADVERSARY'S OBJECTIONS

1. You Concede the Point

It often happens that you agree with an adversary's objection to your question or to your witness' answer. For example, your witness' puzzled look may reveal the wisdom of an adversary's "unintelligible" objection, you may realize that you need to lay a further foundation, or you may agree that your witness' lengthy answer merits a "narrative" objection.

When you concede an objection to your question, you may either wait for the judge's ruling or offer to withdraw the question. By demonstrating your understanding of evidentiary rules, the latter tactic may lend force to your arguments on disputed evidentiary issues.

When you concede an objection to an answer, consider giving your witness a short, polite instruction if you think the witness is likely to repeat the error. For example, you may tell a witness who is prone to narration something like, "I know you're anxious to tell us everything you saw, but to be fair and help us understand your testimony, it's important for you to listen carefully and simply respond to what you're asked. Can you do that?"

2. Arguing Objections

In general, do not argue an objection unless a judge invites you to do so. Not only is this proper procedure, but also the judge might be prepared to rule in your favor. If you want to comment on an objection, say something like, "Your Honor, might I be heard?" Use similar language if you want to ask a judge to reconsider an adverse ruling which you were unable to argue before the ruling.

3. Offering Evidence for Limited Purposes

As you know, evidence is often admissible for one purpose but not for another. For example, an out-of-court assertion may admissible if limited to the issue of the hearer's "state of mind," and evidence of a "remedial measure" may admissible if limited to the issue of ownership (Federal Rule of Evidence 407). In such situations, you may obviate an objection by incorporating the limited purpose into a question: "For purposes of state of mind only, please tell us what you heard Dumpty say just before Dumpty fell off the wall." This tactic can both demonstrate your awareness of and willingness to follow evidence rules, and can avoid an objection that disrupts a witness' story.

4. The Adversary's Objection Is Overruled

Again, do not say "thank you" to the judge. And do not be so flush with victory that you neglect to get an answer to an objected-to question. If the witness does not recall the question, re-ask it or ask the judge to have the court reporter repeat it.

5. The Adversary's Objection Is Sustained

Now, "thank you" is a real no-no! If you want to contest a ruling, you may ask to be heard. Unlike baseball umpires, judges sometimes do change their minds, especially if you can point out that a judge misapprehended the issue to which evidence relates.

If you are uncertain of the basis of a ruling, you cannot mend the problem with further foundational evidence. Therefore, you may want to ask for clarification: "Your Honor has sustained the lack of foundation objection. Might you inquire of counsel as to just what foundational element is lacking?" By artfully phrasing your request in this way, you take the judge off the spot and force opposing counsel to identify the missing foundation.

6. Offers of Proof

Just as an adversary's offer of proof can help you identify a ground for your objection, your offer of proof can help you to overcome an adversary's objection. For example, if the relevance of evidence depends on testimony which the judge has not yet heard, ask to make an offer of proof. If the judge agrees that the expected testimony makes the evidence relevant, the judge can admit it "subject to being connected up." Consider an example:

Q: What time did you awake that morning?

A: About 6 A.M.

Q: What did you do then?

A: I had breakfast.

Q: What did you have for breakfast?

Opp. Counsel: Objection, irrelevant.

Judge: Sustained.

You: Your Honor, might I make an offer of proof? If permitted, the witness will testify he cooked fresh grits for breakfast. He will further testify that the length of time it takes to cook grits means that he could not possibly have been at a meeting across town at 6:30 A.M., as opposing counsel Gambini contends.

Judge: The objection is overruled. You may inquire.

During cross examination, you should make offers of proof at the bench, out of a witness' hearing. You generally do not want adverse witnesses to know in advance the evidence you hope to elicit.

E. WITNESS PREPARATION

Unlike your British counterparts, you can meet with clients and witnesses to prepare their testimony. Despite the cynical "woodshedding" label often attached to witness preparation, your preparation goal is to foster accurate and credible testimony.

Typically, the major witness preparation activity is a mock direct and cross examination. Use the same vocabulary and manner in your office that you plan to use in the courtroom. Both you and a witness should feel comfortable with a story, yet not so structured that questions and answers sound scripted. As some experienced litigators put it, you want to "rehearse testimony over and over until it sounds spontaneous." The following suggestions can increase the effectiveness of preparation:

- Offer advice in response to specific answers, such as telling a witness to elaborate further in response to an open question. In general, comments on specific questions and answers are likely to be more effective than abstract suggestions that might trouble a Broadway stage veteran, such as "Make them like you."

- If a witness' answer is at variance with a prior statement, ask for an explanation and consider incorporating the explanation in the direct testimony.

- To make a mock cross examination more realistic, consider asking a colleague to conduct it.

- If you will offer exhibits during a witness' testimony, or ask a witness to mark a diagram, include that in preparation.

- Remember that any remarks you make to non-client witnesses are not privileged, and can be inquired into by your adversary during cross examination.

Throughout a preparation session, take a witness-centered approach by inviting witnesses to ask questions. Witnesses' concerns that you might not anticipate may affect their testimony. For example, a witness may think a rehearsal session is improper. If so, the witness may get caught in a lie by denying during cross examination that a rehearsal took place. Similarly, non-party witnesses may want to know how their testimony fits into your overall story. Of course, try not to increase a witness' nervousness by giving responses that unmask your own inexperience: "No, I don't know what you call the person who sits in the front of the courtroom and wears a black robe." The general pieces of advice that witnesses often appreciate include:

- "On cross examination, all you have to do is answer questions, and let me worry about whether questions are legally proper. It's my job to protect you from improper questions, so if I don't object assume that it's OK for you to answer." This kind of comment often relaxes witnesses by telling them to concentrate on their testimony and leave the technicalities to you.

- "Don't guess at answers. It's no problem if you momentarily forget part of your story. I can easily refresh your recollection if necessary." Merely putting witnesses at ease over temporary "blind spots" often prevents them from occurring.

- Say something like, "You're doing fine. Just talk to the judge and jury like you're talking to me and you have nothing to worry about." Witnesses who believe in themselves often testify with more confidence and enhance their credibility.

- "Whether you think information is helpful or harmful, I just want you to tell the truth." Witnesses may create inconsistencies by trying to conceal information they believe harmful. For example, an excluded witness in a child custody matter may try to help a parent by denying that the parent ever drinks. Meanwhile, the parent's priest testified that he and the parent get together often to discuss theology over a few beers. The witness' credibility has been damaged in a misguided attempt to be of help.

- "If you're asked on cross examination whether I told you anything about how to testify, just tell them that I told you to tell the truth." This is punishment for a cross examiner who sneeringly asks the hoariest question in the books, "Did the other attorney tell you what to say?"

F. JUDGE OR JURY TRIAL?

Parties have the constitutional or statutory right to a jury trial in "serious" criminal cases and many types of civil cases. Nevertheless, juries are present in less than half of all U. S. trials. This section sets out factors that you and a client should consider when deciding whether to opt for a judge or jury trial. (The frequent importance of this decision, and the fact that you will usually have time to discuss it with clients in advance, means the decision is one which you should leave to clients after counseling whenever possible. ABA Standard for Criminal Justice 4–5.2 instructs defense counsel that their clients have the right to make this decision, perhaps because in criminal cases defendants have to personally waive their constitutional right to trial by jury.)

Lawyers' "conventional wisdom" suggests a number of "default" selections. For example:

- Civil plaintiffs should lean towards jury trials, on the theory that jurors are likely to be more affected by a case's emotional aspects than judges and thus might be more inclined to award damages.

- Criminal defendants should also lean towards jury trials, because the rules generally requiring unanimous verdicts in criminal cases mean that one juror's vote can prevent a conviction. Moreover, a defense that falls on the deaf ears of a judge who has heard it all before may impress a juror hearing it for the first time.

- Parties who rely on "technicalities" (e.g., a Statute of Frauds defense) are better off with judges, who have an institutional interest in enforcing rules that jurors may see as obstructions to justice.

- Parties whose cases are based on scientific evidence or are otherwise factually complex should opt for judge trials. Judges may be smarter than the average juror, and more likely to take a full set of trial notes. Moreover, you can "educate" judges before trial by filing trial briefs.

Do not use these bits of lawyer lore as anything more than starting points for deciding between a judge or jury. Among the other factors you should consider are these:

- Jury trials tend to be longer than judge trials, and therefore may entail greater expenses for clients. (A jury trial is also likely to impose greater costs on your adversary, perhaps increasing your case's settlement value.)

- Losing litigants may have to pay a "jury trial penalty." For example, a criminal defendant who puts forward what a judge considers to be a very weak defense and who puts the system to the time and expense of a jury trial may (unofficially of course) pay for the impertinence with a harsh sentence. And a losing civil litigant may be taxed higher costs because jury trials tend to be more expensive than judge trials.

- Judges tend to enforce evidence rules more strictly in jury than in judge trials, perhaps thinking that they are less likely than jurors to be influenced by evidence of doubtful admissibility. At the same time, because judges necessarily become aware of information that they rule inadmissible, the possibility exists that a judge will be subtly influenced by information that jurors would never know about.

- "One free bite" rules in some jurisdictions (see, e.g., Cal. Code of Civ. Proc. 170.6) allow you to disqualify a judge who you and a client consider unacceptable, even though you cannot prove the judge's actual bias. By contrast, when you cannot show actual bias, rules strictly limit the number of potential jurors you can excuse (see Page 322).

- Judges often have "track records" in particular types of cases that you can investigate through sources such as computer data bases, other attorneys who have tried similar cases and even local legal newspapers that publish "judicial profiles" of sitting judges. You may also be able to gauge a judge's receptivity to your arguments by watching a judge conduct another trial. By contrast, background information about potential jurors is harder to come by, unless a client is able to pay a social science research company to conduct a community survey. (On the other hand, the potential ability to conduct a pretrial investigation of a particular judge may be worth little in localities where any of a large number of judges may be assigned to preside on the day set for trial.)

- If your adversary opts for a jury trial, you'll have one regardless of your and a client's preference.

Once you and a client have decided on a judge or jury, you will need to comply with often-exacting local court rules. For example, to obtain a jury trial in a federal civil action you have to serve a jury trial request on your adversary no later than 10 days after the service of the last pleading. (Federal Rule of Civil Procedure 38–b). You may also have to deposit jury fees in advance of trial.

G. VOIR DIRE EXAMINATION

"Voir dire" has a double meaning. The term refers to pretrial inquiries to potential jurors, and inquiries challenging a witness' qualifications to testify. In either context, you will be hard put to pronounce the term to everyone's satisfaction.

1. Jury Voir Dire

The purpose of jury voir dire is to allow parties to take part in selecting a fair and impartial jury by eliminating potential jurors who may be predisposed to the adversary. You have two avenues for excusing potential jurors:

- Challenges for cause, which assert that a potential juror is legally disqualified from serving. For example, you can exercise a challenge for cause against potential jurors whose answers reveal actual bias or who appear to be too infirm to serve. You are allowed an unlimited number of challenges for cause.

• Peremptory challenges, which permit you to excuse potential jurors based on your or a client's subjective belief from a person's answers, background, etc. that the person is predisposed in your adversary's favor. Peremptory challenges are strictly limited in number. For example, 28 U.S.C. Sec. 1870 provides for only three peremptory challenges in civil cases; Federal Rule of Criminal Procedure 24 provides for three peremptory challenges in misdemeanor cases.

Traditionally, lawyers conducted jury voir dire questioning. However, to curtail the time devoted to voir dire by lawyers who used it as an opportunity to argue their cases, judges often conduct the bulk of jury voir dire. Before those judges, you may be limited to submitting written questions for the judge to ask, or to supplemental oral voir dire.

Since few potential jurors admit to direct evidence of bias, their attitudes and voir dire answers constitute circumstantial evidence from which you may draw an inference of impartiality or predisposition. For example, assume that you represent a defendant in a shoplifting case. A potential juror states that she works for a department store. Based on a generalization such as, "People who work for department stores are likely to believe a security guard's testimony," you may want to challenge the store employee. Of course, like all circumstantial evidence the information that emerges during voir dire may be subject to conflicting inferences. For instance, if you accept a generalization that "People who work for department stores are likely to distrust security guards," you will be inclined to want the store employee on the jury.

Searching for "especially whens" and "except whens" (see Pages 50–55) during voir dire examination can help you choose between conflicting generalizations. For example, assume that you learn that the security staff at the potential juror's store has recently given a training course on how to identify shoplifters. You might infer that this experience would make it especially likely that the employee would believe a security guard's testimony. On the other hand, the employee might believe a security guard "except when" a couple of security guards in her store were recently fired for incompetency.

Unfortunately, you'll rarely have time during voir dire examination to thoroughly explore such topics, and you'll generally have to draw inferences on incomplete data. Two techniques that may help you and a client make a more educated judgment are as follows:

- Ask open questions. When you encourage potential jurors to talk, they often reveal important information that you would not have thought to ask about. For example, you might ask the department store employee questions such as, "Tell me about your experiences with your store's security staff."

- In big-ticket trials, consider hiring a social science research firm to conduct community surveys and produce "profiles" of suitable jurors.

Lawyer lore is embarrassingly filled with stereotypes about the suitability of different social group members to serve as jurors. For example, people of German descent were often said to make good defense jurors. However, modern trial rules outlaw some of those stereotypes. For instance, challenges based on race and gender are forbidden. Anyway, in today's mobile and complex society, such broad social stereotypes are probably poor predictors of potential jurors' attitudes.

Judges rarely grant challenges for cause, even when some aspect of a potential juror's background gives rise to a strong inference of predisposition. So long as potential jurors insist that they can be fair to both sides, judges are likely to deny challenges for cause. For example, assume that you challenge the department store employee's legal ability to sit in judgment of the defendant in the shoplifting case. If the employee says something like, "I won't be influenced by my job; I can give both sides a fair trial," the judge will probably not excuse the employee for cause. To preserve your limited number of peremptory challenges, therefore, you sometimes try to elicit sufficient "evidence" to convince a judge that a potential juror's predisposition is sufficient to constitute a legal impediment to jury service.

For example, assume that you represent the shoplifting defendant, and together with your client have decided that the department store employee is likely to be predisposed to the prosecution. To try to convince the judge to excuse the employee for cause, you may question as follows:

1. Q: Ms. Lynn–Sossin, you said that the fact that you work for a department store will in no way influence you, correct?

2. A: That's right.

3. Q: I appreciate that. But tell me if you could what experiences you've had with the store's security staff.

4. A: I've found them generally pretty reliable. If I put in a call because a customer strikes me as suspicious, someone shows up pretty fast. And they're well trained and don't let problems get out of hand.

5. Q: Is it fair to say that you're pretty impressed with them?

6. A: I'd have to say that's true.

7. Q: And in your experience the security guards you've worked with have been honest and reliable?

8. A: Yes.

9. Q: If you knew nothing about a person except that the person was a store security guard,

how would that affect your belief in what the person had to say?

10.   A: Well, I'd assume they were telling the truth, the same as other people I suppose. But I'd want to hear what everyone had to say before making a decision.

11.   Q: But as compared to someone you knew nothing about, wouldn't the fact that a person was a store security guard make you more inclined to believe that person's testimony?

12.   A: I suppose it's possible, but I can be fair.

At this point, you might challenge the potential juror for cause, arguing that she is predisposed in favor of the prosecution. If the judge refuses to excuse the juror, you and the defendant would then have to decide whether to exercise a peremptory challenge. If you have none, or prefer to exercise them on other potential jurors, you might conclude by committing the juror to her promise of fairness:

13.   Q: So Ms. Lynn–Sossin, if you're on the jury, you'll give both sides a fair trial. You won't believe or disbelieve witnesses for either side based solely on their employment, correct?

14.   A: That's right.

In the voir dire sample above, you sprinkle open questions into the voir dire examination (Nos. 3 and 9). By encouraging potential jurors to talk, you can often draw informed inferences from their choice of words, their body language, etc. about their suitability to sit as a juror. Though hard to convey in text, your manner should also be conversational and polite. You don't want to alienate people who might wind up as jurors-or the friends they leave behind if you excuse them!

Perhaps the two most basic rules of jury voir dire are these:

- You cannot ask potential jurors to "prejudge a case." What this means is that you cannot ask potential jurors to reveal how they would decide a case under an assumed set of facts. For example, in a drunk driving case, you could not ask, "If you were satisfied that Mr. Chivas had only had one beer to drink before getting into his car, will you find that he was not under the influence of alcohol?"

- Voir dire questions must be relevant to predisposition. (This rule is less universally followed than the first.) This rule seeks to confine the scope of voir dire and protect the privacy of potential jurors by preventing attorneys from pursuing remote topics that might pertain only to a peremptory challenge, such as what TV programs a person watches or what they read.

While the "prejudgment" rule generally prohibits you from arguing your case, your voir dire questions can serve to educate potential jurors about arguments they will confront if they are chosen to serve. The key to the propriety of "educating" questions is to phrase them in such a way that they seek assurance that a potential juror is not predisposed against those arguments. Consider these examples:

- Inoculation against an adversary's arguments. While you cannot ask potential jurors to prejudge cases in your favor, you can properly ask them not to prejudge cases against you. An effective technique is to confront potential jurors with evidence favoring the adversary, and seek assurance of open-mindedness despite that evidence. For example, assume that in the drunk driving case you will dispute the prosecution's evidence that your client Mr. Chivas had drunk three martinis before driving. You might ask:

  "Ladies and gentlemen, you'll probably hear testimony from a prosecution witness who claims that Mr. Chivas had drunk three martinis. Without listening to the evidence, do any of you think that you should accept that testimony simply because it comes from a prosecution witness?"

  "If you serve on the jury, you will all agree that it's wrong to prejudge any witness' testimony, and you promise to keep an open mind until you've heard all the evidence?"

  Such questions are proper because a potential juror who refuses to promise to keep an open mind cannot legally serve on the jury. Of course, you expect potential jurors to make such promises. Your real purpose is an educational one.

- Inoculation against silent arguments. Assume that you represent a civil plaintiff suing a police officer for excessive force in making an arrest. A possible silent argument favoring the defendant officer is that "a conclusion that the force was excessive will deter police officers from adequately protecting citizens." During voir dire, you can surface the potential argument and seek a potential juror's agreement not to let it be determinative:

  "The judge will instruct you that in reaching your verdict, you shouldn't take into account the affect the verdict may have on other police officers. Will you be able to follow such an instruction?"

A juror who answered "no" would be subject to a challenge for cause. Thus, though your real purpose may be to educate and inoculate against a potential silent argument, the question is probably proper.

- Emphasize the burden of proof. Without asking a potential juror to prejudge a case, you can emphasize an argument regarding the burden of proof:

  "The judge will instruct you that you cannot vote for conviction unless the prosecution proves its case beyond a reasonable doubt. Are you willing to follow that instruction?"

You wouldn't reasonably expect a potential juror to answer anything other than "yes." However, the question allows you to stress an argument while formally probing a potential juror's fitness to serve.

2. Foundational Questioning of Witnesses

Jury voir dire probes the foundation for potential jurors' fitness to serve. Voir dire of witnesses probes evidentiary foundations. For example, you may ask to "take a witness on voir dire" when you dispute:

- a lay witness' personal knowledge;
- a document's qualification as a business record; or
- the sufficiency of an offered expert's "specialized knowledge." (Federal Rule of Evidence 702)

Whether to permit voir dire is within judges' broad discretion. When you take a witness on voir dire, you interrupt the normal flow of testimony by asking questions before the adversary has finished an examination. In most circumstances, you can simply wait until it is your turn to ask questions to explore the adequacy of a foundation. Then, if you sufficiently undermine the foundation, you can move to strike an exhibit or a witness' testimony. The disadvantage of forgoing voir dire is that delay may permit a factfinder to hear improper evidence. Better to make a voir dire challenge, which may occur out of a jury's presence. (Federal Rule of Evidence 104–c)

For example, assume that you represent the plaintiff in a wrongful death suit involving allegedly negligent highway blasting. You dispute the qualifications of a witness called by the defendant to give expert testimony regarding blasting procedures. Following the defendant's foundational questioning, you may proceed as follows:

Q: Your Honor, at this point I'd like to take the witness on voir dire for the purpose of inquiring into the adequacy of the witness' qualifications as an expert.

Judge: Granted.

Q: Your Honor, may the jury be excused for this portion of the testimony?

Judge: I'll keep the jury here. You won't be getting into the substance of the witness' testimony, and if I rule that the witness is qualified I presume most of what you elicit will go to the weight of the testimony. Proceed.

Q: Now Dr. Vesuvius, you received your engineering degree in Landscape Mountain Blasting from Football Tech about 10 years ago, correct?

A: That's right.

Q: And since graduation, you've been a Professor of Engineering at Southwestern Northern University, teaching clinical courses in blasting techniques, dynamite design and gypsy mythology, correct?

A: Yes.

Q: You've never designed a blasting project, or consulted on an actual project?

A: That's true. However, I've analyzed simulated blasting with students.

Q: Can you describe your publications?

A: Yes, I'm the author of "Blast Trajectory Analysis in a Nutshell." I also recently published a study commissioned by the Army Corps of Engineers, studying alternative methods of leveling the Rocky Mountains.

Q: At this point, Your Honor, I object that the witness is not sufficiently qualified to give expert testimony in this matter. The witness has no actual experience on blasting projects.

Judge: Any further foundation from the defense?

Def. Att: None, Your Honor.

Judge: All right, we'll take the morning recess while I decide on my ruling.

If the judge ultimately sustains your objection, the voir dire challenge prevents the factfinder from ever hearing the witness' opinion.

H. EXPERT WITNESSES

Experts have taken on an increasingly important role in trials. Among the reasons for this phenomenon are:

- Fields of expertise have both narrowed and mushroomed. Experts can tell us "more and more about less and less."

- Federal Rule of Evidence 702, admits expert evidence so long as a judge thinks that an expert's opinion would "assist" the factfinder. As interpreted by *Daubert v. Merrill Dow Pharmaceuticals* (U.S. Sup. Ct. 1993), Rule 702 also compels individual judges to evaluate the reliability of novel scientific evidence.

- Many jurors have come to expect parties to produce experts who can validate claims.

As a result, vast numbers of experts offer their services, often in publications aimed at litigators. And with good reason-a recent survey found that on average, more than four experts testify per civil trial.

The primary function of experts is to deliver opinions based on specialized knowledge. As a reward for pleasing their parents by becoming experts, expert witnesses enjoy several evidentiary advantages:

- Experts are not required to testify from personal knowledge. (Federal Rule of Evidence 703) For example, a medical expert may testify based on information gleaned from hospital records.

- Experts can use their specialized knowledge to deliver opinions forbidden to non-experts. (Federal Rule of Evidence 702)

- Experts can testify to otherwise inadmissible evidence. (Federal Rule of Evidence 703)

- Unlike lay witnesses, for whom testifying is an unpaid civic obligation, experts can demand compensation for using their specialized knowledge.

● In practice, judges tend to allow experts greater narrative freedom than lay witnesses. Also, since experts do not often tell stories, expert witness examinations tend not to follow a chronological format.

Any specialized knowledge may qualify a person to give expert testimony. University degrees and publications are not a requirement. For example, assuming that the testimony is relevant, a Hollywood agent may qualify as an expert on industry customs about movie star billing.

1. You Are the Proponent of an Expert

Experts generally draw conclusions from circumstantial evidence when the generalizations underlying those conclusions are sufficiently beyond everyday experience. For example, assume that you represent the county in a child welfare proceeding. Your expert, Dr. Hans Offe, is of the opinion that the spiral fracture of a child's leg suggests that the leg was intentionally broken. The generalization underlying this opinion is, "People who suffer spiral fractures to their legs have often been intentionally harmed." Lay factfinders lack the specialized knowledge to determine the generalization's accuracy. Hence the need for the expert.

Thus, when you are the proponent of an expert witness, you will typically ask the witness to:

- Establish the witness' expertise by asking the witness to describe the sources of the witness' specialized knowledge. For example, you may ask about formal education, professional experience, professional organizations to which a witness belongs, publications, and previous service as an expert. As suggested above (see Page 295), an adversary may offer to stipulate to an expert's qualifications.

- Testify to an opinion.

- Identify the evidence on which the opinion is based. For example, you'd ask the child abuse expert to identify the evidence suggesting intentional harm.

- Validate the underlying generalization by explaining the basis of the opinion. For example, you would ask the child abuse expert to describe what a spiral fracture is and explain why it is suggestive of an intentional injury. (Federal Rule of Evidence 705 provides that an expert needn't disclose the bases of an opinion. Nevertheless, you should ordinarily elicit this information.)

- Identify "especially whens." Just like any other generalization, you can strengthen the probative strength of generalizations based on specialized knowledge by having an expert identify evidence making them especially likely to be accurate in a particular case. For example, the child abuse expert may testify that a spiral fracture suggests intentional harm, "especially when" the injured child is only two years old. Again, you'd want to validate the "especially when" by asking the expert to explain why the age of the child strengthens the conclusion.

In bygone days, experts had to testify based on information in hypothetical questions. In the middle of trial, the proponent of an expert would provide an expert with "hypothetical" information, and ask the expert to give an opinion based on the assumed accuracy of the information. This practice led to endless squabbles about the correspondence between evidence in the record and information in a hypothetical question. Federal Rule of Evidence 703 allows but does not require hypothetical questions; experts can be given information "before the hearing." However, some attorneys still use hypothetical questions because they can be a dandy way of recapitulating evidence for a factfinder before closing argument.

Like many specialists, experts are prone to use incomprehensible jargon. This is not necessarily a negative; one way to demonstrate expertise to jurors is to show that a witness knows lots of words that they don't. Nevertheless, make sure that an expert explains obscure terms, and illustrates unfamiliar concepts with familiar examples.

2. Cross Examining an Adversary's Expert

The obvious difficulty of cross examining an expert is that you are playing on the expert's turf, which by definition is at least somewhat beyond everyday experience. Fishing is therefore even more hazardous than with non-experts. Thus, unless you also have expertise, you will generally need to rely on your own expert witness, or at least a consultant, to develop safe questions.

One typical method of undermining an expert is to elicit evidence of bias. For example, the size of an expert's fee can suggest that an expert's opinion has been influenced by financial concerns. (Unless your expert is getting even more!) Similarly, evidence that an expert always reaches the same opinion can lead to an inference that the expert adjusts evidence to fit the expert's pre-existing conclusions. (One of the best-known examples is the so-called "Dr. Death," who in one death penalty case after another testifies that the defendant is likely to kill again and therefore fit for execution.)

Second, you can undermine an expert's qualifications-even after a judge rules that the expert is qualified. For example, you may elicit evidence that:

- an expert's professional training is old and stale;

- an expert has forensic training but little or no actual experience;

- an expert is a generalist in a field in which genuine experts specialize;

- the impressive-sounding organizations of which the expert is a member are open to anyone willing to pay the fee; or

- an expert is but a "technician" who operates a machine but has no real understanding of how it works (e.g., a police officer who uses a breathalyzer machine to determine blood alcohol levels in drunk driving cases).

Third, you can attack the credibility of the information on which the expert's opinion is based. For example, recall the child abuse expert whose opinion that a child was intentionally injured was based in part on the existence of a spiral fracture. Evidence that the fracture was not a spiral one would cast doubt on the opinion. As you know, experts often have no personal knowledge of the information on which their opinions are based. Therefore, you cannot usually attack the credibility of such information during an expert's cross examination. However, you can ask an expert to agree that a change in the facts could lead to a different opinion: "Doctor, if it turned out that the x-ray you saw was not of a two year old child, but was in fact of a 98 year old adult, could that alter your opinion?"

The three methods described above allow you to cross examine an expert without confronting the testimony head-on. Often, however, you have to do so. One method is to elicit "except whens" to generalizations underlying an expert's opinion. You can undermine an opinion if you produce evidence of a fact which an expert has conceded would make a generalization less likely to be accurate. For example, assume that you cross examine an expert who testifies that a ship captain's hoarse voice on a recording is an indication that the captain was under the influence of alcohol at the time the recording was made. The generalization underlying this opinion is something like, "People whose voices are hoarse are often under the influence of alcohol." On cross examination, the expert concedes that a hoarse voice may also be due to stress and to a person's just having awoken. Evidence that these factors were present at the time the ship captain's voice was recorded would undermine the expert's opinion. (In some situations, even the possibility of alternative explanations can undermine an opinion.)

Another method to attack an opinion head-on is to attack the accuracy of an underlying generalization. That is, you can demonstrate that other experts disagree with the foundation on which an expert's opinion rests. For example, you may inquire into:

- The limits of knowledge of a field of expertise. For example, in a medical malpractice case, you may ask an expert to admit that no medical test can conclusively rule out a patient's allergy to a particular medication.

- Tests which the expert might have performed to substantiate an opinion but which were not performed.

- If the expert is a non-percipient witness, the value of actual observation to a reliable opinion.

Two common sources for attacking an adverse expert's opinion head on are:

- The conflicting opinions of authors of authoritative treatises. (Federal Rule of Evidence 803–18) If an adverse expert agrees that a publication is "authoritative," you can read into the record a passage that conflicts with the expert's opinion.

- Court opinions in jurisdictions that do not permit expert testimony in the expert's field. For example, assume that you are cross examining an expert on "Child Abuse Accommodation Syndrome." Other jurisdictions do not allow expert testimony on this subject, and their reasons can be effective fodder for cross examination.

I. JURY INSTRUCTIONS

Substantive and procedural rules are the foundations of your arguments and an important component of closing arguments. (See Chapter 10) In jury trials, judges inform jurors of these rules in a series of oral instructions. Traditionally, jurors would have to interrupt deliberations and ask to have instructions reread if they were confused. Supposedly, this procedure prevented jurors from focusing on one instruction while ignoring another that modified it. Increasingly, judges permit jurors to take the written instructions into their deliberations.

Many instructions are "boilerplate," and judges take them from court-approved books of jury instructions. However, you can submit proposed jury instructions, and may want to do so for the following reasons:

- You want to rephrase instructions in "plain English" that jurors can understand. The language of many jury instructions makes insurance contracts seem entertaining, and you may facilitate jury understanding by preparing user-friendly versions.

- Apart from the vocabulary, another way to make instructions understandable is to "tailor" them by substituting case-specific references for abstract language. For example, assume that an instruction that might be given in a criminal case reads as follows:

"Any person who carries concealed upon his person or concealed within any vehicle which is under his control or direction any pistol without having a license to carry such firearm is guilty of a misdemeanor."

Incorporating the evidence in a case, you may ask the judge to substitute this "tailored" instruction:

"In order to convict Mr. Dillinger, the State must establish each of the following elements beyond a reasonable doubt: That Mr. Dillinger carried a revolver on his person when he attended the movie on May 6; that the revolver that Mr. Dillinger carried was completely concealed from view; and that Mr. Dillinger did not have a license to carry the revolver on May 6."

- You want the judge to give an instruction that the judge may not otherwise give. For example, you may want the judge in a criminal case to instruct on a lesser-included offense. Or, you may have found appealing language in a dictionary, a law review article or a nutshell treatise.

Anxious to avoid reversal, many judges prefer to give only pre-approved instructions. However, judges have discretion to give your proposed instructions so long as they conform to the law and the evidence.

J. SUBPOENAS

A subpoena is a court order requiring a witness to appear in court. A subpoena which directs a person to produce documents as well is a "subpoena duces tecum." In some jurisdictions, courts issue blank, pre-stamped subpoenas which you can complete and serve.

You should subpoena even the friendliest of witnesses. If a witness you are counting on is ill or otherwise unable to attend when needed, the success of your request for a continuance may depend on your answer to the judge's question, "Is the witness under subpoena?" A witness may regard a subpoena as an indication of distrust. However, you can maintain rapport by assuring witnesses that the practice is routine, and even in the witness' best interests. For example, a subpoena can protect an employee who has to miss work to attend court.

Most jurisdictions have "on call" procedures, which allow witnesses under subpoena to go about their daily business until their testimony is needed.

K. PACKING FOR TRIAL

Your proficiency at handling documents inside the courtroom can serve as a "silent argument" (see Chapter 5). The credence that a factfinder gives to your factual arguments and that a judge gives to your evidentiary contentions can be affected by your ability at managing documents. Thus, before leaving your office organize your files in such a way that you can readily access documents during trial.

A "trial notebook" is a traditional organizational tool, though one that is increasingly being supplanted or supplemented by laptop computers. A typical trial notebook is a three ring binder in which documents are grouped and separated by differently colored index tabs. Your trial notebook may contain the following materials:

- Copies of court documents, such as pleadings, answers to interrogatories, trial briefs, pre-trial orders, written motions in limine, and the like. You may want to prepare a separate notebook for voluminous court documents, and an accordion file for documents that will not fit easily into a notebook, such as depositions and exhibits. (Do not punch holes in documents that you will offer into evidence!)

- A Chronological Story Outline, which summarizes the overall story that you are trying to convince a factfinder is accurate.

- Argument Outlines, which list the arguments on which you rely to convince a factfinder of the accuracy of your overall story. For example, the outline of an inferential argument might identify the "embryonic argument," the "especially whens" strengthening the argument, and the "except whens" undermining the adversary's counter-argument (see Chapter 4). To further the usefulness of argument outlines, you might annotate them by identifying the documents or witnesses which are the source of the evidence.

- Direct Examination Outlines, which list the important evidence you expect to elicit from each of your witnesses and which you can have in front of you as you conduct direct examinations. Direct examination outlines can also refer to the exhibits that you plan to offer during a witness' direct examination, and refer to any documents you can use to refresh a witness' recollection. (Some attorneys prepare actual "scripts" in question-answer format. Important downsides of detailed scripts are that they may impair your ability to respond to unexpected answers, and you may focus attention on a script instead of a witness.)

- Cross Examination Outlines, which resemble direct examination outlines but list the important evidence you expect to elicit from adverse witnesses.

- Opening Statement and Closing Argument Outlines (you may want to keep these in separately-tabbed sections.) These outlines should highlight what you plan to say without being so detailed that you will be tempted to read them. However, you may write out the exact text of an important jury instruction or a witness' of critical testimony.

- An Exhibits List, so you can keep track of which exhibits have been received into evidence. You may want to bring to court a list of all your expected exhibits. Checking off each as it is received into evidence is a good way to avoid the embarrassment of forgetting to offer an exhibit into evidence.

- Jury trial documents. For example, you may want to prepare an outline of topics you want to cover during jury voir dire. Also, you may have plain sheets of paper with pre-printed squares (numbered 1–12, if a panel will consist of 12 jurors) in which you can record information pertaining to each juror.

- Copies of any written stipulations.

- Witness information sheets, including subpoenas and data such as telephone, pager and fax numbers for each witness. If you suddenly need to locate a witness who is "on call," this information may be very necessary.

- A copy of the latest issue of a scientific journal, preferably with an unpronounceable title. This will cause your adversary no end of worry.

L. MISCELLANEOUS CUSTOMS AND PRACTICES

1. Sitting and Standing

Unlike weddings, courtrooms don't come equipped with ushers. To find your place in an unfamiliar courtroom, look for the jury or witness box. Plaintiff's counsel table is usually the one closer to the jury or witness box. If you are still uncertain, ask the clerk or bailiff.

To show respect to the court, stand whenever you address a judge, whether you are making an argument or interposing an evidentiary objection. In many courtrooms, you are also required to stand behind a lectern while arguing or examining witnesses. In some courts you can remain seated while examining witnesses, but many attorneys prefer to stand up anyway.

You normally cannot approach a witness unless you have reason to do so, such as to point out a relevant portion of an exhibit. Ask the judge for permission to approach, unless the judge advises you that you need not bother to do so. Return to your "mark" when the reason for approaching a witness has expired.

2. Promptness

One of Murphy's unwritten laws is that the judge always takes the bench at the scheduled time when you are late. If for any reason you expect to be late, call the clerk promptly and give a realistic time for your arrival. Better yet, be on time.

3. Approaching the Bench

Ask to approach the bench whenever you want to make a statement or objection that you do not want a witness or jurors to overhear. Judges prefer bench conferences to the more time-consuming alternative of excusing jurors. Whenever a judge is likely to make an evidentiary ruling during a bench conference, or you or opposing counsel is likely to make statements you want on the record, request the court reporter's presence at the bench as well. Hope that the judge has a long bench.

4. Converse in the Triangular

One of the stranger customs of trial is to address all comments to the judge, even though opposing counsel, the real target of your remarks, is standing right next to you. For example, assume that you want to inform a judge that opposing counsel is unfairly attempting to back out of a stipulation. Do not talk to counsel directly: "Why are you trying to get out of the stipulation we agreed to three days ago?" Instead, address the remark to the judge: "Your Honor, Ms. Boland agreed to this stipulation three days ago and now, after the witness has been excused, is suddenly attempting to withdraw it."

(Fortunately, the custom is not pursued to its logical conclusion. The judge will not pretend that neither counsel can hear what the other said and repeat everyone's remarks!)

5. Observe Courthouse Etiquette

Proper trial behavior extends beyond courtroom doors. Never discuss a case in a public area of the courthouse when you might be overheard. Public areas include elevators, corridors and bathrooms. In addition, avoid corridor conversations with jurors, as anything more than a smile and "good morning" might be interpreted as an attempt to influence the jury. (Either the judge or you should advise jurors that the attorneys are not being unfriendly, but simply following required procedures.) Of course, once a verdict is rendered, most jurisdictions allow you to discuss a case with any jurors who are willing to talk. And if appropriate, you can smile.

6. Handling Client Distractions

Some clients are wont to tug at their attorneys' sleeves in the middle of trial with proposed questions or arguments. One way to avoid this distraction is to furnish clients with a notepad and pen, advise the clients to write down their thoughts, and promise to review what they've written before concluding testimony or argument. (This ploy will not work if the client is trying to tell you that your briefcase is on fire.) Another effective method that some attorneys use is to seat clients away from counsel table, perhaps even in the spectator area.

However, do not automatically regard all clients as potential distractions. Clients may assist you in a variety of ways, such as by:

- taking notes while you conduct direct examinations;
- advising you of their reactions to potential jurors during voir dire;
- observing jurors' reactions to testimony.

Not only will such activities make a client feel involved in a case, but also your conferring with a client can serve as a "silent argument" that a client is responsible and trustworthy.

7. Note–Taking

A trial task that will flood your mind with happy memories of student days is note-taking. A court reporter's recorded tape or machine markings is no substitute for a personal set of notes. For example, notes will help you:

- make or respond to objections;
- frame cross examination questions;
- refer to specific testimony or an adversary's opening statement during your closing argument.

The task may at first seem daunting: "I'm supposed to be alert for possible objections, observe a factfinder's reaction to testimony, watch out for inconsistencies with prior testimony, and take notes?" However, rather than being an extra task, note-taking may "keep your head in the game," helping you perform the other trial tasks. Following tradition, you may keep notes on yellow pads with vertical lines drawn down the center. To the right of the center line you take down testimony; to the left, remind yourself that an assertion is one you want to return to during examination or argument. Laptop computers are increasingly popular, though somewhat less traditional.

M. THE DIRTY TRICKS HALL OF FAME

By now, if you hoped to find in this book a collection of courtroom "tricks" guaranteed to win verdicts no matter the validity of your arguments, you are no doubt sorely disappointed. As an apology, I present a few tricks that lawyers are said to have tried at one time or another. Some of them may be apocryphal, and in any event you should consider them only for whatever entertainment value they may have.

- The Magic Cigar. Clarence Darrow would draw attention away from an adversary's evidence by sticking a length of wire down the middle of a cigar. When he lit up, the wire caused the ashes to remain on the cigar. The jurors were so fascinated by the mysterious ashes that they paid no attention to the evidence. (A trick which manages simultaneously to violate ethical, evidence and health rules!)

- Ripped van Winkle. Listening to the direct testimony of an adverse witness who is providing devastating evidence, counsel leans back and appears to doze off, hoping to fool the jury into thinking that the testimony is of no consequence.

- The Ancient Novice. Finishing closing argument with an emotional appeal, the attorney humbly prays that the jurors will not hold the errors of a beginner against the client. The wily attorney is, of course, a veteran of 75 trials.

- The Paper Chase. In the middle of an aggressive cross examination, the attorney pauses, searches for and carefully studies a piece of paper. Holding the paper and smiling, the attorney asks, "Isn't it true that . . ." The shaken witness, assuming that the question is based directly on whatever is written on the paper, agrees to whatever the question asserts. The attorney then discards the previous day's shopping list.

- The Fertile Octogenarian. Sorry-wrong book.

- The Unreliable Informant. Again in the middle of an aggressive cross, the attorney's associate rushes into the courtroom and whispers the latest stock market quotations into the attorney's ear. The attorney smiles and turns to the witness. The witness admits to anything in the next question.

- The Religious Zealot. Representing a defendant charged with first degree murder in front of a jury with a number of Catholics, William Fallon (a flamboyant 1920's New York attorney) instructed his client to wear a rosary in his breast pocket while testifying. On a signal from Fallon, the witness caused the rosary to "accidentally" fall out of his pocket. The defendant was acquitted.

- The Kitchen Sink. Earl Rogers (a flamboyant Los Angeles contemporary of Fallon who represented Clarence Darrow in Darrow's jury-bribing trial) is the source of a number of tricks:

- Representing an alleged thief who stole a ring worth only about $3.00, Rogers had the thief dress for court wearing fancy jewelry. The jury voted for acquittal, figuring that a rich man would not stoop to such a petty theft. After the trial, Rogers returned the jewelry to the pawnbroker from whom they'd been rented.

- Cross examining an eyewitness to the theft of a horse, Rogers engaged the witness in friendly conversation about farming. In the meantime, Rogers had the defendant quietly change places at counsel table with one of Rogers' associates. Asked to identify the thief, the witness pointed to the associate and the case was dismissed.

- In a murder case, a professional gambler was shot and killed by one of two young men with whom he was playing cards. Rogers' client was charged with the murder. The witness was the other young man, who said he stood by unafraid while the defendant drew a gun and shot the gambler. During closing argument, Rogers started screaming angrily. He suddenly drew a gun, and everyone in the courtroom ducked for cover. The jurors voted for acquittal, figuring that the prosecution witness had lied about standing by unafraid.

- For descriptions of some of the most noteworthy lawyer pranks depicted in courtroom films, see Bergman, "Pranks for the Memory," 30 University of San Francisco Law Review 1235 (1996).

INDEX

___

References are to pages

___

LITIGATORS
Need to use adversarial techniques, 10
Personal characteristics of, 5

"MENENDEZ TRIAL" REFERENCES, 194–196, 219–220

MIND SET, 34, 89, 132, 183, 236

MOTIONS IN LIMINE, 63, 297–298

MOTIVE
See, Bias

NARRATIVE QUESTIONS
Direct examination, use during, 118–122
Expert witnesses, 334
Objecting to, 121, 308
"Pseudo-narrative" questions, 121

"NO, NO, NO" TECHNIQUE, 122, 212–213

NORMATIVE ARGUMENTS
See generally, Chap. 5
Closing argument, adressing during, 269, 291
Defined, 58
Direct examination, addressing during, 137
Factors underlying, 59
Historical arguments, contrasted with, 57
"Pseudo-normative" arguments, 269–270, 291
Reason to forgo cross examination, 217–218

NOTE–TAKING, 349

OBJECTIONS
Additional remedies, 304
"Arguing outside the record," 276
Arguing adverse ruling, 312, 313
"Argumentative," 186, 204, 208, 211, 233–234, 309
"Asked and answered," 308
"Assumes facts not in evidence," 309
Can't we all get along?
"Character evidence," 307
"Compound," 186, 307
"Counsel is testifying," 126, 142
Continuing, 302
Diagrams, 172
Ethical concerns, 298–300
Form objections, list of, 307–310, 311

†